# Putting a Face on AMERICA
## The Great American Journey

# LYN HANUSH
*with Joni Balog and Samantha Gruver*

WINEPRESS **WP** PUBLISHING

WinePress Publishing (PO Box 428, Enumclaw, WA 98022) functions only as book publisher. As such, the ultimate design, content, editorial accuracy, and views expressed or implied in this work are those of the author.

ISBN 13: 978-1-57921-882-9
ISBN 10: 1-57921-882-2
Library of Congress Catalog Card Number: 2006934488

Printed in China.
APC-**FT4702**

# DEDICATIONS

### To God

Who gave us the idea for this Journey, and gave us the courage to get out there and do it, and the strength to take each step. He faithfully met each of our needs and helped us persevere in every situation.

"All the nations may walk in the name of their gods; we will walk in the name of the lord our God for ever and ever" (Micah 4:5).

To God be the glory!

**Lyn, Joni and Sam**

### From Lyn

To my husband, Dave, who didn't just say I could go on this walk; he believed with me that God was leading. Without his love, encouragement, and support this Journey could never have happened. He was there through thick and thin, cheering me on. He spent tireless hours keeping our family and friends informed of the walk's progress, and gave of himself so much to make this all possible.

I love you!

**Lyn**

And, to my children, Alyce-Kay, Laurie, Russ and Darrol, and to their spouses, and to my grandchildren—for their prayers, letters of encouragement, and sacrifices made so that we could keep moving. Thank you.

With love,

**Mom/Grumman ("Grandma")**

### From Sam

To my sister, Lois, who cheered me on across the states. Thanks for the time you spent with me during our Christmas break talking, laughing, and being my friend, as well as my sister.

With love,

**Sam**

### From Joni

*To my daughter Beth, son Paul and his wife Lori, and grandsons, Scott, Ryan and Kyle, for your loving support, letters and care packages to encourage me to keep on trekking.*

*With love,*

**Mum/Nana**

*To Lyn, who dreamed the impossible dream of the Great American Journey and made it possible.*

*Your sister in the Lord,*

**Joni**

### From Cassie

*To all our drivers who let me sit in the air-conditioned van, and to all the veterinarians who showed compassion as they stitched me up and gave me shots.*

*With thanks,*

**Cassie Woof-woof**

# TABLE OF CONTENTS

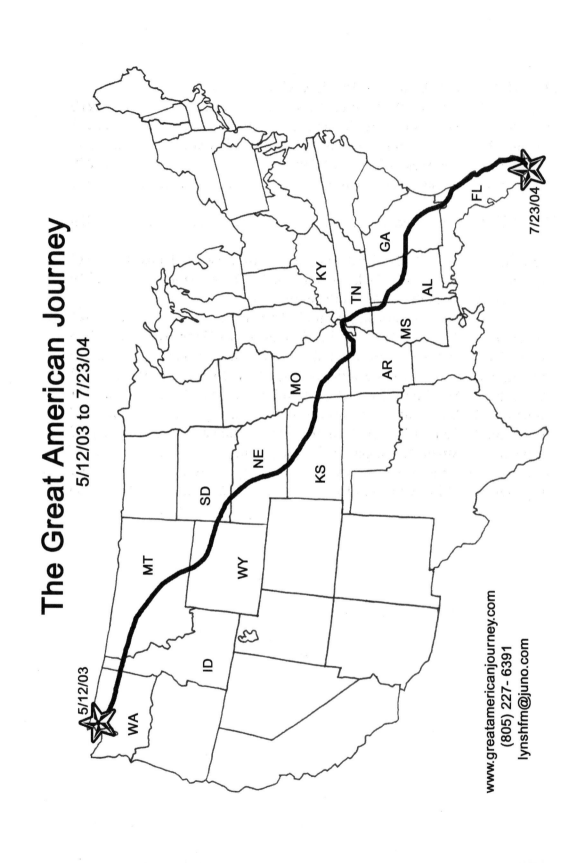

# The Great American Journey

## 5/12/03 to 7/23/04

5/12/03

7/23/04

WA
MT
ID
SD
WY
NE
KS
MO
AR
KY
TN
GA
AL
MS
FL

www.greatamericanjourney.com
(805) 227- 6391
lynshfm@juno.com

# FOREWORD

Not many of us would have the desire or capability to undertake such a significant expedition as described in *Putting A Face On America*. These women walked across America, representing each one of us. On this trek, they had unique opportunities to meet an amazing variety of fellow citizens throughout rural America.

Their experiences, related in this book, of meeting and sharing their faith really "puts a face on America." As Lyn, Joni and Samantha describe their personal encounters with transparency, honesty and candor, you, too, will begin to understand the rural people of America. You will laugh with them at the humorous experiences—and cry with them, as you see God's provision.

Put on your walking shoes and go across America one experience at a time. You, too, can continue these encounters by adding your prayers for those the ladies met along the way. (See Appendix 11 and 12 for the prayer lists.)

I especially appreciated the examples and guidelines that each of us can follow to pray for the Lord's leading and guidance for unknown people. Just picture waving at every car, truck, and train, and with each wave goes a prayer for the driver and occupants of that vehicle. Or to pray for a specific town: for its leaders, schools, youth, and safety for all.

"To God Be The Glory" was their theme as they traversed this great nation. They humbly proclaim that only through God's direction, planning, strength and provision were they able to accomplish this Journey. Many times throughout the Journey, God changed their plans. Lessons were learned as they set "their" plans aside and acquiesced to God's superior plans.

They walked these 4,026 miles for you and for me. I couldn't walk that far—not even across California—but I can meet this multitude of people and get to know them through the encounters described in *Putting A Face On America*.

—Dave Hanush

# ACKNOWLEDGEMENTS

Marilyn Anacker and family

Atascadero Bible Church

Jeff and Shirley Beaumont

Edgar and Dorothy Black

Dellie and Charles Chapman

Gail and Jerry Chehock

Wayne and Maggie Clark

Kelli Clifford

Ernest and Bernice Cobb

Colechin family of England

Cassie and Gary Conner

Debbie Corona

Judi Cox

Carol Crouch

Roy and Charlotte Derksen

Diversified Marketing Network

Tony and Patti Dowden

Don and Adrienne Durfee

El Camino Bible Church

Pat and Daryl Fahey

FairWeather Four

James Feld

Charlie Ferrell and our Sunday School class

Earline Ferrell

Pastor Tom Ferrell

Anne Foster

Delbert Franz

Penny Fuentes

Chip Gruver

Happy Wanderers Hikers

Ron and Chris Harder

Coni Harris

Jim and Betsy Hawkins

Lynn Hixon's ladies' prayer group

Jeff and Penny Hoops

Betty Jackson

Russ James

Jahde Family

Steve and Susan King

John and Lois Kyle

Dick and Cathy Lampman

Meredith Lewis

Anthony and Doris Limbrick

Geoff Lyons

John Matson

Roger and Susan Matters

Valerie McCallum

Carol Mervyn

Bob and Bernice Miller

Doug and Deanna Millsap

Joan Moore

Floyd Newhall

Henrique and Vickie Ott

Luis Palau

Pathfinder Hikers

Dick and Mary Pearson

Jeff and Connee Potter and Reece

Ingeborg Rayham

Jean Ridley

Al and Marilyn Roberts

Gary and Melody Runstadler

Lois and Stan Salapka

Mike and Helen Salapka and children

Ronni Schoch

Steve Schumann

Robert & Lilian Schunneman

Robert and Tara Schaefer

Ron Smith

Nancy Steussi

Clayton Thomas

JoAn Thomas

Ike and Janice Tiner

Janice Uhler

Kathleen Uhler and family

Larry and Lori Willardson

YWCA Hiking group in San Jose

*To the inspiring people we met as we journeyed* . . . the churches we visited, and to myriads of others who gave so much of themselves, so we could meet the people of America. You kept us warm in the winter with your gifts of crocheted caps, scarves, socks, and gloves. You blessed us with gift certificates and care packages filled with goodies (especially chocolate). You helped with mechanical problems, and you sent money and gifts to make sure we had a special Christmas away from home. And most important, you prayed for us day after day after day. You were all wonderful and we love you all—or y'all (depending which part of the country you're from).

### To Our Artists

~   **Josh Beaumont**, thank you for your delightful illustrations in the introductory section of each state. I trust it will be a great help to our readers as they follow our route across America.

~   **Diane Cobb**, Lyn's niece, your illustrations set into the story are beautifully detailed, and fit in so nicely. How grateful I am that you allowed us to use your artistic talents.

*May God bless each and every one of you.*
**Lyn, Joni and Sam**

# INTRODUCTION

## *In the Beginning*

This is the tale of three women and their amazing journey. From May 12, 2003 to July 23, 2004, Lyn Hanush, Joni Balog, and Samantha (Sam) Hanush-Garrett (now married, she is Sam Gruver) walked from Blaine, Washington, in the northwest corner of the United States, to the southernmost point in Key West, Florida. Lasting 438 days (14 ½ months), the walk of 4,026.5 miles went through 15 states. We walked well over 8,000,000 steps, and we took more than 30,000 digital pictures.

Our walking adventure began as a dream over 50 years ago. When I was 11 years old, a friend and I talked about bicycling across America. Later the cycling dream changed to walking. At that young age it was just a dream, but I later realized it was a seed planted in my heart by God—a seed that would grow over time. Gradually that dream began to come into focus.

When I was around 40, my mother had a stroke and moved in with us. I would take her for long walks in her wheelchair. Over time our walks increased until we were going ten to fifteen miles at a time. I enjoyed the challenge that walking gave me, and I remembered my childhood dream.

In 1982 I hesitantly asked Dave what he would think about the possibility of my walking from Mexico to Oregon along the California coast. He responded that if I could get someone to walk with me it would be OK with him. My daughter, Alyce-Kay, and her future husband, Mike Garrett, both wanted to join me on this venture. On June 27, 1983, we began walking the California coast, finishing the distance of 1,037 miles on August 23. It was a beautiful experience.

I then began to plan other long distance walks. In 1984 I led my first San Jose to San Francisco walk. We walked fifty-six miles in four days, and finished by walking across the Golden Gate Bridge. This has been an annual walk now for more than 20 years, increasing to six days and approximately 100 miles.

In 1993 a hiking friend, Sue Dunaway, joined me to walk along the coast of Oregon and Washington to complete the walk from Mexico to Canada. We finished at the Peace Arch on the border between the United States and Canada, where ten years later the Great American Journey would begin. The Oregon-Washington walk, from June 21 to August 7, 1993, was a total of 773 miles.

Initial planning for our "Great American Journey" began in early 2001. Then came September 11, 2001, when terrorists crashed into the World Trade Center and the Pentagon, and Flight 93 went down in Pennsylvania. Right away, Dave and I knew this next walk had to be a walk of prayer for our nation. As we emphasized the urgent need for prayer, we began to get a little more interest from other people. Then one day a hiking friend, Joni Balog, expressed a desire to walk the full distance with me, but didn't know if she would be able to. We began to make this a matter of prayer.

Soon two others, JoAn Thomas from Hamilton, Ontario, Canada, and Anne Foster from Bear, Delaware, were considering becoming a part of the team. I asked Joni, JoAn, and Anne to prayerfully consider making a firm commitment to walk with me.

My granddaughter, Brenda, and friend, Marilyn, went with Joni and me to a quiet beach one day to talk. As we walked, Joni told me she was ready to commit to joining me for the Great American Journey. Together we knelt on the beach, with Marilyn and Brenda standing beside us, and prayed, committing ourselves to God for this Journey, and committing the Journey itself to God. Soon after this, JoAn and Anne both wrote that they would commit to starting the Journey, but weren't sure how long they would be able to participate.

We set our start date for May 12, 2003. Initial planning began by placing a yardstick across a map of the United States from the northwest corner to the southeast corner and drawing a line. Mileages and times in each state were calculated at an average of 15 miles a day, five days a week. The back road route would help us "Put A Face On America."

After I spoke at the Paso Robles Rotary Club, Jeff Hoops offered to donate a motor home to be used as our living quarters for the Journey. We also had a shuttle van. After being introduced to Judi Cox, I shared about our need for a driver for the shuttle van, and she offered to drive the first month for us.

On May 5, 2003 our team left California to drive to Blaine, Washington, where we would begin our Journey across America. The evening before we began, our team met for prayer.

*Dear Father, thank you for the privilege we have of participating on this Journey with You. Prepare the way for us, and may we be sensitive to Your leading each day. Give strength to our feet and legs, and wisdom to our minds. Fill us with Your love for this country, and may we be able to share that love with many people across this great land. Lord, we're excited about starting this Journey. Help us to step out tomorrow, and each day of this Journey, with much enthusiasm for the work You are giving us to do. And now we ask for a good night's rest so that we'll be ready for our big day tomorrow.*

**In Jesus' precious name,**
**Amen.**

# WASHINGTON STATE

## —Traversing the Cascades—

Began Walking in Washington ..............................................May 12, 2003

Finished Washington .......................................................June 30, 2003

Actual Days in State ........................................................ 50

Walking Days in State ...................................................... 31

Total Mileage for Washington and for the Journey to Date..............417.5

Capital.................................................................. Olympia

Admitted to Statehood .......................November 11, 1889 ~ the 42nd state

Population ................................................................. 5,894,121

Highest Point....................................................Mount Rainier ~ 14,410 feet

Lowest Point ...................................................... Pacific Coast ~ Sea Level

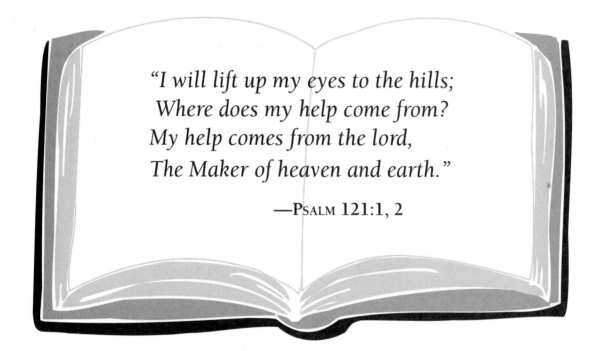

"*I will lift up my eyes to the hills;*
*Where does my help come from?*
*My help comes from the lord,*
*The Maker of heaven and earth.*"

—PSALM 121:1, 2

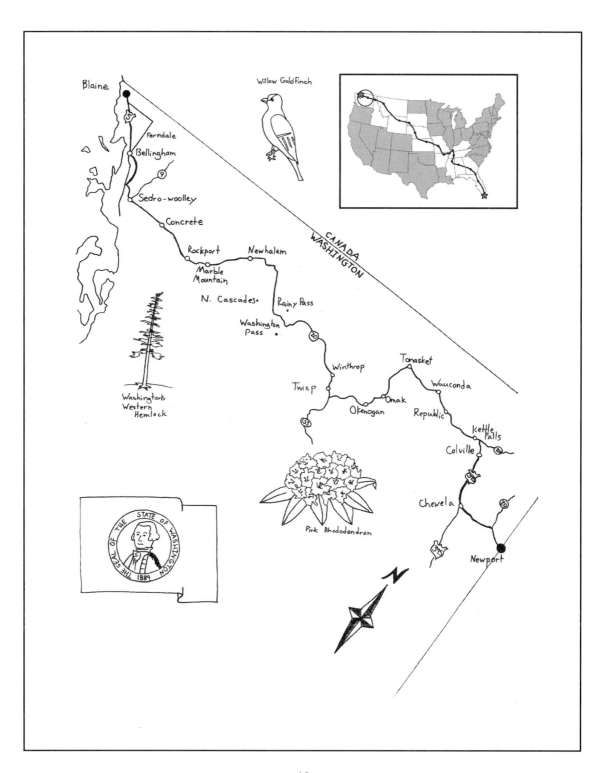

Blaine

Willow Goldfinch

Ferndale
Bellingham
9
Sedro-woolley
Concrete
Rockport     Newhalem
Marble
Mountain
N. Cascades•
Rainy Pass
Washington
Pass
20

CANADA
WASHINGTON

Tonasket
Winthrop        Wauconda
Twisp
Omak        Republic
Okenogan
Kettle
Falls
Colville

Washington's
Western
Hemlock

Chewela

Newport

THE SEAL OF THE STATE OF WASHINGTON
1889

Pink Rhododendron

*Chapter One*

# YOU'RE WALKING WHERE?

**Lyn**

Alligators, armadillos, manatees, rattlesnakes, pronghorn, bison, moose, elk, bears, badgers, Bengal tigers, and many other creatures. Over the next fourteen months we would see these and more up close and in abundance. But today was May 12, 2003, and we were just beginning our adventure. Besides the many animals there would be people of all sizes, shapes, and color. We were embarking on a Journey that would open our eyes and hearts to an America we had not known before. Soon we would see the faces of people in different states and regions. And these faces would be indelibly etched in our minds.

Walking across the border through the Peace Arch from Canada into the United States, we began the realization of my 50-year dream. Besides me, our team included Anne, JoAn, Judi, Joni and her dog, Cassie.

The long months of planning were over, and our Great American Journey had officially begun. Once through the Peace Arch, we stopped to take pictures, then called our homes to let family members know that the walk was now in progress.

Our route took us inland to the town of Custer where the local post office came into view. We stopped in at Toni's Tavern to use restrooms. Some of the locals were interested in what we were doing, and cheered us on after we shared about our Journey of prayer.

Continuing to the outskirts of Ferndale, it appeared that our road would wind around the town to get to our destination. Looking for a more direct route, we spotted a pathway to the south that looked promising. A young man, John, was working nearby on a railroad signal, so we asked him about the path.

As we explained what we were doing he responded with enthusiasm, "That path goes about half a mile to a ditch. There should be a plank crossing the ditch. This will take you to Malloy Road, which will take you to Main Street and on through the town."

We thanked him for his help, and he wished us well as we continued on.

Arriving at the ditch, we were surprised to see John standing there to help us cross and get us headed in the right direction. He was the first of many "angels" we would encounter in the months ahead.

## Joni

I saw Ferndale as a quaint town with old wooden homes and picturesque churches. Cute little shops lined the streets and enticed the tourists. It was a great day, with sunshine and scattered clouds as we worked our way slowly through the town and crossed the overpass to our motel. Our first day ended with a total of 16.8 miles. Now we were ready for a good night's rest.

Our feet crunched noisily on the small gravel path beside Bakerview Road as we entered Bellingham. Bright flowers bloomed amidst vines and shrubs along our route. A man working on phone lines saw us and asked how far we had walked and where we were going. When we told him we were walking across America, praying for the nation, he asked if we prayed for servicemen.

"Yes," we assured him, "we do."

His 23-year-old son, David, was in the army in Afghanistan, and he asked us to pray for him. This was the beginning of a long list of military personnel we would pray for as we crossed the nation.

## Lyn

On our third day out it began to rain as we walked on a narrow road heading south out of Bellingham. After walking a few miles my cell phone rang. It was Dave telling me that he and Russ, our son, were nearby with the 30-foot motor home that was to be our living quarters for the duration of the Journey. Soon they arrived and we all got in, marking in our minds where we had stopped walking. We went back to Bellingham to meet Judi where she was parked in the van.

After lunch we drove to Eagle's Nest RV Park at the edge of Concrete. This would be our campsite for the rest of May. We had been looking forward to having this thirty-foot motor home as our roving headquarters. The next day-and-a-half was spent settling into our new home, which we quickly dubbed the Castle.

There were many things to learn about the RV. Russ James of Atascadero, California had taught Dave how to handle this large vehicle. While Judi, JoAn and Anne took a day off for sightseeing, Dave passed on to me what he had learned, since I would be the one to drive. Dave and my son also taught Joni and me how to maintain it.

After a good practice session I drove 23 miles through a heavy downpour to Sedro Woolly. Peering through the rain, I saw a truck heading my direction. It looked to me as though we would collide. I screamed! Dave said, "Don't panic. The truck driver doesn't want to hit you any more than you want to hit him." He taught me how to be sure I was in my lane. In the months ahead I would be thankful about learning to drive in these less than desirable weather conditions, as it gave me confidence for driving in all kinds of weather across the nation.

Russ and Dave went to get the propane tank filled, which in itself was quite an experience. It took a while just to find where it was positioned on the underside of the vehicle. While it filled, a mobile RV repairman, Louie Goldner, came along. He promised to come to our campground Sunday afternoon to talk with us about repairs that needed to be done. Louie was a welcome help when he came that Sunday. In a hard rain we had already discovered a bad leak that soaked the closet, and we needed to learn about dumping the holding tanks. He helped us with these things and more, making the next months of our Journey much easier.

The next day Dave, Russ and his dog, Loki, had to say good-bye and start their drive back to California. They had driven up in the motor home and were returning in Joni's car. It was very hard for me to say good-bye and watch them drive down the road. I knew I wouldn't see Dave again until September, and we had never been apart that long. I also wasn't expecting to see Russ until I returned home, but, thankfully, he was to return to help us a couple more times. (For Russ' thoughts on this first portion of our Journey, see Appendix 1. Dave's thoughts are included in Appendix 7.)

Our days began to settle into a routine of breakfast, prayer time, loading the day's supplies into the van, and heading out to start walking. Judi met us with snacks, water, and whatever else we needed. She also did the shopping, prepared most of our lunches, found nice picnic spots, and transported us between these places. In the evening we returned to the Castle, where we had our dinner and time for sharing, journaling, and evening prayers. At some point during the day we each had personal time with our Bibles and notebooks as well.

One morning we woke up to find it had snowed in the night, leaving patches of snow on the ground. The surrounding mountains looked beautiful as they sparkled in the morning sun.

Sunday morning, May 18, we attended Concrete Community Bible Church. We were all wearing newly acquired matching shirts, which caused people to ask if we were some sort of group. When Pastor Rob Thomas found out what we were doing he asked us to share about our Journey. This was the first of many times we shared in churches across the nation. A soloist then sang the song she had selected before ever hearing of our trek, "Keep On Walking." (Coincidence or God-incidence?)

Most of the way through Washington we walked along Highway 20. Sedro Woolley had a lovely "Welcome" sign, and we stopped to take pictures. JoAn wanted hers from a different angle. She walked out to an island in the road and began to take the picture. As she did so, a policeman drove up, stopped, and put on his flashing red light. JoAn finished taking her picture, and crossed back in front of the police car to where we were standing. He turned off his light, then drove on. We all laughed as we realized that he had just nicely stopped all the traffic so JoAn could get her picture without cars driving in front of her camera. This was our first of many encounters with especially kind policemen across the nation.

During our stay in Concrete we had a call from a cousin. Gary and Melody and their two children, Angelica and Crystal, were in Sedro Woolley and wanted to spend some time with us.

It was very exciting to have our first guests in the Castle. We put on our team shirts, and they took photos to share at their church.

## Joni

While treading a footpath between Sedro Woolley and Concrete we spotted some trailside berries. As we wondered aloud what kind they were, a voice called out to us, "Those are salmonberries."

We conversed with our unseen friend through the hedge, learning that the berries were not yet ripe. His dog, Lady, pushed through the bushes to greet us as we told the man about our Journey across America. His shocked reaction was, "You gotta be kidding?!" We laughed and talked some more, then said good-bye and continued on our way.

Our trail wound through dense groves of pine, fir and aspen. Bridges crossed over meandering streams lined with ferns. The trail, often misty and rainy, looked predominantly green. There were lots of little farms along the way, with cows and horses, and gardens filled with azaleas and rhododendrons. Dogs cheered us along with their happy barking, while snow-topped peaks of the Cascades loomed in the distance. A man with his children stopped and pointed out a bird in the bushes, telling me it was a Red Breasted Sap Sucker. The pathway, hard-packed dirt and gravel, was easy walking. Cassie especially liked this path, as she could run freely. It worried her if our group didn't all stay together, and she sometimes ran back and forth trying to herd the others back into line.

This 23-mile trail eventually ended in the town of Concrete, where we were camping. A sign informed us: "Some of the richest deposits of limestone needed in the manufacture of cement are found in this area. The process: limestone, clay and water were mixed and baked in kilns to produce clinkers that were then pulverized into cement."

From here we began to climb on our way through the beautiful passes of the Cascade Mountains.

*Chapter Two*

# BREAKDOWNS AND REPAIRS,
# BLISTERS AND DUCT TAPE

---

### Lyn

Walking past Rockport we were attracted to a house with rock walls and chimney. Its owners, sisters Beth and Joyce, had lived there since the 1950s. In front stood a lamppost covered in small stones and topped with a mossy toadstool-shaped cover. Behind it were steps, which appeared to be large slabs of stone. Rock pillars held up a porch overhang attached to the house. Low walls of stone wrapped around the garden areas in front. Beth and Joyce were outside as we admired their home. They allowed us to take a picture of them in front of their place by the lamppost. They had seen us earlier and were quite curious to know what we were doing. While Joyce was talking with us, Beth went to get some water for Cassie, who drank her fill.

### Joni

Blisters! The scourge of hikers. Duct tape—the prescription for all maladies and insanities. Most people think of duct tape as a staple for every household repair job, but for blisters?

Cassie was a good walker, and loved splashing in lakes, creeks and rivers. I had a problem with blisters, so Lyn tried to take Cassie's leash in hope that would put less pressure on me. However, Cassie made it clear that she wanted only me to hold her leash. Anyone else would find themselves in a virtual tug o' war with Cassie. Eventually she let others take the leash, as long as they followed me rather than going in front. When Cassie got hot and tired she rode with Judi in the air-conditioned van.

In the town of Marblemount we spotted Clark's Skagit River Cabins with a small restaurant in front. On the lawn were rabbits running everywhere. They were so tame we could almost walk up and touch them. Thankfully Cassie was in the van at the time.

Across the street was a small wayside chapel, the "Chapel of the Wildwood," with space inside for one or two in each of six small pews. We sang "O Come All Ye Faithful," then prayed, giving thanks for the good day's walk.

Ten days into the walk I woke up feeling very sick, and my blistered feet were so painful I couldn't possibly stand on them. I insisted that the others go on without me so that I could rest for a few days until I could move comfortably. This was a very hard decision to make, but eventually I urged the others on so they wouldn't get behind schedule. Had I known then what delays were ahead of us, I wouldn't have been so insistent that they continue without me.

## Lyn

The rest of us walked that day in rain. We decided to eat lunch inside at Howie's Diner in Marblemount. After ordering our food and explaining to Howie what we were doing, he took our order in to be filled. A few minutes later he returned with his wife, Johannah. She asked a few questions, then told us our meal would be on the house. We gave her one of our cards, and she asked us all to sign our names on it—our first autograph signing!

Newhalem had a path winding through the area and back out to Highway 20. We enjoyed tumbling waterfalls, bubbly streams, views of the snow covered mountains ahead, and brightly colored flowers all around as we headed up through the Cascades.

After two days of rest Joni decided she was ready to try walking again. Anne suggested wrapping her feet with duct tape. She had learned this technique while hiking with another group in Florida. Joni put Vaseline on her sore and tender feet, then wrapped duct tape around them as a tough protective covering. This lubricating and wrapping would be a tactic we used often on our walk. Joni remarked, "I feel like a home repair job with all this duct tape wrapped around me."

As we walked through the scenic wonderland on our way up the mountain, Judi drove Lady Van Go, the name we gave our shuttle van, into the lower peaks of the Cascade Mountains. The engine overheated, and Judi waited for us at Diablo Lake Overlook with the hood up. A couple stood nearby looking at the scenery. We went to talk to the man, hoping he might have some ideas about what to do.

After introducing ourselves and explaining about our walk of prayer across America, we told them about the problem with Lady Van Go. Ken introduced himself and his wife, Gayle, then went to get a bottle of water from their car. While Judi went with Ken, Gayle asked us questions about our Journey. She told us they were Christians, and they really appreciated knowing we were praying for the country. When Judi and Ken finished with the van, they came back and we all held hands while Ken and Gayle prayed for our safety, our health, our vehicles, and for the prayers we would be praying for America.

Sunday, May 25, we attended Marblemount Assembly of God Church. We were introduced and had the opportunity to share with a few individuals after the service. They had a guest speaker from India, Samuel Mohanraj and his wife, Elizabeth. Samuel shared a great message, and Elizabeth sang a beautiful solo. Afterwards we went to lunch at the Eatery, where the owner, Tootsy, talked with us. The pastor and his wife, along with the Mohanraj's, came in while we were there, and we talked with them again.

We encountered our first deep snow at Rainy Pass, altitude 4,855 feet. From Newhalem three days earlier, at 509 feet, it had been quite a climb. The beauty at the top of the Pass was stunning.

Cassie walked across some ice, breaking through to the water flowing in a small drainage ditch along the road. We all laughed when she jumped back and looked quizzically at the ice, wondering what had happened.

The next day we took a day off from walking to move our Castle to the KOA in Winthrop. Here we took another day to get the overheating problem taken care of in Lady Van Go. Laurie, a staff member at the campground, lined up a mechanic for us. We took the van to Winthrop Auto where Dan was assigned to work on her. He put in a new thermostat while we explored this quaint western town. It gave us the opportunity to meet several people and get to know the town better.

After visiting a few shops, we were ready for some lunch at the River Road Café. Paula, the cook, and Caroline, the server, eagerly listened to our story as we sat on the rustic patio overlooking the tree-lined Methow River.

Later we stopped at a sports shop. Looking around, we spotted hiking sandals and decided to try some on. Rita, a clerk, helped us, as Joni, Anne and I each decided to buy a pair. Later I wished I had bought several pair of these extremely comfortable sandals. Hiking sandals of any kind were hard to find in most places.

Rita phoned the local newspaper and I talked with Carol, a reporter. I answered her questions about each of the walkers, the purpose of the walk, the timing, and the route.

A few days later as we were walking along the road, we noticed a man on a hillside taking pictures. We looked around to see what he was photographing. The scenery was all very pretty, so as we got closer we asked him if he was taking pictures of the scenery.

He said, "No, I'm taking pictures of you ladies." He then explained that he was the editor of the Methow Valley News. Carol had told him about our walk and he thought it was worth more than just a back page item. Our story ended up on the front page. This was our first news write-up of the trip.

As Judi drove up Rainy Pass she breathed a sigh of relief, believing that the overheating problem was now taken care of. Now continuing to Washington Pass at 5,477 feet, we felt dwarfed by the mountains on either side. The highway below curved in a huge circle, with the snow-covered mountains glistening all around. Under a vivid blue sky, the beauty of it all was breathtaking.

The steep walk down brought us into beautiful Upper Methow Valley, full of signs of spring. Young foals nursed while lively colts romped nearby. Mares grazed in the green pastures and watched their young. From time to time we saw deer running in the woods and meadows. Larkspur bloomed in the fields, and some gardens produced English poppies, iris, and dahlias.

On Sunday, June 1, we were in Winthrop and visited the Friendship Community Church. Pastor Allen Abbott asked us to share about our Journey. After the service we talked with many people and several gave us prayer requests. Preston and Laurie Hobart invited us to come out to the Prayer Center where they work. We would do this later.

After Winthrop we left Highway 20 to walk the east side of the Methow River on Castle Road. We enjoyed walking beside this wide river. Along this route we saw a number of interesting mailboxes made from old pieces of farm equipment. There was also an unusual silo with an old abandoned car nearby.

In a pen near the town of Twisp we spotted a large sow with five little piglets, which we promptly named "Breakfast, Lunch, Dinner, Bacon and Sausage."

Judi drove us into Twisp to eat lunch at the Antlers Tavern, which served a delicious meal. When she took us back to where we had stopped walking, we spotted some yellow-bellied marmots running in the field and watched them play for a while. Finally we walked out to Highway 20, our route for the next several weeks.

On June 3, Joni and I drove to Chewelah in eastern Washington where my sister lives. Samantha (Sam) Hanush-Garrett, my 15 year-old granddaughter, had arrived there the day before and was planning to hike with us the rest of the way. She was a home-schooled student and would certainly be getting a unique educational experience in the months ahead.

We headed back to Winthrop, where the others had enjoyed a free day of resting and exploring. They were sound asleep when we arrived at camp around midnight.

Our first day of walking with Sam was on the eastern side of Loup Loup Pass, and into the town of Okanogan. Sam hadn't had time to do much training, but we had to laugh as we realized she was in much better shape than we were. We had trouble keeping up with her.

Driving back over the Loup Loup Pass at 4,020 feet to Winthrop, Lady Van Go had begun overheating again, so the next day we went back to see Dan at Winthrop Auto. This time he put in a new radiator, while we did some more walking around the town. By now we knew quite a few people, and some recognized us from the news story or from church. Several gave us prayer requests, and we concluded it must have been in

God's plan for us to be back in town for repairs. We ate lunch at the Riverwalk Café again, then walked back to the Castle.

Anne drove Joni and me in her car to visit the Prayer Center that the others had seen a couple of days earlier, while we went to pick up Sam. What an incredible place this was—a retreat for people to just pray and meditate. The main prayer room had a lighted globe in the center of the floor—downstairs that same globe was in the center of the ceiling.

Preston, the Prayer Center director, put on a CD while we knelt beside that globe and recommitted ourselves to God for this Journey. The first song that played talked of God preparing the pathway ahead of us. Wow!

The next day we moved the Castle to Omak, finding a nice campsite at the fairgrounds. Being the driver of the RV, I had decided that we would only camp where I could drive the motor home into a pull-through space. Here we were at the third campground of the trip, and there were no pull-through spaces available. It was the only campground around, so we went for it. I looked it over, figured out my maneuvers, then backed into it with confidence.

One day while I sat in the Castle working on the computer, two motor homes pulled in on either side of ours. As they set up camp I overheard one man reading aloud the words on the side of our Castle: "Praying for America." Then he continued, "That thing's gonna need prayer to make it across America." A little later the couple on the other side joined their friends to sit in chairs between our two RV's. Once again I heard the same man announce in a loud voice to his friends, "Look at this, it's really gonna need prayer if they expect it to go across America!"

I decided it was time for me to go share with our new neighbors, and let them know what we were doing. Grabbing two of our information cards I opened the door and greeted them with a smile. Introducing myself, I explained our Journey. The man's wife and the other couple were quite interested and asked questions. But the one man just couldn't get past the thought of trying to get our old motor home across the United States. Still, we enjoyed the opportunity to share with these temporary neighbors.

A friend from California, Rosie, joined us in Omak for a few days. She brought care packages from friends and family, so we had a time of celebration as we sifted through the bags and boxes to see what was in them.

The next day we walked from Okanogan to Omak. Early in the day we saw a beautiful stone church off to the side, and detoured to take a look. A small lively lady saw us taking pictures and came to talk with us. She was the pastor, and had a ministry to the homeless in this old church. Several Sunday School rooms had been converted into small apartments that were now occupied by homeless people. They were just heading out with her to the Farmer's Market, but waited for Pastor Maggie to give us a tour of this historic building.

After walking the short distance into Omak, we packed some things into the van and headed east to Chewelah for the weekend. There were seven of us with our visitor from California. We were going to visit my two sisters. Lois and her husband Stan live in Chewelah, where Gail and her husband Jerry were visiting them. Lois and Stan's two children, with their spouses and children, all live on the same acreage appropriately named "Cozy Acres."

After spending the night we went to the Evangelical Free Church of Chewelah with them on Sunday, June 8. Lois introduced us and asked us to tell about the Journey. Afterward we spoke with members of the congregation, and some gave us prayer requests.

In the afternoon we all had lunch on the "Cozy Acres" hill, then stayed to visit and have Reece, my nephew, help us download pictures onto the computer. All too soon it was time to leave. Gail and Jerry were also leaving, taking Judi and JoAn with them to Spokane to catch their planes for home the next day. Rosie left at the same time. We were sad to see them leave, but grateful for the time we had them with us. (Judi's recollections are in Appendix 2. JoAn's are included in Appendix 9.)

## Joni

With Judi gone, I had a solution for a driver. Having missed a few days of walking already, I offered to drop the walkers off at the start each day, drive ahead while they began walking, park the van, and walk back with Cassie to meet them. Together we could walk on to the van and repeat the process. Lyn was against this idea at first, knowing that I had planned to walk the full route, but after much discussion I insisted that this was what needed to be done.

## Lyn

With a heavy heart I gave in to Joni's plan. It worked well, though my preference certainly would have been all of us walking together all the time.

Anne stayed with us another couple of days as we walked into the high desert area. This was our first day with Joni driving. The weather was great except for a strong wind. Certain now that our van troubles were behind us, we were ready to walk. Our legs felt strong and ready to be stretched, and Joni was even a bit excited about her new role in this Journey. As we walked past Riverside Joni pulled up beside us in the van. She told us she would go ahead to park and walk back to meet us. As she pulled away we noticed some coolant on the ground. Our hearts sank, we felt certain it was from Lady Van Go.

# Chapter Three

# HITCHHIKING IN ONE EASY LESSON

### Joni

We decided to walk to Riverside and stop for lunch. But as I was driving I noticed the van heating up again. Spotting a side road, I pulled off and parked behind a hill and raised the hood. Walking back I soon saw Anne, Lyn and Sam coming toward me. Once we met we walked to the van and I explained that the temperature gauge had suddenly shot way up.

As we all stood by the raised hood of the van a man drove up to see if he could help. He advised us to take it to the local Ford dealer. Their schedule was filled and they suggested we take it to the "Auto Doctor" in nearby Omak. We made an appointment with Nelda in the office to bring the van in the next day. She was very interested in our prayer walk.

The rest of the day we spent running errands and reorganizing our Castle. Anne was leaving in a couple of days, so she began packing things in her car, and we prepared the Castle for three people and a dog. A lot was accomplished, but we found it very discouraging to keep taking time off for van problems.

### Lyn

Early on the morning of June 10 we took the van in, and Nelda told us she had shared about our Journey with her prayer group the night before. Later that morning Nelda called to let us know they had used a pressure test and found the problem. It would take a seventeen-dollar part that they had to order. The part would be in the next morning, and they would call us as soon as it was ready.

We met some of our neighbors in the campground, Russ and Betty. They had their "kids," the "fur people" with them. Their four schnauzers "pray" with heads bowed and paws up. They also wave good-bye, roll over, give a high-five, and a few other tricks.

Russ and Betty invited us inside their RV to see what they had done to save propane. They bought an electric two-burner hot plate to use in place of the gas stove. It is flat, and just sits on top of the regular stove. When in camp the RV is always plugged into electricity, which is included in the camp fee.

Another suggestion was for the water heater. When it is fully heated turn the flame down to pilot only. The water will remain hot, and propane is not wasted. These ideas worked great for us. (When winter came, however, we found we needed to leave the gas flame up for the water heater, it just didn't keep it warm enough in the freezing temperatures we encountered.)

## Sam

I had shared about my Teen Mission experiences with a twelve-year old girl in the camp. She wanted to hear more about my time in Germany, Malawi, and Uganda. I was able to encourage this girl in her Christian faith and walk. Cool!

That evening we took Anne to dinner at the Breadline restaurant in Omak as she was leaving us the next day. It was a fun evening with great food, a delightful waiter, John, the friendly owner, Paula, and a co-worker, Annie. They had just read about us in the paper, and were very interested in our walk.

## Lyn

Early on the morning of June 11, Anne and I woke up and had our Bible times while Joni and Sam slept. Then Anne hugged me. I wanted to wake the others, but she refused to let me, and drove away heading home to Delaware. Anne hoped to return to walk with us another time, but it just didn't work out. She was a good walker, and a great companion. We would miss her. (For Anne's story see Appendix 3)

Nelda called to say the van was ready. We were surprised it was ready so soon, and we quickly dressed and walked over to get Lady Van Go. This was indeed the end of our overheating problems.

Often we go through life with the same problem coming back again and again. No matter how hard we try we can't seem to shake the difficulty, or find a solution to it. Like our van when we couldn't find the answer to the problem, we went from place to place seeking help. We tried a new thermostat and a new radiator, before finding someone with the right diagnostic tool who knew how to use it. The solution was simple, and it was the only answer. Once we knew what was wrong it was fixed with one little part.

Like our van, life has its difficulties. We go about our daily lives in search of a solution, a change. Are we willing to have God diagnose our problem, and help us with it? He makes it clear that He is our solution, and there is no other.

It was still early enough to get some walking in, so we headed out just after lunch and walked over 15 miles that afternoon.

## Joni

Walking the last two miles to Tonasket I saw a huge tent with a sign reading, "Gospel Meeting Revival." When Lyn and Sam arrived at the tent we talked with John, the evangelist who introduced us to Cameron, a speaker from Australia. They were enthusiastic about our Journey and invited us to come to the meeting that night, "and bring the dog with you," said John.

So we finished the day's walk and returned by 7:00 P.M. to attend the meeting. Cassie was so exhausted from the day's walk that she slept through the whole evening until the closing song. Then she sat bolt upright, and to my relief did not sing along.

As the three of us and Cassie began walking the next day from the top of Wauconda Pass down to Republic, I commented that it was such a beautiful day to walk I wished I didn't have to go back and get the van. I just wanted to walk all day. Lyn and Sam looked at each other and said, "Then do it." We were sure we could find someone in Republic who would take us back up to Lady Van Go. It was mostly downhill that day and so beautiful. We were happy to all walk together.

At 4:30 we walked into town. We had started that morning at 11:00 and had brought only snacks and water with us. Stopping at a store to ask about a good place to eat we were given several suggestions. We decided on Esther's Mexican Restaurant. Finding that the restaurant had outdoor seating we asked about taking Cassie to the patio to sit with us. They agreed, and we got seated in a nice little corner by ourselves.

After placing our order and explaining to the waitress what we were doing, we asked her if she knew of anyone who was going back over Wauconda Pass. She didn't, but suggested we make a sign and stand on a corner, assuring us we would get a ride. A lot of people were in town for Republic's Prospector's Day celebration.

Our waitress brought us marking pens, and we wrote on a piece of cardboard, "Need ride to Wauconda." When we left the restaurant we headed for a major turn in the road and held up our sign.

I decided that Lyn and Sam could hitch a ride easier if Cassie and I were not there, so I sat on a bench not far away. Within minutes they had their ride. Maybe this hitchhiking business was easier than we thought it would be. It was a man driving a small jeep. I took a photo of the car as the other two got in, "just in case."

Sam climbed over camping gear and squeezed in the back, Lyn got in the front and off they went. It took only about thirty-five minutes and they were back with Lady Van Go. They told me the man's name was Jess Story. Living up to his name he told them stories all the way up the mountain pass. They learned he lived in Grand Coulee and was on a camping trip. We were all very grateful for this good Samaritan who was willing to pick up "two strange hitchhikers."

## Lyn

In Omak we attended Cornerstone Community Free Methodist Church. It was June 15 and the pastor had just returned from Russia and was not ready to preach that Sunday. Rene Scott, the Children's Minister, gave a very good message in his place.

She spoke of her vision for the children and what she hoped to achieve. Rene brought up the idea that each of us have been given a vision, and that we need to follow through to bring that vision to reality.

That afternoon we went to McGoo's Café for lunch in Omak. The food was good, and Sam had a chance to talk with our waitress about our walk. She gave Sam a prayer request that we added to our prayer book. We never knew who God might bring into our lives to talk with and listen to, but our goal was to always be ready when those times came. Sam had the opportunity here to be sensitive to the needs of this young woman, and she was ready.

We moved the Castle to a place at the Colville fairgrounds with hook-ups for everything but dumping. However, we were able to get a spot close enough to the dump station that by buying a longer dump hose dubbed "Slinky," we could pull Slinky over to dump at anytime without having to move the RV.

On Tuesday the sliding door of the van wouldn't open, so we had to find a locksmith to get it repaired. We walked around Colville and met a lot of wonderful people. While talking to the owner of a book store we found out she had a brother who has a restaurant near my home in Paso Robles, California—small world. As we visited the shops in town many expressed their gratitude for our prayers.

There were so many delays. If the van wasn't overheating, we were having door or window problems. It seemed there was always something. A lot of time had gone into planning every detail of this Journey. There was no time for the inconvenience of vehicle breakdowns. Then one day it dawned on us—each time we had a delay God brought us into contact with someone who gave us a prayer request or told us they were praying for us, or encouraged us in some way. We always learned some lesson on those days of waiting. "In his heart a man plans his course, but the LORD determines his steps" (Prov. 16:9).

Finally we got back to Republic, took some pictures of this very picturesque town and stopped in at the Town Hall to see if the mayor was in. We met the deputy clerk, Margo Sattler, and a council member, Linda Hall, but the mayor wasn't in. Still we passed on greetings from Mayor Frank Mecham of Paso Robles.

We walked over Sherman Pass at 5,575 feet. Walking through a seven-mile long area that had been destroyed by fire, we learned that it had been started by a lightning strike in 1998. Over 20,056 acres of White Mountain had been burned. The stark barren trees stood as a memorial to that awesome firestorm.

Many logging trucks went by us every day. Truck drivers often waved as they passed. One stopped and asked what we were doing. He had seen us walking for weeks and had to know what it was all about.

It was raining and very windy as we came into Kettle Falls. There was a big wonderful bridge crossing over the Columbia River into the town, and we took lots of pictures. At this point we were wearing ninety-nine cent ponchos—you know, the bright colored disposable ones? The wind was blowing so hard that we looked like colorful balloons bobbing across the bridge. That made us laugh, and we had to get pictures in our wind-tossed ponchos.

There is a Historical Museum in Kettle Falls along our walk route, so we stopped there to take a look. This was a nice break from the weather, and by the time we left the rain had stopped.

Small stones had peppered Lady Van Go's windshield and a crack was spreading across it. Our insurance company gave me the name of a local repairman and we called him to check it out. Later John and his wife Lynn came to the campground to get the van to replace the windshield. We asked them about a church, and they invited us to join them at the Colville Free Methodist Church on Sunday, June 22.

When we arrived John and Lynn introduced us to Pastor Greg Knox who asked us to write down our prayer needs for the Journey and put these requests in the offering. They had a prayer time during the service when all who wanted prayer came forward to kneel at the altar. We were asked to come forward at this time as well. Others from the congregation came up and prayed, then the pastor went down the row praying for each one of us.

We will never forget his beautiful prayer that revival would sweep across this land, beginning in the northwest and blowing across the nation, and that our prayers would be a real part of this revival.

It was a very humbling and beautiful experience. That Sunday was a tremendous highlight of our Journey, and one we thought about often in the days ahead.

There was a baby dedication that Sunday as well. Pastor Greg asked the congregation to pray for Larissa in the years ahead whenever she came to mind. As part of the congregation that day, we agreed to pray for her as well. When we returned to our Castle we wrote Larissa's name down in our prayer request book and have continued to pray for her regularly. (In the summer of 2006 my husband and I had the privilege of attending a service at this church again. We made it a point to meet three-year old Larissa, and what a joy that was. She is full of life, and her parents told us that both she and they need lots of prayer. We also met her big brother who is a big help in running after Larissa.)

Pastor Greg talked in his sermon about how God wants to use each of us in an incredible way. He asked those of us in the congregation to make ourselves available for His use in any way He chooses. It was certainly our desire that God would use us on this Journey according to His plan.

Colville was our next community to walk through. Here we left Highway 20 to walk on Highway 395 through Chewelah, where my sister and family live. From there we would be heading over the Flowery Trail for our final days in the state of Washington.

As we walked through Colville, Diane and Maggie, friends of my sister joined us for lunch at a restaurant, then walked through the town with us as we prayed for the community.

The Flowery Trail Road was under major construction with blasting taking place during the week. We had talked with the highway department and came to an agreement about the best way for us to work that part of our route. Bypassing the construction area for now we made plans to return on Saturday to walk over the pass when the blasting was on hold.

Driving around to the east side of Flowery Pass to continue walking I suddenly screeched to a stop. "Sorry," I said to the others as we all gawked ahead at the moose darting across the road in front of us. What a surprise! None of us had thought about the possibility of encountering a moose. We had thought about bears and other smaller wildlife, but moose—never! That added some real excitement to our day.

That Saturday my sister, Lois, and Maggie drove up to join us as we returned to walk over Flowery Trail Road on the construction portion we'd had to skip earlier. We were able to park a car at each end of our route so that the five of us, and Cassie, could all walk the full day together. It was a great time of walking, with no traffic or construction for the day. At the end of the walk Diane joined the five of us for a meal at a Chewelah restaurant. It was fun to spend time visiting with these ladies, especially since it would be the last time Lois and I would be together for more than a year.

## Joni

The next week we drove to about four miles outside of Usk to start our hike. It was very hot again. Cassie refused to walk and I knew she was not feeling good. I left her in the van under a tree with the windows open and walked to meet Lyn and Sam. We walked across the bridge over the Pend Orielle River (pronounced Ponderay) and saw some pylons in the water. A man at the store told us that from the 1920s to the 1950s there was a wood mill operating in Usk. The pylons used to keep the logs separated before going into the mill.

Sitting there on one of the pylons was a Bald Eagle. Martins darted over the water from their nests under the bridge, so we stayed quite awhile trying to get a good photo of these birds.

The town of Usk, population 108, consisted of a post office, a store, a bar, a few houses, and a wooden "mall" the size of a mid-size barn. The sign on top of the "Usk Mall" proclaimed "Laundromat, Taxidermist, Video rentals, Notary Public."

We then continued on the Le Clerc Road, beside the Pend Oreille River. I drove ahead to a shady spot near the Skookum Grange and Community Center. Sitting down on one of the wooden seats out front, I waited for Lyn and Sam.

## Lyn

Finally we were finishing the state of Washington. On June 30 we walked through the border town of Newport. Perhaps you will enjoy their Historical marker.

---

The town began as Newport, Idaho, in 1889 when Mike Kelly erected a log store building on the bank of the Pend Oreille River at a point south of the present Old Town bridge. In 1890 a post office was added to Kelly's store, and mail was brought in by team and buckboard from Rathdrum, Idaho, by way of Blanchard. The site of Newport, Idaho was the center of commerce, with thirteen steamboats conducting commerce on the river.

In 1892 the Great Northern Railroad built a line through Newport, a boon to homesteaders who could more easily access the lands of the Pend Oreille Valley. The first depot, a simple boxcar, burnt down in 1894. A new depot site was selected three blocks across the state line in Washington. As rail business grew the riverboat businesses began to wane. Mike Kelly and his brother Tom were the first to move their stores along with the post office closer to the railway depot. Others followed and the town became Newport, Washington. The remaining town in Idaho became known as Old Town.

---

We stopped at City Hall to see if the mayor was in, but he wasn't. Continuing on to the Chamber of Commerce Visitor's Center, we talked with Diane Gerking, the office manager, and Francis Olson, a volunteer at the Chamber and a former mayor of Newport, from 1982 to 1990. Francis called the present mayor, Fred Anderson, and he bicycled over to greet us. We passed on our greetings from Paso Robles Mayor Frank

Mecham, chatted with the three of them, and took pictures together. Then we said good-bye and headed on our way.

Now we walked the final steps across the Pend Oreille River and into Idaho. (Pend Oreille is French for ear pendant. The Calispel [sic] Indians of this area wore earrings back when the French were here, and thus the name Pend Oreille.) Our first state was finished—only fourteen to go! It was time for a little celebration! So far, we had walked a total of 417.5 miles, taking two weeks longer than originally planned because of the many repairs needed on Lady Van Go.

The next day we took off to just relax and watch some DVD's we'd rented for the occasion. We had not had a day off, except for repairs, and were happy to just sit and relax for a day. We decided then and there that we would celebrate the end of each state with a day off, but in reality this was the only time we did so.

In a few days we would be celebrating the Fourth of July with some wonderful people, and watching fireworks from the banks of the Pend Oreille River.

# IDAHO

## —Special Provision—

Began Walking in Idaho ...........................................................*July 1, 2003*

Finished Idaho ........................................................................*July 8, 2003*

Actual Days in State ....................................................................... 8

Walking Days in State ................................................................... 5

Total Mileage for Idaho ............................................................*63.9*

Total Journey Mileage to Date ..................................................*481.4*

Capital .................................................................................... *Boise*

Admitted to statehood ...................................*July 3, 1890 ~ the 43rd State*

Population ......................................................................... *1,293,953*

Highest Point .............................................................. *Borah ~ 12,662 feet*

Lowest Point ......................................... *Snake River at Lewiston ~ 770 feet*

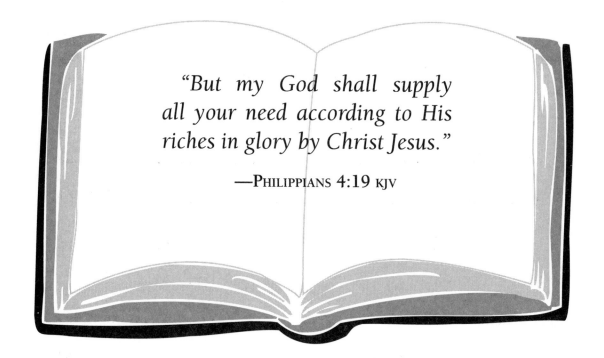

*"But my God shall supply all your need according to His riches in glory by Christ Jesus."*

—PHILIPPIANS 4:19 KJV

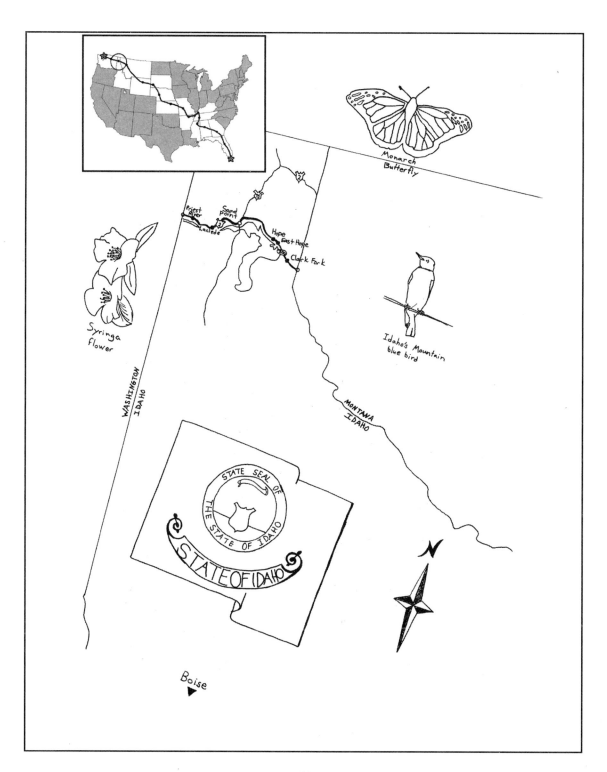

Monarch
Butterfly

Pojert
River
Sand
point
Laclede
Hope
East Hope
Clark Fork

Syringa
flower

Idaho's Mountain
blue bird

WASHINGTON
IDAHO

MONTANA
IDAHO

STATE SEAL OF
THE STATE OF IDAHO
STATE OF IDAHO

N

Boise

# Chapter Four

# MOVING BEYOND HOPE

### Joni

As we entered Idaho I spotted the Pend Orielle Veterinary Clinic. Cassie had been having troubles with her stomach. She was listless and not eating much, so I needed to get her to a veterinarian as soon as possible. Once they checked her over, and prescribed some special food and medication, she was soon on her way to recovery. We all were relieved and happy.

### Lyn

Our first Sunday in Idaho was different from anything we had yet experienced. First, a little background. For the past few days we had been quite concerned about our finances for the trip. The amount we were each putting in would not be enough to fund all our expenses, especially considering repair bills and other unknowns that kept coming up. On Saturday we had a lengthy discussion about this subject. Finally we realized we needed to turn it over to God in prayer.

Sunday morning we drove off in search of the church we had picked, "House of the Lord." Heading down a road I thought was the right one, we saw a sign for "House of Prayer." As I drove up, we realized it wasn't the church we were looking for. I began to turn around when the others said, "They're motioning us to come in." We had been spotted and they were urging us in, so we made a quick decision to stay.

This church was up in the hills above Old Town near Priest River Road. It was a wooden building that they were fixing up. Two old couches, a collection of chairs in a semi-circle, and a wooden pulpit made up the furnishings inside the church. A beautiful picture of Christ hung on a wall.

The congregation of twelve welcomed us in, and listened to the story of our Journey across America to pray for the nation. They burst into applause and praise to God. The service consisted of singing, interspersed with Scripture reading and praise, as we sat in a circle. We were truly humbled when Pastor Deborah asked if it would be OK for her to anoint our heads and feet while Pastor Dennis and others prayed over us. We gladly accepted. It was an incredible experience.

## Sam

Later Pastor Dennis prayed that God would begin a revival in our nation, beginning in the northwest and working its way across the nation as we walked. We shared about the pastor of the previous Sunday praying the same thing over us. It was really awesome.

Now Grumman (my name for Lyn) shared about our theme verse being from Micah 4:5. "All nations may walk in the name of their gods; we will walk in the name of the LORD our God forever and ever." She shared that while people from many nations have brought their gods here and are worshiping them, it is our goal to walk in the name of our God across this land and share His love with all we meet. Next we all held hands and had a prayer time together. We had been in this service for almost four hours.

Following this we were invited to stay and eat a meal with them. They were very friendly, and we felt like we had stepped back in history to the time when the disciples gathered in homes to pray, sing, worship and eat together. At some point during the day Pastor Dennis felt God leading him to put a basket out to collect a love offering for our Journey. We were overwhelmed with gratitude.

Joni expressed her concern about Cassie not feeling well, and they encouraged her to bring Cassie inside. As she brought her in, Pastor Dennis said, "That's who I have been praying for, Cassie!" God had laid it on his heart to pray for someone with stomach problems. It wasn't until he saw Cassie that he realized it was a dog, rather than a person he was praying for.

When we were back at our Castle talking about the incredible day we'd had, we knew God had heard our prayers of the night before. While we didn't know how all our expenses would be met, God had it all under control. We only had to trust Him with our needs.

## Lyn

At last we began walking in Idaho, our second state on this fifteen state Journey. One of the first things we saw was a sign that announced "Interstate Trucks Secure Trip Permits—Muzzy Fast Stop." We saw this sign several times, and always wondered who and where was Muzzy. We never found him, but we were sure the truckers all knew where he was. Our route through Idaho was on Federal Highway 2 to Sandpoint, then on State Route 200 to the border of Montana.

The first town we came to was Old Town, with a population of 190. Most towns in Washington had not had the population on their signs, so we were happy to see the numbers here. Our prayers for the communities were often said as we came to the town sign, and it was nice to have an idea of how many people we were praying for.

Another thing we had begun doing before we left Washington was to wave to all the people driving toward us, and with each wave went a prayer. Our prayer was for their safety on the roads and that they would be blessed with a personal relationship with God.

The Albeni Falls Dam had a nice museum and visitor's center. It was in a beautifully wooded area on the south side of the road. We didn't spend a lot of time there, since we were anxious to get through Idaho.

Priest River was our next "large" town with a population of 1,754. This seemed really small, considering that the three of us had all lived in San Jose, California. While Joni still lived in San Jose, now Sam and I both lived in communities with populations of about 25,000. In our minds that number was small, but over the months ahead, we began to see that towns with one thousand or more were large. Priest River was a nice town with old style buildings.

Suzi of the Priest River Times had asked us to stop by the office when we got into town so she could interview us. Earlier she had taken pictures as we walked. After our interview we asked if anyone was heading back to Newport, where we had left our van. Suzi checked around, and a few minutes later the manager of the paper, Teri, came out and said she was going to Newport. I rode back with her while Sam, Joni, and Cassie waited at the park. Teri works on a project with the Chamber of Commerce, where she puts together backpacks full of things for small children who have been rescued from drug busts. These children sometimes have nothing, so the packs provide clothing, a blanket and other small items.

By the time I drove back to get the others, it was early afternoon, and we needed to eat some lunch. We stopped in at the "Joodle Bug" in Priest River and ordered sandwiches and ice cream sodas.

After lunch we arrived at the Chamber of Commerce just as a lady was going in. Following her in, we asked if they had any pins for the city, since we were collecting these for our hats. They didn't have any for Priest River, but they did have Idaho pins. We took these and left. The lady followed us out and locked the door. Only then did we realize they were not open, and that we'd just happened by as she was stopping in to get something she had forgotten. She said nothing and was very kind to us.

We walked beside the river for a while, then between some rocky outcroppings. Here Joni and I each found an interesting rock to add to our collections. We planned to collect at least one rock from each state to include in our backyard landscaping at home. Later, when Joni had driven ahead, Sam and I saw a duck with about fifteen young ducklings. They scurried along as though we were chasing them. The mother duck kept trying to sidetrack us by flying away. We stopped to take a few pictures, and as we did one of the little ones ran up to me and looked up as if to say, "Are you my mother?"

We were staying at the River Country Motel and RV Park, next to the Mangy Moose. Both were very nice campgrounds. A couple of men staying at the Mangy Moose had come over to visit with us a time or two after finding out what we were doing. One told us he had been thinking a lot lately about getting back into a church. We told him we would be praying for him.

The owners of our camp, Al and Karolyn, had been very nice to us, and we stopped to talk with them frequently. As we were driving out one day, we saw Al and Karolyn working on their paddlewheel boat, the "SS Puff'n." This was set up in front of the camp away from the water. They were fixing it up to use as a special room for motel customers, and invited us in to see how it looked. We saw that they had put a lot of work into making it very authentic. Al said they wanted to be sure to get some pictures of us to put into their scrapbook, so we arranged to do that the next morning.

Joni became somewhat of a team ambassador, since she couldn't always walk with us these days. Sometimes she drove to small towns on side roads to find out about the area. Other times she stopped at stores, libraries, city offices, or visitor centers to get information for us.

As Sam and I walked through the town of Laclede, past the Klondike Café one day, we heard a voice calling to us. We looked around and saw a man on top of the Klondike. He asked if we were the ladies walking across America. It seems Joni had been at the city offices in Priest River and told the clerk, Mitzi, about our Journey. Mitzi told Joni to make sure we all came to the Fourth of July picnic, and also stop to meet Bruno at the Klondike Café. They weren't open when we walked past, but Mitzi had told Bruno about us, and he spotted us from where he was working on the roof and asked about our walk. He also invited us to the July Fourth celebration.

During our time in Idaho, Joni found some great places for us to enjoy our lunch. Frequently we drove to a place by the river or the lake and set up our folding canvas chairs to relax in while we ate. Most of the time for the next several months, we ate crackers with cheese or peanut butter or canned pink salmon for lunch. This was simple to prepare, simple to pack up, and we all enjoyed it. We figured we at least had a little more variety than the Israelites had when they ate manna in the wilderness day after day. In fact, we started calling lunchtime our "manna break."

As we approached the small town of Dover, Joni and Cassie met us and led us to an asphalt bicycle trail we could walk on right into Sandpoint. The highway we had been on was pretty busy, so this was a great relief. Joni and Cassie walked with us for a while, then left Cassie with us while she went back to get the van to meet us at Sandpoint. Cassie was OK with us once Joni was out of sight.

On July Fourth we spent some time with Al and Karolyn and another couple, Ben and Betty, taking pictures. Then we drove to Sandpoint, a town of 6,835 people, to begin walking. When we arrived we discovered that their Fourth of July parade had just finished. (A few weeks later we learned that a friend, Cathy Lampman, from California, had been at that parade. We were all disappointed we hadn't known and been able to get together.)

We walked around Sandpoint and looked in several shops searching for our Idaho souvenirs. Joni was collecting Italian charms for her bracelet. I was collecting earrings from each state.

We walked beside the Pack River for a while, where we saw herons and a variety of other critters. After a while we quit for the day so we could get back to the Klondike for the Fourth of July activities. Serving us extra amounts of food they said, "You need lots of energy."

They had us stand to be introduced to the crowd. Several came over to talk with us while we ate. We stayed for an hour or two, then headed back to camp to take care of our evening duties before dark. As it began to get dark we joined the other campers by the river to watch the fireworks on the island. It was a beautiful day and a fun evening.

On Highway 200 a bridge has been built over the edge of the Pend Oreille to bypass the towns of Hope and East Hope. We chose to get off the main highway and walk through these little communities.

The towns of Hope (population 79) and East Hope (population 200) may be small in size, but they are rich in history. We learned that David Thompson founded the town in 1809, though the Kalispel Indians had occupied the area for a long time. The Kullyspell House was the first structure, and was a meeting place for Indians of various tribes once a year. The "Mary Moody" was the first steamboat on the lake in 1866, and the railroad began construction there in 1881. Highland House, a Northern Pacific Railroad Hotel, was built around this time, and later East Hope Hotel was built to house twenty-five mill workers.

We continued walking and saw a sign for "Beyond Hope" RV Park just a mile-and-a-half off the main road. Soon after this we arrived at the Clark Fork Drift Yard where large booms divert floating debris from the Clark River and keep it from entering Lake Pend Oreille. People are welcome to collect any of the driftwood they want.

Our last Sunday in Idaho we attended a small white chapel with a steeple and a cross on the top. The Community Church of Laclede was close to where we attended the

July Fourth picnic. In many ways it reminded me of the church I grew up in at Visalia, California. We were introduced as visitors and a few people talked with us afterwards. Some had seen us walking during the week.

On Tuesday, July 8, we walked the last twelve miles of Idaho. The town of Clark Fork was on our route and was home to about five hundred and thirty citizens. A beautiful stone slab sign welcoming us to Clark Fork was erected at each end of town. The signs were the work of Anthony Trunnell as an Eagle Scout project in 2001. At the Montana sign we stopped to take pictures entering one state and leaving the other. We now had just thirteen states to go.

# MONTANA

## —The Big Sky and the Rockies—

Began Walking in Montana..................................................... July 8, 2003

Finished Montana ....................................................... September 9, 2003

Actual Days in State.................................................................64

Walking Days in State...............................................................47

Total Mileage for Montana....................................................651.1

Total Journey Mileage to Date..............................................1,132.5

Capital ..............................................................................Helena

Admitted to Statehood.............................. November 8, 1889 ~ the 41st State

Population.........................................................................902,195

Highest Point........................................ Granite Peak ~ 12,799 feet

Lowest Point.........................................Kootenai River ~ 1,800 feet

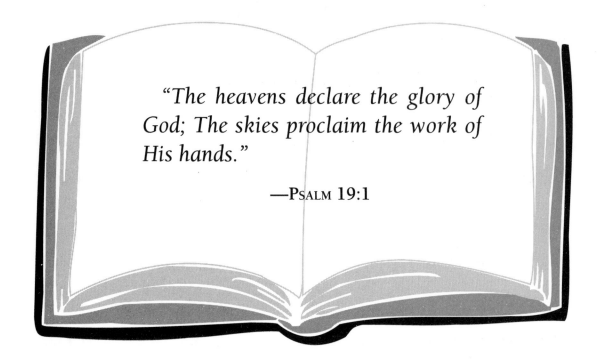

"*The heavens declare the glory of God; The skies proclaim the work of His hands.*"

—PSALM 19:1

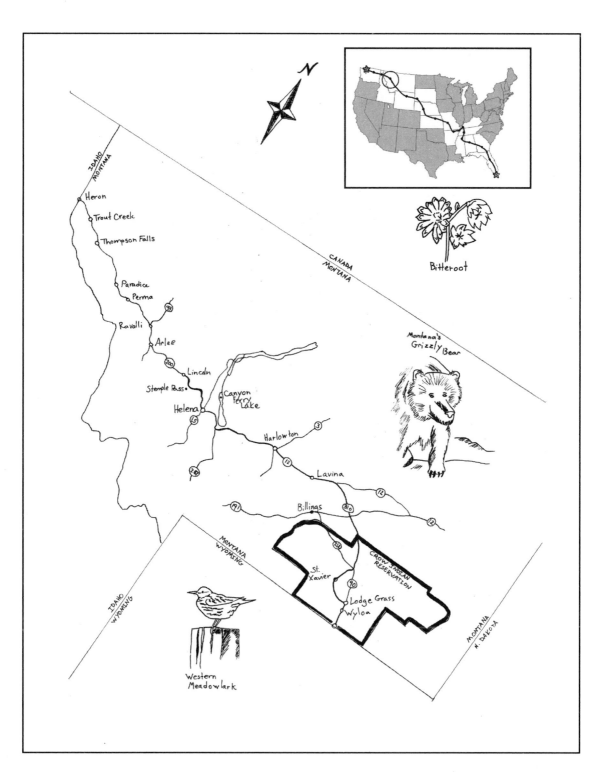

Heron
Trout Creek
Thompson Falls
Paradice
Perma
Ravalli
Arlee
Lincoln
Stemple Pass
Helena
Canyon Ferry Lake
Harlowton
Lavina
Billings
St. Xavier
Lodge Grass
Wyloa

IDAHO
MONTANA

CANADA
MONTANA

MONTANA
WYOMING

IDAHO
WYOMING

MONTANA
N. DAKOTA

CROW INDIAN RESERVATION

Bitteroot

Montana's Grizzly Bear

Western Meadowlark

# Chapter Five

# FACE TO FACE WITH A BEAR
# AND TWO TIGERS

## Sam

The sudden splash of water startled me as it ran down my face, arms, and legs. I spun around to find Grumman and Joni holding empty gallon water jugs. We all laughed. We had finished Montana! It had been a long journey through the large and beautiful state whose people were so diverse, each group interesting in its own way. The experiences of our 64 days in Montana had taught me a great lesson on not judging other people.

Come with us as we go back to the beginning of Montana and hear the stories of our walk through this great state. There was plenty of sunshine and a canopy of blue sky above us. Our path for the first few weeks in Montana was on State Route 200. We looked forward to lots of time in this state, and to its vast expanses. The Clark Fork River bounced along beside us for many days, and we were fully enjoying the freedom of being out on the road.

This was the third state we walked through and was, by far, the most rewarding. Our first Montana campground at Thompson Falls was in beautiful country surrounded by the Lolo National Forest. It was the beginning of many delightful experiences.

Our first encounter with the people of Montana came only ten miles into the state. We stopped in front of a lonely house on a rural highway to take pictures of life size wooden bears in the yard. Suddenly, a voice in the bushes said, "Would you like to see some real bears?!"

Startled, we said, "We'd love to." As Barbara opened her front door for us, we saw she was in a wheelchair. She explained to us that years ago she had lost the use of her legs.

We discovered we had entered a private wild animal rescue service. What a great assortment of wild animals: tigers who slept on her bed, a beautiful baby deer just getting his antlers, and an obese mountain lion who, when petted, purred like a giant kitten! In her yard were many large cages, where we met her friends like the black bear, who had been in captivity in a zoo for so long he would not last in the wild. There were peacocks, llamas, goats, chickens, tigers, deer, bobcats, and many others. We were amazed at how friendly and hospitable she was, and we all enjoyed watching her wheeling herself around the obstacles in the yard with great ease.

## Lyn

We were delighted at the sight of two large Bengal tigers, named Mork and Mindy. They paced inside a large cage and paused near the front, as Barbara reached inside to give them a pat or two.

With Cassie safely contained on the front porch, Barbara gave us a tour of her large home, where we saw a variety of animals she and her husband, Gene, had rescued. Shasta, the overweight mountain lion, purred noisily as we approached her in the main room. Barbara told us Shasta was on a diet. The bedroom had a bed big enough to accommodate Mork and Mindy, along with Barbara and Gene, as they watched television together each evening. Outside, Spirit and Sabrina, the bobcats, watched as we neared their enclosure. Sabrina rubbed her cheek against Sam's cheek through the chain link fencing, then reached out with her furry paws to hug Sam. The shaggy llama was named Mr. Whiskers, and we christened a long-haired goat with the name of Moses. Taz, the black bear, stood on his hind legs while we took turns feeding him chocolate puffs. Many of the animals come freely into the house and sleep on the beds, or sit in the rocking chairs, and roam around the rooms.

Along with the living animals, their home is filled with a variety of stuffed animals. We learned that they used to do a lot of hunting, but have now dedicated themselves to rescuing animals instead of killing them.

As we talked, Gene pointed outside and said, "A wild bear has just walked into the back yard, if you'd like to see it."

Barbara showed us to a room where we could safely watch through the window, while she took some bread out to feed him. We were told that they have cared for many injured bears in the area, then released them back into the surrounding forests when they were well. Now many of these bears come back regularly to enjoy the day-old bread obtained from local stores. Sometimes several bears come at once, and if they get into a fight over the tasty morsels, the one who started the fight is sent to the shed for "time-out." Picturing a bear sulking in a chair in the woodshed made us laugh in delight. As we prepared to leave, Barbara told us she has never had to have one stitch because of an injury caused by an animal. We were amazed at how adept she was at caring for these animals from her wheelchair.

## Joni

The weather was a sweltering 110 degrees for several days. In an effort to avoid the hottest part of the day, we began getting up and out by 6:00 A.M., and sometimes even as early as 4:30 or 5:00. These early mornings were still cool enough to wear a light sweater. By mid-morning it was very warm, and we wore sleeveless shirts and shorts as we hiked along. We were thoroughly enjoying our Journey with its day-to-day encounters.

As Sam and Lyn plodded along, I drove across a one lane bridge spanning the Clark Fork River, and on into the tiny town of Heron about two miles south of our route. There was a general store in the midst of beautiful scenery.

This became a pattern, for me to drive into small communities that were just off our route. I enjoyed talking with people in these areas, and often had interesting experiences to share with Lyn and Sam when I returned to meet them.

## Lyn

Walking into Thompson Falls under a cloudless sky and a hot sun, we were stopped by a young woman as she pulled up beside us in her car. In response to her questions, we told her we were walking across America, praying for the nation. She exclaimed, with tears in her eyes, that she was overwhelmed we would do such a thing for our country.

Continuing on through the town, I wished I had asked the young lady if she had any special prayer requests. She was gone, so there was really nothing I could do about it. Still, it bothered me that I hadn't asked her.

Thompson Falls had lots of cute little shops, and we took the time to explore some of these. Then we found a nice little restaurant where we could get some lunch. With the hot mid-day temperatures, we took a break and went to the library to check our e-mail. Joni took Cassie back to the Castle to rest, while Sam and I continued at the library computers. When Joni and Cassie came to get us we all went for ice cream. As we walked to the van we saw the young lady we had seen earlier in the day walking our way. I immediately went over to talk with her.

I told her that since we met her this morning, I wished I had asked if she had any special requests that she would like us to be praying for. She began to tell me about her mother's illness, then finally got to the core of her need when she told me about the

55

situation of her son on visits with his dad, and how difficult it was when he returned from those visits. I sat with her at a picnic table under the shade of a huge tree and talked. Taking her hand and praying, I assured her we would enter this information in our book to pray for her throughout the Journey. We were so thankful God brought her back across our path. I learned a valuable lesson—to listen closely when people talk, and when I sense they need prayer to follow through right then.

Back at our Castle that evening we had a call from Gary and Melody, the cousins who had visited us in Concrete, Washington. They were in Thompson Falls and wanted to know if it would be OK for them to come out to our campground. We had a good visit and they told us they would join us to walk part of a day.

About two miles east of town the next day, Gary and Melody drove up and stopped. We took a little time to talk while the girls gathered rocks and played. Then they walked about half a mile with us. Gary went back for their car, while Melody and the girls continued walking. When Gary came with the car, we said good-bye and watched them drive off on their vacation. It was great fun to have visitors.

East of Thompson Falls we still walked beside the Clark Fork River, flowing rapidly past small islands covered with trees and grasses. Opposite the river were small rocky mountains.

We were now entering Big Horn Sheep country. Apparently they are here in great abundance during the winter months, but go back into the hills for the summer. We saw a sign that told us there were Big Horn Sheep for the next ten miles.

On Sunday, July 13, we went to Trout Creek to attend Cabinet Mountain Bible Church. Many greeted us, including Pastor Happ Cheff. His wife Sandy was away, so we didn't get to meet her. We were asked to share with the congregation about our Journey. The response to our sharing was good. A few had seen us during the week and had wondered—who were those happy women waving to everyone that came along?

At the close of the service we all sang a benediction to the tune of "Edelweiss." The words blessed us so much that we asked if we could get a copy.

> "May the Lord, Mighty God, Bless and keep you forever.
>   Grant you peace, perfect peace, courage in every endeavor.
>   Lift your eyes and see His face, And His grace forever.
>   May the Lord, Mighty God, Bless and keep you forever."

## Sam

Montana is filled with many little towns with clusters of homes, a library, a post office and a general store. There are not many large cities. These small towns were our favorites—ones if you were to drive through, you would hardly realize they were there.

Our route brought us to a small town named Wild Horse Plains. Most referred to the town simply as Plains. When we saw the City Hall across the railroad tracks, we decided to see if the mayor was in. He actually came in while we were talking with Linda, the clerk, Cathy, the deputy clerk, and Ron, the acting mayor. We gave him greetings from Paso Robles, California Mayor Frank Mecham, took a few pictures, and were soon on our way again.

## Joni

At about 8:00 A.M. we started walking toward Paradise through rugged, craggy mountains, with the Clark Fork River and the railroad to our right. The sun was already hot, but it was great hiking. After about three miles of walking with Lyn and Sam, I turned back to get the van, hoping to meet up with them to walk through Paradise. I thought I would take the trail beside the tracks to get off the highway and away from the logging trucks for a while. After an hour I realized the trail followed the train tracks, but not the road. It took me quite a distance out of my way.

Eventually I had to climb over a barbed wire fence, then another fence, to hook up with a different trail. Coming to a large lake I let Cassie have a swim. There I had a choice of returning to the tracks or climbing still another fence to walk through a cornfield where a sign proclaimed, "No Trespassing." Finally I headed through the field toward the road and hopped one more fence into someone's garden. As I walked past the house I watched for someone to apologize to, but seeing no one, I continued up a steep slope to the road. The hour it took me to walk back would have taken fifteen minutes on the road. But it was fun. I saw some deer, but no humans or trucks.

## Lyn

Meanwhile Sam and I had reached the town of Paradise. We waited by the side of the road for a while, since we liked to enter towns together. After about half an hour, with the sun heating us up and no place to sit down, we walked into the town where we could at least find a little shade under the large trees that lined the street. John and Phyllis were just setting up their lemonade stand. Finally Joni came along, and we all enjoyed a glass of huckleberry lemonade. Ummmm, very refreshing!

Walking through this quiet little town we were surprised to see a cool 1931 Chevrolet sitting in front of a house. A few minutes later we met the owners, Johnnie and Carrie, walking toward us. At Johnnie's urging we all took turns sitting in the driver's seat and the rumble seat, while the others took pictures with our cameras. Ed, who lived at the same house, came out to see what was happening.

Johnnie gave Sam a bouquet of wildflowers, then told us about a spring we would see as we headed along the road. He claimed it was the freshest, nicest drinking water around. When he heard that Joni would walk awhile with us, then come back to get the van, Johnnie suggested that she walk to the spring. He would then meet us with his All Terrain Vehicle and give her a ride back to the van. Joni protested, but Johnnie prevailed.

The spring water was indeed wonderful, so we filled our drinking bottles. Then we saw Johnnie coming. He wanted Joni to drive the All Terrain Vehicle back, while he rode behind her. This time Joni prevailed and rode behind him while he drove. While Joni went back for the van, Sam and I enjoyed watching people coming and going to the spring. They brought a variety of containers to fill with water. One man, after filling two very large containers, proceeded to wash his cowboy boots and a pair of jeans, as well as a chamois. We watched in awe and laughingly wondered if we should suggest to my husband, Dave, that he could find a nice spring to wash his clothes in during the months while I am on this Journey.

As we continued walking, we passed one of many rock quarries in this area. The owner told us there was a herd of long horned sheep on the hill behind the quarry and encouraged us to go through the gate to see them. He also told us that if the sheep ran away, we should just pick up a few rocks and shake them together. This would get their attention and they would turn to see what we're doing.

There were 25 to 30 sheep in the herd. Cassie immediately started to chase them, but it was too steep for her to climb. We picked up some rocks and rattled them, and the sheep turned around and took a few steps toward us. We took several pictures of these beautiful, majestic creatures then went on our way.

Our second campground in Montana was just outside of Missoula, at the Jellystone RV Park. This was a very nice camp spot for us and we enjoyed the nightly social at the pavilion, where they served a choice of huckleberry or vanilla ice cream. I enjoyed a "Diet Coke float" each night with the huckleberry ice cream. Sam and Joni usually had a scoop of each, and Joni shared hers with Cassie. Sometimes the server put in a little extra vanilla for Cassie.

Sitting back with our ice cream, I began to think back to the time a cowboy tried to teach me to throw a lasso. The only thing I lassoed at the time was a large rock. Soon we three would all find ourselves herding several head of cattle back to their watering hole, but without a lasso.

*Chapter Six*

# HERDING CATTLE

---

### Sam

Everyone in the town of Perma came out to see us—there were only three inhabitants! "Sheriff Bill," "Mayor Harold" and "Resident Buster" really held none of these offices. This was all in fun, since they and their homes were far apart. But we enjoyed talking with each of them for a while.

Buster invited us in to see the home he was building out of tree trunks (the support beams were actual trees with branches). It was certainly unique. Crooked trees stood gallantly as pillars holding up the porch roof. Inside he had a place for a hot tub. Another tree held out graceful branches for draping towels over. An old wagon wheel hung from the ceiling with railroad lanterns spaced around it—a dramatic chandelier. We took lots of pictures, then thanked Buster for the fine tour and headed on down the road.

### Lyn

As we walked we often found a variety of coins. Most of them were pennies, but from time to time we found nickels, dimes and quarters. Sam even found a twenty-dollar bill once. The money we found went into a special fund that we called our "Furry person fund." This simply meant it was to buy special treats for Cassie. In actuality, we bought treats for us and shared them with Cassie.

Our route continued on through Dixon, Ravalli, and Arlee. Dixon was a very quiet town—almost too quiet. It seemed rather eerie to us, so we prayed that God would bring life to this community.

Ravalli had a few shops and a tiny post office next to a small farmer's market where we bought some fruit. Joni needed stamps, so when the clerk finished with our fruit purchases she put on her "post-mistress hat" and went into the post office to take care of that purchase. Truly a small town atmosphere.

Continuing on to the cute little town of Arlee (pronounced more like Ah-lee), we bought some chocolate, which we proceeded to eat right away. With temperatures soaring well over one hundred degrees each day, we couldn't let chocolate stay around very long.

On July 20 we attended the Arlee Alliance Church. Unfortunately we arrived about twenty minutes before the service finished. The sign out front told us the service began at 11:00, but they were on a summer schedule and started at 10:00. At least we were able to catch most of the message on "God's Amazing Love."

We met Reverend Corey Tilroe after the service and talked with others as well, including Red and Barbara. Barbara was especially excited about our Journey of prayer, and shared with us about some of the things happening in the area. When we mentioned our plans to cross over Jocko Pass just outside Arlee, they cautioned us to be aware of our surroundings in this lonely, deserted place. After quite a while we said good-bye and drove to Ravalli for lunch.

That afternoon we drove to St. Ignatius, a beautiful Mission established in 1854 by Jesuit missionaries on the Flathead Indian Reservation. The original mission burned down and was later rebuilt. Oh, how different from the California Missions we're used to. Many stairs led up to the large brick building with modern stained glass windows. Fifty-eight beautiful original murals adorned the inner walls, ceiling, and altar. Upon entering we saw paintings of the Salish Lord and the Lord's Mother, both portrayed as native Indians.

Next came a nineteen-mile drive through a National Bison Preserve along the Flathead River. Driving very close to large herds of grazing bison, we saw huge males, with their woolly heads seemingly disproportionate to their bodies. Calves stayed close to their mothers as we shot many photos. We also spotted some pronghorn deer. It was a glorious Sunday, and we enjoyed having the time to relax.

A two-hour drive through the Bison Range took us up to an elevation of 4,700 feet, with a panoramic view including the Mission Mountains of the Rockies. Arriving back at the Castle at 9 P.M., as the sun was setting, the temperature was still over 100 degrees.

From our campground just outside Missoula, we sometimes went into the "big city" to shop. To help Sam celebrate her 16th birthday on July 21, we drove her into the city for an evening of pizza. This was a special treat for us all since most of our meals were simple things we could put together in the Castle. Our actual walk, however, did not take us through Missoula.

The day after Sam's birthday we turned off State Route 200 and headed over Jocko Pass—paved for a short distance, but mostly a gravel and dirt road. There was very little traffic, and Cassie loved the freedom of running free in this heavily forested area, hunting for small critters.

Some people had warned us of pockets of satanic activity over Jocko Pass, so we had really prayed about whether or not we should change our route. However, we had a real sense of peace about walking through there, and never felt threatened as we plodded over the dusty road. In fact, we had a very real sense of God's peace as we continued through and prayed for the area. It was also a great relief from the hot sun pounding down on us day after day. Our worst enemy on this route was the dust as the infrequent car sped over the dirt road. After a while we learned to hold our bandanas over our nose and mouth whenever a car came along. Fortunately we were at a campground with excellent showers during this time, being covered with dust at each day's end.

Jocko Pass was actually fun when we would occasionally meet people stopping to find out what these crazy ladies were doing walking on this lonely, out-of-the-way road. Ted and his friend were out picking huckleberries. They showed us how to find the best berries and told us they planned to take their "pickin's" to a neighbor, who would bake them a huckleberry pie. We sure would have enjoyed a piece of that pie fresh from the oven.

From time to time we saw cattle grazing among the trees, and a few times met up with some of the bovines on the road. Once a small herd of cows with calves marched ahead of us for a mile or two, making us feel like real cattle herders. When one mother got separated from her calf, she mooed at us loudly, then ran past to walk beside her calf. They finally headed off on a trail that led down to a reservoir.

Later we met Mike and Mark with a load of lumber they were delivering. They gave us a thumbs-up when we told them what we were doing. In fact, they were astonished at the monumental task we were attempting. At last we turned off Jocko Pass, onto State Route 83. This took us south to once again connect with State Route 200 heading east.

The time came to move on from Jellystone RV Park. Although reluctant to leave the wonderful showers and laundry room, we were also happy to be making progress. Spring Creek RV Park in Lincoln, our next destination, had an abundance of trees and plants, with deer and rabbits running freely.

Diane E. Wright
6×9 1978

The campsite we had reserved had not been vacated, due to an emergency, so they had prepared us a place in back where they let us hook up to electricity with a long extension cord. We had water hook-up, but would be sharing the sewage dump with our neighbor. We enjoyed our neighbors, Timberwolf, Three Feathers and their granddaughter, Jessica, from the Blackfeet [sic] and Aquaila tribes. Before they left, several days later, we were able to buy some of the beautiful feathered crafts made by Three Feathers.

On Sunday, July 27, we attended the Blackfoot Valley Bible Church in Lincoln. The pastor was away and David Barndt had come from the Lolo Community Church to give the message during his absence. He spoke about Deborah and Jael from the book of Judges, both women, and how they won a war for the Israelites. The message seemed to be for us as women praying across America. God often uses women for His purposes.

We talked with a few people after the service, then went to lunch at the PondeROSE'S Restaurant. The afternoon was spent working on a variety of necessary little chores at our Castle.

After several days camped in Lincoln, we walked into the town. Stopping at the city limit sign to pray, Joni noticed a large rock nearby and picked it up. She brought it over to the sign and set it down saying, "This stone is a memorial to the fact that we prayed for the town of Lincoln." We had been sharing about memorial stones in the Bible that the Israelites placed at various spots on their travels to remind them of some special event. We all thought this was a great idea and decided from then on to place a stone when we prayed at each town.

Walking through this area we had sensed very little enthusiasm from the local people. There seemed to be an oppressive feeling here, so we prayed with extra zeal for the people of this community. While a few people were very nice and expressed their gratitude for our prayers, others seemed to respond with indifference.

At last we came to Stemple Pass where we crossed through the Rocky Mountains and the Continental Divide. The dirt and gravel road (another dusty day) climbed to an elevation of 6,376 feet. People had told us that moose, grizzlies and rattlesnakes were a danger on the Pass, so we kept watching for them here. The only animals we saw all day were squirrels—a bit of a disappointment, since we wanted to see one of the larger animals.

### Joni

The last two miles of Stemple Pass were very steep. As we got to the last quarter mile from the top Lyn was not feeling well from the heat, over 100 degrees, and the altitude of 6,349 feet. I decided to help her out by putting Cassie's leash around her neck and

The Peace Arch between Canada and the United States

Clayton Thomas saw us off at the start of our Journey

Russ, Dave and Loki brought the Castle to us

Two sisters, Beth and Joyce, in front of their fascinating house

A policeman held the traffic back so JoAn could take a picture of this sign

Our scenic route through the Cascades

Breathtaking view in the Cascades

The full team just before three left for their homes
- taken at Cozy Acres where the Salapkas and Potters live in Chewelah, WA

JoAn "Just Walking in the Rain"

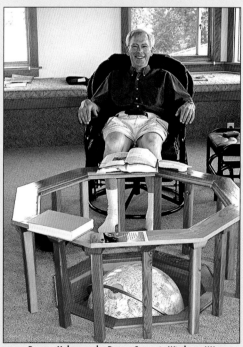

Preston Hobart at the Prayer Center in Winthrop, WA

We had to walk the Flowery Trail Road on a "non-blasting" day

Jess Story gave Sam and Lyn a ride back to the van at the top of Wauconda Pass

The Usk Mall had "almost" anything you might want

Campground owners, Al and Karolyn, with our team in front of our Castle

Our first Idaho church - The House of Prayer in Old Town

Whenever possible we brought greetings to the local mayor from Mayor Frank Mecham of Paso Robles, California - Here we're with the mayor and a councilman in Paradise, Montana

Gary, Melody and their two children, Angelica and Crystal enjoyed walking with us a short distance

Sam sits in the rumble seat of Johnnie's 1931 Chevrolet as Carrie looks on

Buster's unique home in Perma, Montana

We "herded" these cattle to the watering hole

We had a great time walking around Canyon Ferry Reservoir between Helena and Townsend, Montana

It was great to meet Mike and Mark as they delivered lumber to a home along Jocko Pass

Timberwolf, Three Feathers and Jessica were our neighbors at our Lincoln, Montana campground

Saint Joseph's Church was moved to this spot to make way for Canyon Ferry Reservoir

We attended a small "Home Church" in Helena, Montana - Here the congregation consists of Clark and Ruby, Chris and MaryEllen and their children, plus our team

The Wheatland County Courthouse in Harlowton, Montana

Saint Mark's Episcopal Church in Big Timber, Montana

Lyn had to put her feet into the cold waters of the Yellowstone River
- Edward gives her a hand

Nancy prepared a great meal for Edward and the hungry team

Dr. Bob of Lavina, Montana walked a bit with us after preparing
and serving us his special pancake lunch

Our newly rescued pup, later named Waliluke, was too weak to walk the day we found him, so Sam gave him a helping shoulder

Lyn sets up "Slinky" and "Slunky" at our campsite in Hardin, Montana

Jerry FlatLip wore this full headdress for a re-enactment of some Indian wars

Lyn, Joni and Meredith after church in Sheridan, Wyoming

Oliver was a Crow legislator who told us a lot about his people
- shown with his grandson

Waliluke's fear of these statues in Sheridan, Wyoming was quite obvious

This class from Three Peaks Christian School was studying Memorial Stones, so they came to where we placed our stone to pray with us

Meredith came to cook for us for a week, then joined us for some walking as well

Joni's friends, Ingeborg and Nancy, joined us for a few days of walking and sightseeing

Lyn was happy to have Dave come for a visit and to walk his mile and a half beginning at the little town of Spotted Horse

pretending to pull her along. This was fine for a few minutes, until her legs buckled under her and she gracefully slumped to the ground. Sam and I dragged her to the shade of the trees. I hiked quickly to the van at the crest and got cold water and Tums for her. She soon felt well enough to walk the rest of the way to the top. I felt very bad that I had put the leash on her and apologized. Lyn brushed it off, saying she thought it was funny.

At the top of the Pass we sat on benches, ate cheese and crackers, prayed for the valley below and wrote on a stone saying we had prayed for the community. We took pictures of a sign at the top telling us we were now at the Continental Divide. From there we returned to the Castle.

Our meals were often very interesting! Lyn had a Lean Mean Grilling Machine along, so we sometimes grilled hamburgers, chicken or steaks (the steaks were more for celebration meals). Right after shopping we had pretty good meals, but as our supplies ran low, and we didn't have a Wal-Mart close by, we resorted to what we called our "Castle concoctions." An example of this was when we had rice with onions and seasonings, beans with bacon bits, and canned chicken with seasonings all mixed together. Sam and Lyn enjoyed this special mix, but I wasn't so sure.

Making our way down the other side of Stemple Pass, we saw lots of old, abandoned log cabins. The surrounding scenery was magnificent with pines, firs and wildflowers. When we came to County Road 279 we headed southeast. Once over the Pass, the scenery changed to rolling hills burnt golden by the very hot sun. Gradually the firs and pines disappeared until there were just barren hills and farmlands.

I had been apprehensive about hiking down the eastern side of the Pass because of bears and rattlesnakes, but we saw neither, just a lot of cows.

We arrived at Canyon Creek, a tiny community of about 150 residents. The Country Store also served as local post office and gas station. We spotted some purple hued rocks on the hill beside us. Lyn and I, collecting rocks from each state, got quite excited by these beautiful specimens and added some to our collections. Sam often chided us that the Castle would soon be so full of rocks there would be no room for anything else!

## Lyn

Approaching Helena, the Capital of Montana, we walked on local back roads to bypass the city. We did take time to drive into Helena, tour the capitol building, and even tried to get an appointment with Governor Judy Martz. Though we didn't expect her to have room in her schedule for us, we knew we had to try. We did walk around the capitol and prayed for the state of Montana at the four corners of the building.

In Helena we enjoyed one of our favorite treats, hot fudge or caramel sundaes at McDonald's. Sometimes people gave us gift certificates for McDonald's, which we used either for ice cream sundaes, or for breakfast.

On this particular day we ordered our sundaes and, as usual, we asked for extra sauce on the side in a separate container. This had to be specified carefully, or we ended up with the extra sauce in the sundae itself. We stood there talking while they filled our order and were shocked when they brought our sundaes with two full cups of extra hot fudge on the side. This was more than enough, but they couldn't put it back, so we had a lot left to take back to our Castle refrigerator for later use. It took care of my chocolate cravings for a while.

At last it was time to move from Lincoln to our next campground. This move put us in The Silos RV Park about eight miles west of Townsend. We chose a spot with a view of the meadow, but near many old motor homes like ours. It was a comfortable feeling not being surrounded by massive RV's that were at least twenty years newer. We loved our "antique Castle," but sometimes felt a little out of place surrounded by the newest, most modern motor homes.

The Silos was an old park, but everything was clean and well cared for. The staff and the campers were all friendly and helpful. Throughout the fourteen-and-a-half months of our walk, we remembered this as one of our favorite campgrounds.

# Chapter Seven

# WALKERS STOPPED FOR SPEEDING

## Lyn

At the AAA in Helena I asked for maps of local back roads. The clerk laughed, "Honey, this is Montana, we don't have back roads." She did give us a map of Helena and the surrounding area and told us Highway 12 would not be so busy once we got past Townsend. We found a route to bypass Helena and walk alongside Canyon Ferry Reservoir. This was safer and more scenic than U.S. Highway 12, which was under construction.

## Joni

On August 3 we attended Faith Baptist Church of Townsend. Some rather interesting circumstances helped us find this particular church. Let's go back to Friday, August 1st. That day when we finished walking, we scouted the route ahead in the van. This brought us into Townsend, and we decided to drive through the town to find a church for Sunday. We spotted a few, but weren't really settled on one.

Heading back to our campground, we were in deep conversation as I drove through the construction zone. Then I noticed a patrolman make a U-turn and pull up behind us and turn on his red light. I pulled over, and the very nice officer asked where we were headed. I told him where we were going, and about our Journey. He pointed out that the speed limit in the construction zone was 35mph, and we'd been going 60 mph—oops.

We told him about our Journey of prayer for America, and that we were praying for their community. He stood there in deep thought, stroking his chin, then told us he appreciated our prayers. He let us go with a simple warning.

Lyn asked him, "Do you live in Townsend? Could you recommend a church for us in this area?" He suggested Faith Baptist Church, gave us the address, and told us he was the pastor! I quickly assured him we would be there on Sunday.

Pastor Mike Wenzel introduced us to his congregation as three women he'd stopped for speeding through the Highway 12 construction zone on Friday. When the congregation found out we were walking, someone asked, "If they were walking how did you stop them for speeding?"

The message that morning was from Psalm 119:97–104. Pastor Mike talked about the importance of loving God's Word, loving God, and loving people.

When church was over we asked about a good restaurant for lunch and were directed to the Horseshoe Café. When we arrived, we discovered about half of the congregation was already there. The meal was delicious, and we had a good time. We spent the rest of the day relaxing.

## Lyn

We enjoyed walking the lovely road winding around Canyon Ferry Reservoir. This lake is fed by the Missouri River. A beautiful hawk circled lazily overhead, and osprey sat in their nests watching for a good catch to feast on. We walked across the dam and along the east side of this large lake. There were sections of road construction, but not much traffic. Often the road crews talked with us as we passed by. The deep blue sky appeared to go on forever. We understand now why Montana is called the "Big Sky Country."

While walking deep in thought, I passed close to an angry rattlesnake. At the sound of its rattle, the first indication that it was even there, I jumped about ten feet into the air (perhaps a bit of an exaggeration). Following the initial shock, I skirted back around the snake and zoomed in with the camera for a few pictures of this coiled, hissing creature.

For several days we had been plagued with grasshoppers of all sizes and colors. Hundreds of them lay squashed in the road to be feasted on by their still living relatives. Frequently we were hit on the face, neck, arms or legs as they jumped or flew across our path. It was impossible to avoid them, there were just too many.

On a hill on the east side of the road stood a small Catholic church. The sign told us,

---

### Saint Joseph's Roman Catholic Church

Men who are close to the soil are traditionally close to God. For this reason the pioneer residents of the fertile Canton Valley turned early to the task of erecting this community house of worship. Built in 1875-76 by popular subscription, it was attended by Fr. Paladino, one of Montana's first priests. In 1954, as the reservoir of the newly constructed Canyon Ferry Dam was to be filled, the building was moved to the present location where it has continued to serve the community for church services and ecumenical activities.

---

It was a small, simple building. We were hoping to look inside, but it was tightly locked and the windows were covered with shutters. The view of the reservoir from the church was awesome. Our imaginations wandered back in time to picture a scene without the lake, and the little village in its place.

## Joni

One day we decided to take a scouting trip through the Big Belt Mountains to find a shortcut to Highway 12. Stopping our walk at Confederate Gulch, we drove up into the mountains to see if the road led out to the highway. The scenery was stunning from this narrow dirt road, with a small river running alongside through thick vegetation. Suddenly a tree "reached out" and scratched the side of the van! Lyn was very quiet, perhaps afraid to say anything.

Then I had to drive the van through the river. I was fearful of getting stuck in the middle, but I could see the water was shallow. (Lyn's and Sam's eyes were closed as they held on tight.) We made it OK!

A group of men was panning for gold. Apparently this was a big mining area, with millions of dollars worth of gold having been taken out in the 1800s. We eventually reached Highway 12, but by now Lyn had decided it added too many miles and harrowing experiences. So we would stay on the main roads to Harlowton.

Back in the Castle that evening, a windstorm blew through the RV Park. With lightning and thunder all around I wondered, "Do they have hurricanes in Montana?" We all looked out the windows to see if people were evacuating. The power went out, but all except us, the California gals, were cool, calm and collected. Following the storm the sky turned beautiful shades of orange. This was the most gorgeous sunset we had ever seen, so Lyn and I grabbed our cameras and dashed outside. Later we would say this was the best one of the whole walk!

## Sam

After several days of walking south beside the lake, we turned east through the Smith River Valley. The Big Belt Mountains were just ahead, with the Castle Mountains beyond them.

Beginning our second day on the Big Belt Mountain Pass, Cassie ran into the brush, barking frantically. I went to see why she was so excited and glimpsed the back side of a young bear running away. It stopped and turned to take a look at Cassie, then continued running up the hill. This was the closest we had been to a bear in the wild.

After walking through the heavily wooded areas of the Pass, we reached the top, and there the vegetation suddenly changed. Now we were walking over rolling hills alongside fields and pastures, but no trees. Herds of pronghorn grazed nearby.

## Lyn

On August 10 we joined nine others at a small home-church on the west side of Helena. Pastor Chris Thompson had invited us when we met him earlier in the week. The congregation was made up of his wife Mary Ellen, their five children, another couple, Clark and Ruby, and the three of us. The service was very interesting, and afterward we were invited to stay for a lunch of bratwurst, potato salad, fruit salad and punch. It was delicious and the fellowship was great.

Chris told us he worked two jobs—part-time at Wal-Mart, and also as a chaplain for the local emergency services. His main goal is to make a difference in people's lives. If his church grows as a result, that will be great, but it is not his basic aim. Ending our time together in prayer, we promised to add them to our prayer book.

## Sam

The next day was a long drive—over the Big Belt Mountains, then through the Castle Mountains, to begin our walk heading toward Lennep and Martindale.

Soon we came to a junction where we turned south. A creek meandered through low bushes on the east side. Suddenly I saw a small animal racing along the ground. "Grumman, what's that?" I cried. It stopped briefly to turn and look at us.

"I think that's a badger!" she said. Then it jumped into the creek and disappeared. (Remember, I refer to my grandmother, as Grumman.)

Another day we watched several bulls in a field as they kicked the ground, raising huge clouds of dust. Then, snorting loudly, they ran at each other banging heads together. As fascinating as it was, we were thankful for a good sturdy fence between us.

## Lyn

Heading east on County Road 294 we saw a man unloading a backhoe from his truck. He told us he was heading into the back country, where his cattle were ranging. As we continued walking our imaginations went wild. We pictured "Montana Tex" (our name for him) rounding up his cattle with a backhoe and herding them to market. An interesting mental picture.

Further along on one side of the road was an abandoned substation. A brand new one stood opposite. It was an intriguing contrast. We stood there considering the past and the present styles. A car stopped beside us and Warren Fagen asked if we were also walking across America. He had met two Methodist ministers a few days earlier who were walking across the nation, but he had no more information about them.

Warren also told us that the power stations on top of the hill marked the Montana Central Divide. Here the Smith River from the northwest, the Shield River from the south, and the Musselshell River from the east come together.

An old railroad bed lay to our left. Sam and I thought it looked like it would be a nice trail to walk on. There was no way of knowing how far it would take us, or if it would stay along the route we needed to follow. We decided to chance it and found it to be a pleasant change. There were no signs telling us to "stay out," and it seemed quite open.

Soon we saw Joni walking toward us on the road. We hollered to her and she and Cassie crossed the field and climbed the bank up to where the tracks had been. Suddenly I realized that a trestle had been removed, leaving a large gulch between us. Joni laughed and asked, "How are you going to get out of this mess?" Sam and I finally found a way down the steep side of the track bed and crossed to the other side.

Coming to an old signal, the wires and electrical parts had all been ripped out. We could not resist seeing who could climb the highest on the swaying signal ladder. Joni and I began singing "I've Been Working on the Railroad," with much gusto as we danced along the railroad bed, while Sam snapped pictures of us crazy ladies.

When we drove back over the mountains to the Silos Camp for the final time, we were rewarded with a delightful display of lightning. We sat at the top of Big Belt Mountain Pass with our digital cameras set on video, trying to photograph the lightning streaking across the sky. Later we found that one of the videos actually had captured a strike.

Our last evening in the Silos campground we had a real treat—watching a training session of a fire-fighting helicopter with rope and bucket. The large bucket was filled at the lake, then dumped onto the grassy area nearby. This was repeated several times.

We had camped at the Silos in Townsend for eleven days and really hated to leave. It was such a peaceful spot, so open, and so many friendly people at the campground, but it was time to move on. Our neighbor, "Big G" and his dog Josh, came over to say good-bye. He showed us photos of himself in his "mountain man" suit made from elk skin. In the picture he was holding a musket that he fires in competitions and re-enactments of the civil war. Now we packed up our stuff and prepared to move on to the next part of our Journey.

Before leaving the campground we checked the oil and tires, and noticed the tires were in pretty bad shape. Driving to Townsend, we stopped at K.C.'s to get new tires. We left Lady Van Go at K.C.'s, walked to the Creamery for some ice cream, then continued to the library to check our e-mail. When the van was ready we headed out, much later than we had hoped.

Our drive to Big Timber took us over the Bozeman Pass at almost 6,000 feet. The motor home did not like the steep climb and rebelliously slowed to 35 mph. At last we passed over the crest and headed down the other side to our destination.

When we finally arrived it was close to 6 P.M. Setting up went smoothly as we all set to work on our assigned tasks. The campers next to us watched in amazement and asked, "Is it just women in your group?" We explained to them what we were doing, then laughed at their stunned expressions. They were very nice and told us they come here every year with their grandchildren.

The campground at Big Timber was far from our route, so driving to our start point each day would take us an hour or longer for the next week. During long drives like this Sam often read to us. Presently she was reading from the book, "Hinds Feet in High Places" by Hannah Hurnard. If you've never read it, we highly recommend this wonderful allegory. We could easily relate much of it to our Journey. The main character is "Much Afraid," and some of her enemies are "Pride," "Bitterness," "Self Pity," and so on. "Much Afraid" is escorted to the High Places by "Sorrow" and "Suffering."

Driving to our starting point one day, we had to stop for road construction between Lennep and Martinsdale. Dick Toews, the flagman, asked where we were heading. While we waited, we told him about our Journey. Dick attends the Christian Missionary Alliance Church and promised to share about our walk with his prayer group that evening. We always appreciated this kind of response.

Three days later we were walking along U.S. Route 12 east of Harlowton, when we saw a car stopped on the side of the road. Noticing a man sitting in the front passenger seat, we nodded and said, "Hello," and asked if he needed help. He told us they'd had a blowout and help was on the way. Telling him about our walk, we asked if we could take his picture. When I asked his name, he said he was Harry Toews. I asked if he was related to Dick Toews and learned that Dick was his son. What a small world!

*Chapter Eight*

# ATTACKED BY GRASSHOPPERS

## Lyn

Through this part of Montana the temperatures were soaring to over 110 degrees daily. Joni was careful to meet us every two or three miles with the van to give us extra water.

With the heat so bad, Joni couldn't get Cassie to come out of the van to walk. It was too hot to leave her in the van without air conditioning, so Joni drove into towns and took Cassie for walks on shady streets. She often met townspeople and told them about our Journey. Though Joni wasn't able to walk with us at these times, she got to see people and places of Montana that Sam and I didn't see.

## Joni

"Two Dot. World Famous Bar," boasts the sign at the edge of the road. I had to find out about this "World famous bar," so I drove into the town just off the main highway. Except for the bar all other buildings were either falling down or in need of repair. It reminded me of a ghost town.

According to a couple of men there, as well as the lady who owned the bar, Two Dot (population 29, at 4,900 feet elevation) is named after the colorful early day cattleman, Two Dot Wilson, whose cattle carried the Two Dot (. .) brand. As far as I know, the bar's claim to world fame was just somebody's idea for a sign that would attract attention.

Mr. "Nobody" (he didn't want to give me his name) owned the bank next door to the bar. As this brick building had been gutted, he told me I was welcome to take one of the loose bricks from the building as a souvenir. From Two Dot I drove to a marshy area thick with cattails, picked a bunch, and took them back to decorate the Castle.

The grasshoppers were alive and well everywhere we walked. They continued to hit us in the face, arms and legs as they jumped and flew about. These grasshoppers were of all sizes and colors, and we tried to get some pictures of them sitting still, which they seldom did. A news article claimed there were about forty grasshoppers per square foot, but we felt sure it must have been eighty. The fields were full of them, and we were concerned about the poor farmers' crops.

Then there were the bees on this stretch of highway, and each of us was stung at least once. These nasty stings caused swelling and burning, even after the stinger was removed. We made a paste of baking soda and water to sooth the burning sensation.

## Lyn

Sam and I talked with a father/son duo, who had stopped to see if we needed help. Both wore cowboy hats, and the young boy, about eight years old, held a sucker in his mouth as if it were a piece of straw. After we shared with them about our walk, the boy said softly, "It's gonna git hot." Then they drove off.

Harlowton was one of our mail stops. What fun to go to the post office and find a huge pile of letters waiting for us! We were so grateful to all who wrote and sent us care packages and could hardly wait to open our mail.

The locals call Harlowton "Harlow." This was a cute little town with lots of personality. Near the center an electric locomotive was on display—the last of the electric locomotives to be used. "Harlow" was quite a booming town until the train stopped running, and many shops and stores were boarded up.

Next to the Montana National Guard Armory was a war memorial to honor the men and women of Wheatland County who had given their lives in World Wars I and II, and the Korean and Viet Nam wars.

## Joni

In Harlowton, Cassie and I walked beautiful tree-lined streets, finding some very well-kept older homes with lovely gardens. Two young boys who wanted to pet my dog were very excited when I shared with them about "Cassie's walk across America." Learning we were from California, one of the boys got even more excited, saying he and his family had just recently moved to Montana from Napa, California.

The library had a book sale and I purchased four books. Joan Smith, the librarian, asked lots of questions about our walk. We took photos of each other to put in our scrapbooks.

## Lyn

August 17 was a Sunday, and we had chosen St. Marks Episcopal Church, built in the 1850s, for our Sunday services. We entered the small stone structure through a bright red door and sat on wooden pews. There were padded stools to kneel on. The Vicar, Reverend Kenneth Truelove, introduced us to the congregation and afterwards we talked with many of them during a time of socializing. Edward and Nancy Clement invited us, including Cassie, to ride in their car and join them for lunch and the afternoon at their ranch.

On the way to their place we stopped at a market, and Nancy went in to pick up a few things. While Nancy was inside I looked across the parking lot and noticed four men dressed alike. Unable to resist, I went over to ask them if they were a Barbershop Quartet. Sure enough, they were. I told them my husband was also a Barbershopper. After taking their picture, I gave them one of our cards with the information about our walk. They decided to sing for us. What a delight, as we walkers stood in the parking lot at the market, being serenaded by a Barbershop Quartet.

The wall of the market was a beautiful mural. A painted sign told us,

---

### Clark on the Yellowstone ~ Thursday, 17 July 1806

The horse's feet were sore and the party had just spent the night, having no tent, in the rain, hail, thunder and lightning. Dawn brought fair weather to Captain William Clark, ten men, Sacagawea and her child, 49 horses and a colt. They broke camp and headed east passing through an area Clark called 'Rivers Across' (Big Timber) because the Boulder River and Big Timber Creek fell into the Yellowstone near each other. Clark also noted the surrounding mountains and kept moving for they were in search of Cottonwood Trees large enough to make canoes to aid a speedy return to the states.

---

At Nancy and Edward's ranch they gave us a tour of the house, which was listed in the National Register of Historic Places by the United States Department of the Interior in cooperation with the Montana Historical Society. It had originally been the John Otto Spannring Family Farm. The family had arrived in Montana in 1902 and homesteaded this land. The final addition to the Spannring holdings came in 1943, bringing their total acreage to 2,286 acres. In 1988 Edward and Nancy Clement of Salisbury, North Carolina, purchased and meticulously restored this historic property. (This information was taken from a plaque hanging in the home.)

While Nancy prepared our meal, Edward drove us around the ranch, known as the Yellowstone Bend Ranch Preserve. There were 3,030 acres in this preserve bordered by the Yellowstone River. In the 1900s the land was used mainly for growing wheat and alfalfa. Surrounded by the Sweet Grass Mountains, the Beartooth Mountains, the Sarka and the Crazy Mountains, it is now used to graze cattle. Edward however, prefers it as a prairie with the shrubs and grasses. That day the ranges were barely visible, as nearby fires had filled the sky with smoke. Deer, pronghorn and a variety of smaller animals roam this acreage. Trout swim lazily in the river.

Edward drove to a high bluff overlooking the Yellowstone River, then on down to the river, where we each picked a stone for our personal collections. I couldn't resist the opportunity to put my bare feet into the chilly Yellowstone River in the same area where William Clark had passed, after he and Merriweather Lewis split up for the return trip to the states.

Back at the house we sat down to a delicious meal of grilled asparagus, a Tuscan torte (made like a quiche) and garlic cheese grits. For dessert we had Peach Melba with a white chocolate chip cookie, served with peach tea. This was our first time to taste grits, and they were wonderfully prepared with a mixture of cheeses, garlic and cream. Edward and Nancy live in North Carolina during the winter months and in Montana in the summer.

Continuing our walk on Highway 12, we passed through the tiny towns of Shawmut and Barber, heading toward Ryegate. Sam had to use her inhaler quite a bit through this area, as we had to put up with smoke from nearby wildfires.

### Joni

Arriving at the small town of Ryegate, I drove up the one small street taking photos. There were no more than a dozen homes, two churches, and a gas station/grocery store. Large wooden woodpeckers, about eighteen inches tall, were nailed on the sides of trees and houses everywhere, but we didn't see a place that sold them. After buying gas and coffee, I asked the clerk if she knew where I might find these brightly painted woodpeckers. She told me I could buy them right there. They were made by a one-armed man who lives in Ryegate. I bought one each for Lyn and myself.

A large wooden sign announced that this was where Chief Joseph had made his final attempt to get to Canada. As Chief Joseph of the Nez Perce Nation tried to lead his people away, the U.S. army stopped him in Montana Territory, just shy of the border. There he made his famous declaration, "From where the sun now stands, Joseph will fight no more forever."

### Lyn

At the post office in Roundup I asked the postal clerk if he knew of Bob McNary in nearby Lavina. He handed me a phone book, where I found the number and called Doctor Bob. I had an article about him that Dellie Chapman from my hometown had given me. He had walked from Lavina to New York, and we were hoping to meet him.

When Dr. Bob answered the phone, I told him what we were doing, and that we would be walking through his town the next day. "Would it be possible to get together?" I asked. He said he would love to meet us. Figuring we would arrive in Lavina just before noon, he invited us to come for lunch. He planned to make his special pancakes. I told him we'd be delighted.

As Sam and I walked into Lavina, Joni drove the van to the side street by Dr. Bob's house. She planned to park it there and walk back to meet us, then we would all walk to his place together. However, he spotted her when she parked the van and went out to talk. As a result, when Sam and I came walking up to his home, Dr. Bob was out front taking pictures of us. It was a real thrill for us to meet him. He prepared thick, tasty bacon and his special pancakes, with a mixture of wheat and corn flour—delicious!

Dr. Bob showed us pictures and souvenirs, including a special quilt, of his walk across America. Then he showed us the flag he had carried on his long journey. There was also a large sign painted on a sheet by students at a local school that proclaimed, 'Welcome home Dr. Bob from the Big Apple."

He had many questions for us. We took several pictures, then he walked with us awhile before saying good-bye. I asked if he would mind if I said a prayer for him and his town. He was most appreciative. It was exciting for us to meet Dr. Bob and to have him serve us lunch in his home.

Our next move was to the town of Hardin. After leaving the Big Timber campground we headed into Laurel, Montana, to an RV place where we could pick up a new "Slinky" for dumping sewage. We also asked about the handy stands to place "Slinky" on. We had seen many other campers using these, and I really wanted one. They told us this stand was called "Slunky" (we kid you not). We now had "Slinky" and her cousin, "Slunky." You may smile, but it did make sewage dumping easier for us happy campers, especially for me, since that was my job. It sure didn't take much to make us happy! That evening when we set up camp at Hardin, I gleefully set up "Slunky" and "Slinky" to do their work.

Water is scarce in this part of Montana. Those living outside of town have to buy their water and haul it in huge plastic tanks. They keep these tanks in the backs of their trucks and periodically go get water to bring back for drinking, cooking, bathing and other uses. The campground in Hardin had to haul their water, because they were a mile outside town, and they asked the campers to be conservative in their use.

When we arrived at our walk point the next morning, a car drove into the parking spot next to us. To our surprise it was Dr. Bob, coming to walk with us. He told us he had read all the literature we left him the other day (walk reports and such) and posted some on his front window. His front window is like a community bulletin board for others to read. Dr. Bob walked with us for a while, then said good-bye before heading back to his car. We hoped he would be able to come another time or two to walk before we got too far away from this area.

The skies were still filled with smoke from the many wildfires burning throughout this part of Montana. It was a great relief one day, when we began walking and could actually see blue sky with beautiful white, puffy clouds. A breeze was blowing, and the pungent odor of smoke was no longer stinging our nostrils. We later heard that the fires were under control for the time, and we prayed they would all be out soon. Walking past fields of hay and grain in their varying shades of gold and brown, we wondered if any fields like this had been caught in the fires.

Frequently we took advantage of our time in the van, while driving to or from our walk route, to explore for better routes, or check mileages we had already covered. One day we decided on a short detour to see the historical landmark, "Pompey's Pillar." When Lewis and Clark's expedition returned to the East from their exploration of the West, they split up in this area. William Clark had come this way, and on July 25, 1806, he carved his name into the rock pillar, now framed in glass to help make it visible for generations to come.

My son Russ and his dog Loki arrived on August 23 to help us with fix-it needs and driving for about a week. He chose a good site to set up his tent and his telescope. Mars was in a good position for viewing during that week. We took turns looking through the telescope and tried to get some good pictures through the lens. The nights were balmy and the skies clear.

On August 24 we enjoyed Sunday services at Hardin's Open Bible Church. They had a guest speaker and their District Superintendent was also there. Because of a special meeting afterwards for the church members, we didn't have much time to talk with people.

Back at camp we prepared a veggie omelet for lunch. Russ joined us and stayed to see some of the pictures we had taken so far on the walk.

The first day Russ and Loki walked with us, it was just for a short distance, then they headed back to the van and into town to do a little publicity. Within a very short time, a Montana News car drove up and stopped in front of us. Donald and his son, also Donald, got out and introduced themselves. They told us they were with a Christian Internet News program going out to twenty-two million people and wanted to know if they could interview us live on their program.

He asked each of us several questions, but seemed to favor Joni with her British accent. Sam and I were quite delighted with this, since Joni usually didn't want to talk and was trapped into talking now. We were surprised she didn't just faint "dead-away" at the prospect of talking live to so many listeners. Actually, she did an excellent job.

Once Donald and Donald left, we continued our walk, but within a short distance we saw two men cross the road ahead of us and begin taking pictures. They were from the Billings Gazette. As they finished their interview, two more men arrived and began setting up a TV camera for "Fox News at 9" on channel 6. After a pleasant interview, we again continued walking.

The next day, August 26, we walked through Billings—a time to celebrate walking 1,000 miles so far. We spent a lot of time meeting people. Several who had seen us either on TV or in the paper shared their appreciation for what we were doing.

Doug introduced us to his dog Buster and told us about his building on the corner, Buster's Antiques and Collectibles. It was the oldest building in Billings. We enjoyed some pictures of how it looked originally. It now had a new facade, but the original building was still there. Doug also owned the building next door, the second oldest in Billings, and was painting it in shades of blue with gold trim—quite beautiful, and very appropriate for the style.

Walking on as far as the local Chamber of Commerce, we noticed several of our cards set out on the counter, along with copies of a news article about our walk. Russ had obviously been here ahead of us. We visited with the friendly volunteers at length. One of them wrote cowboy poetry under the name of Stacey Sue. Outside the Chamber stands an impressive cattle drive sculpture, with a sign stating:

---

### Great Montana Centennial Drive—September 4–9, 1989
The Montana Centennial Cattle Drive Bronze is dedicated to every child who dreamed of being a cowboy . . . every cowboy who dreamed of clear water and rolling prairies . . . every traveler who gazed at the Montana mountains and knew they were home . . . and all the Montanans who hold the dream of our precious heritage in their hearts.

---

Russ stayed at the campground a couple of days to do some repair work on the Castle. He had asked us to make a list for him of things we wanted done. What a blessing that he could do these repairs for us. Russ' stay with us would involve more than driving and making repairs. It would also involve an encounter with a furry critter that none of us would ever forget.

# Chapter Nine

# CASSIE'S NEW PUPPY

**Lyn**

One day when Russ was at the campground, and we were getting ready to walk southeast of Billings, an intense argument broke out between the three of us gals. When we finally started walking, it was about 10 A.M. Joni drove ahead to think and pray, as Sam and I walked and prayed about the situation we were all struggling with.

**Sam**

After we turned onto Hardin Road we saw a cute little dog sitting by a fence. At first we thought he was caught, but looking closer we saw he had been chained to the fence with a short chain around his neck and a metal clip. He could barely move, and could not even lie down, only sit. We checked at the only house around and asked the man there to call animal control. He told us that people were always dropping dogs off there, though he had never seen one chained like that. We waited for a while, then decided to take the dog with us. The poor pup was too weak to walk, so we took turns carrying him. He was heavy and awkward, and soon we had to rest. He was obviously hungry and thirsty, so we searched our packs to see what we could feed him. He quickly gobbled down a bagel and a raspberry nutri-grain bar, then drank water from our cupped hands.

As we sat beside the road with the dog we had temporarily dubbed "Journey," a car went by, then returned a few minutes later. The woman asked if we needed help, and we explained our mission, as well as about the dog we had with us. She parked and she and her four young children got out. Kari home schools her children, and they were all so concerned about this precious little pup. She and the children sat with us beside the road, and we all prayed about what to do. Then they reluctantly got back in their car and drove off to make a planned hospital visit.

As we continued walking I carried "Journey" over my shoulders. Soon Kari and the children (whose names we now learned were Kenton, Kieran, Karson, and Katriel) returned to give us a bag of corn on the cob, a bottle of water, and a check for our walk. We had a hard time saying good-bye to this lovely family, and we prayed that

God would especially bless them in the days ahead. When I held the ear of corn out to "Journey," he grabbed it and ate it right off the cob.

When Joni drove up she was shocked to see me with an animal draped about my neck. Realizing it was a young dog, she quickly got out of the car to help us get him into the back seat with Cassie. The two seemed happy to see each other, and Cassie even allowed "Journey" to nurse, though she had no milk to give him. Cassie gently licked the poor pup and seemed to understand that he needed her help.

Joni and "the kids" drove on ahead while Grumman and I walked. Animal control never came, which suited us fine. When we finished walking for the day, we took "Journey" to the Sugar Factory Veterinarian near our campground and had him checked over, then took him to stay at the Castle with us for the night.

The next day we talked of the hard times we had been having lately, and how "Journey" came at a time that was perhaps one of our lowest points emotionally. When we began to put our focus on caring for this pup, our spirits lifted and our day was brightened. We felt that God had put us in the right spot when "Journey" needed us, and we needed him.

The more we talked, the more we realized that we wanted to adopt this adorable little dog. At the end of our day we took the pup back to see the veterinarian to make arrangements for a full check up, shots, neutering, and whatever else we needed to do. The receptionist was so excited. She had told us from the beginning that she believed we were supposed to keep him.

After talking with my mom, Alyce-Kay, it was agreed that at the end of the Great American Journey I would take the dog home with me. Appropriately, we had found him on August 27, my little brother, JonMichael's fifth birthday. I thought it would be good to give "Journey" a Crow Indian name, since we had found him near the reservation we would begin walking through the next day.

## Lyn

We entered the Crow Indian Reservation on a road undergoing major construction. This gave us some great opportunities to talk with the construction crew, all of whom lived there. We asked them for ideas for a name that means "walking" or "travel" in the Crow language. Over the next few days we talked with several more of the Crow people and came up with three different names. They didn't have written words for the names they gave us, so we spelled them the way they sounded to us.

First was Bishke, which means "Dog." Then someone suggested Owashta, meaning "Traveling." For a while we called him Owashta, but weren't totally set on that. Finally someone suggested Waliluke meaning "Walking." For his official name we put all three names together, Owashta Bishke Waliluke meaning "Traveling Dog Walking."

Waliluke was the name we would use. Often that came out as just "Wali," or even "Walls," which is actually very appropriate, since he was often so hyper in the Castle that he literally seemed to bounce off the walls.

We met so many wonderful people on the Crow Reservation—all with interesting names, such as Not Afraid, Little Light, Flat Lip, Belly Mule, and many others. Several people here gave us prayer requests, which we gladly wrote in our book to pray for on a regular basis.

We met Jerry Flat Lip who invited us to come that afternoon to a re-enactment of some Indian wars, where he would be portraying a chief in full headdress. It was to be at Chief Plenty Coups State Park. We did attend and found it to be a wonderful experience. One woman was making papooses to be used in the re-enactment, and also special hairpieces for her boys who were participating in the afternoon event. Jerry Flat Lip came by in his full headdress so we could take a picture of him. What a delight!

Montana, and especially the Crow Reservation, was changing the glasses through which we viewed people. Little by little we were letting go of our preconceived ideas of how people looked and lived. We were learning to view others as they were, without judging them first.

Sunday came again, and we chose to attend Christ's Evangelical Reformed Church in Hardin. The pastor's wife, a delightful woman, greeted us at the door. We told her what we were doing and gave her one of our cards. She must have told her husband about us before the service began, because he introduced us and asked us to share about our Journey. After the wonderful service, we joined them downstairs for a coffee time. There we had the opportunity to talk with almost everyone and take plenty of pictures.

This was the first time we'd left Cassie and Waliluke together in the van alone. Apart from the pup eating Russ' beef jerky, all seemed to be OK. We took Sam and "the kids" back to the Castle, where Sam chose to stay with them. Russ, Joni and I went to eat lunch at the Purple Cow. After lunch the three of us went to the fascinating museum in Hardin, a small town of yesteryear, with a boardwalk connecting all the town buildings.

## Joni

On our next walking day Russ drove the van, while I walked with Lyn and Sam. We walked twelve-and-a-half miles along the road from Pryor, going toward Saint Xavier. It was very hot, without trees or any kind of shade. Throughout the pasture lands of the Crow Reservation, large rolling hills were covered with colorful rocks and dirt, ranging from purples and reds to yellows and greens. Though seemingly barren, the land here is quite beautiful, and we really enjoyed walking through the area. Cassie and Waliluke happily swam in the streams we came across from time to time.

While we were still camped in Hardin, the receptionist from the veterinarian's office left some of her fresh vegetables at our Castle, including red potatoes, cucumbers, squash, bell peppers and an onion. So that evening Lyn grilled some steaks, Sam prepared the potatoes, and I grilled some of the vegetables. What a great meal we enjoyed that night at the table prepared by Russ. It was a wonderful evening, and we sat and visited until the mosquitoes came out.

## Sam

Walking through the town of Hardin we met shopkeepers and local residents. We had been asked to speak at the middle school in town. The first group we shared with was an alternative studies class, made up of students who were discouraged about school. They had little interest in their studies, because of the lack of job potential on the Reservation. These students listened intently as we shared with them about our Journey. The three of us then talked with different students in small groups, showing them our maps, with the routes marked on them, and encouraging them to dream big—to hang onto their dreams. Their excellent questions revealed a keen interest.

The second group was a health class, where we were given about ten minutes to tell them our story and answer their questions. We took pictures of both groups and asked the students to write their names on a paper. Later we added these names to our prayer book. This was our first experience of speaking in a school, and though we didn't go to many schools, we did find that we loved speaking to students.

As we continued walking through the reservation, people stopped to thank us for sharing with their sons, daughters, nieces and nephews. It is our hope that we were able to give these young people some encouragement for their futures.

## Lyn

Moving day from Hardin was exciting for us, since we would be moving our Castle into the state of Wyoming—though we still had several more walking days in Montana. Our first Wyoming campground was a KOA in Sheridan with a most hospitable host couple. Russ set up his tent here for a couple of days before heading back to California.

As we continued walking through the Crow Reservation, Oliver Costa, a member of the Crow legislature, stopped to talk with us. He shared about his people and their difficulties. An important election would be held in November, and they were now working on balloting procedures and laws. He told us there were 11,000 Crow on the Reservation, with 6,000 of them 18 or over, which is voting age. Oliver shared about the drug problem and how they are trying to handle it. We also learned that evangelists came frequently to hold services, resulting in many of the young people becoming Christians.

A little later two ladies drove up and asked if we were the women walking across America. The driver's nephews had been in one of the classes we shared at in Hardin. The ladies told us they were so grateful for our prayers. They also told us about the bear problem in that area, but we had seen no sign of bears. It surprised us that bears were even in this open area devoid of trees.

Russ took us out to a steak dinner the night before he left for California. It was a nice evening, and we said our good-byes before going to bed, knowing we wouldn't see each other in the morning. It was hard for me to see Russ go, as he had been a tangible link to home. (Russ' thoughts about his time with us in Montana are in Appendix 4.)

We passed through St. Xavier and headed for Lodge Grass. It was a sunny day with a comfortable breeze. Cattle dotted the pastures all around, and once in a while they were even on the road with us. Seeing a dead cow on the road, we asked a rancher about it. He said it belonged to him and that his cousin had hit it a week earlier. Though it had totaled his car, the cousin was not hurt. Scott told us he loses at least one cow a month in road accidents.

On September 7 we attended Cornerstone Community Church in Sheridan, Wyoming. We still had a little more walking in Montana, but since we were now camped in Wyoming, it was easier to go to a church close by. They hold their services in an old, beautifully renovated theater. The historic architectural style outside was quite impressive.

Pastor Tony Forman had us stand at the prayer time, introduced us, and told the congregation about our Journey. Then they prayed for us and our venture. Anna Flint invited us to join her for lunch and we gladly accepted. She told us her husband had died several years earlier. Anna was born and raised in Rhode Island, and had moved to Wyoming in 1949. She had six children, twenty-three grandchildren, and eight great-grandchildren.

One gentleman stopped us on the road as we were nearing Lodge Grass. He had talked with us earlier on his way into town. Returning, he stopped only long enough to hand us each a bottle of ice water.

Right after he drove off, another man stopped to ask what we were doing. After our response, he said, "There's a storm coming. You might want to take a break—until spring." We thought this was hilarious and laughed about it for quite a while. He then wished us well, thanked us for praying, and asked us not to take a picture of him, since it was against his religion.

In Lodge Grass we stopped at the post office to mail some letters and had a nice chat with the postal clerk. He reached out to firmly shake our hands as we left and said, "Thank you for praying for us."

Leaving Lodge Grass, we turned onto County Road 451, our last road in Montana! Ron and Clarisse pulled up beside us and asked what we were doing. We told them we were walking and praying for America, and they immediately began sharing with us some prayer requests.

"Many of our people (the Crow Indians) turn to drink instead of to God. Our youth really need your prayers. This road you're walking on has many accidents, most caused by drunk drivers, and many are killed in these accidents." His final words to us were, "America needs to turn back to God."

It began to rain, which soon turned to sleet. Waliluke didn't quite know what to make of this stuff that kept hitting him on the back and head. He tried to walk in the high grasses to get away from the sleet, then he lay down to show us his displeasure at walking in this weather. It didn't last too long, so he was soon happy to be walking again.

We continued walking until we came to Wyola, a town of about 100 residents, and our last town in Montana. They have a flour mill, a small housing area and the railroad running through. As far as we could tell there wasn't much more to the town. We left Memorial Stone number 20 there and called it a day. This was a record-breaking mileage day for us; our total was 23 miles!

As we would soon be leaving the Crow Reservation, I began reflecting on our time there. I thought a lot about the commitment I had made to God for this walk. Then I thought about the people we had met along our route, especially those on the Crow Reservation. So many of these wonderful people had expressed their gratitude to us for our prayers for them. There were the school children who had been impressed enough to share about our Journey with their families, and others who believed in what we were doing enough that they gave us donations to help us along. What a blessing these people were.

On September 9, as we began our last day of walking in Montana, Keith Blackhawk stopped to talk with us. He told us he was heading out to get his son to come help him repair his pickup truck. Keith was the last of the Crow to talk with us before we left the reservation.

Before leaving this state, we talked with five men who were working on an agreement between the Burlington North Santa Fe Railroad and the Montana highway department on accessibility rights to replace a railroad bridge in 2004. After an enjoyable time of sharing with them we continued on to the border between Montana and Wyoming!

We had been in Montana 64 days rather than the 56 we had originally estimated. It had taken 13 of those days to walk through the Crow Indian Reservation. This was an incredibly joyful time for us, and we celebrated by pouring water over each other at the state line. The dogs looked at us like we were crazy, as we screamed and hooted, both from being ecstatic at finally reaching this border and from the icy cold water pouring over us.

For about an hour we celebrated, took pictures, and prayed for the state we were leaving as well as the one we were entering. We prepared Memorial Stones number 22 and 23 to leave at the state signs for Montana and Wyoming.

*"The LORD is exalted over all the nations,*
*His glory above the heavens."*
        **—PSALM 113:4**

# WYOMING

## *Wide Open Spaces*

Entered Wyoming ................................................................ September 9, 2003

Finished Wyoming................................................................ September 29, 2003

Actual Days in State................................................................20

Walking Days in State................................................................15

Total Mileage for Wyoming ................................................................233.4

Total Journey Mileage to Date................................................................1,365.9

Capital ................................................................ Cheyenne

Admitted to Statehood................................................................July 10, 1890 ~ 44th state

Population ................................................................501,242

Highest Point................................................................Gannett Peak ~ 13,804 feet

Lowest Point................................................................Bell Fourche River ~ 3,099 feet

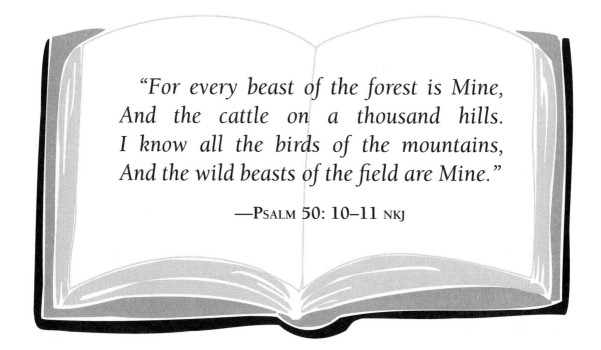

"For every beast of the forest is Mine,
And the cattle on a thousand hills.
I know all the birds of the mountains,
And the wild beasts of the field are Mine."

—PSALM 50: 10–11 NKJ

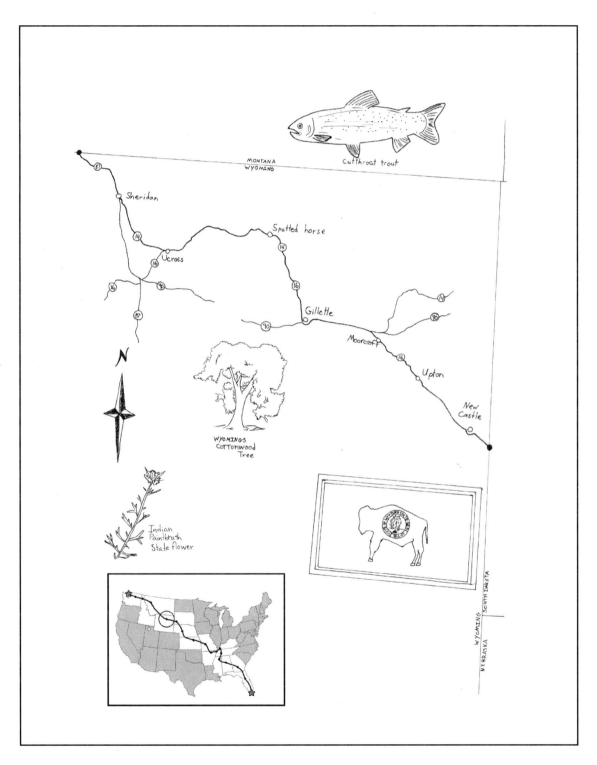

cutthroat trout

MONTANA
WYOMING

Sheridan

Spotted horse

Ucross

Gillette

Moorcroft

Upton

New Castle

WYOMING'S COTTONWOOD Tree

N

Indian Paintbrush State flower

WYOMING   SOUTH DAKOTA

NEBRASKA

*Chapter Ten*

# LITTLE OLD LADY ON A FLYING TRAPEZE

### Sam

Waliluke barked like crazy at the strange creature. In his short life he had never seen anything like it. Several similar creatures lined the street, and Waliluke reacted to each as we came to them. It amused us to see him so agitated.

Only three days earlier on Tuesday, September 9, we had begun walking in Wyoming. The weather was turning cooler, and we felt the urge to move south more rapidly. In fact it was cold as we walked through Parkman. I could see snow on some of the high mountains. The sun warmed us some, but the wind swept down from the peaks, keeping us cool enough to dress a little warmer.

Deer, geese and ducks dotted the valley's green landscape as we walked. A train with three engines on front and another at the end whizzed by. More than two hundred boxcars filled the space in between.

### Lyn

On our first day in Wyoming we walked only eight miles, since we needed to do some scouting of our route. Just before we quit walking, we noticed a red car go past us, then turn around and come back our way. The car pulled up beside us, and someone inside asked if we were the women walking across America. Learning we were "those women," they began handing us dollar bills and coins, telling us, "It isn't much, but it's all we have."

It was very hard for us to take their money, but it would have been an insult to turn them down. While we talked with the five people inside, they continued digging into the ashtray and between the seats, pulling out more coins and handing them to us. They waved to us as they drove off, but returned a few minutes later holding out another one-dollar bill they had found. What a humbling experience. It is our prayer that God will bless these wonderful people abundantly for their kindness to us.

While we were camped in Sheridan, Meredith Lewis arrived from Paso Robles, California to spend a week cooking dinners for our hungry team. She set right to work preparing a delicious dinner of grilled salmon, red potatoes, fresh corn and strawberry shortcake. This was certainly a better meal than we had eaten in a long time. For the next week we looked forward to our evening meals with great anticipation.

On September 11, our route took us through Sheridan where Russ had arranged for us to stop at the Sheridan Press for an interview with Pat Blair. This was an especially appropriate day for an interview, just two years since the terrorist attacks in New York, Washington D. C and Pennsylvania. It was following these attacks that we had decided to really push for this Journey of prayer for the nation.

Following the interview I received a call from Dave, telling me that Mirek Koudelka, a genealogist and good friend of ours, had e-mailed from Czech Republic. He had been thinking back two years to the terrorist attacks and wanted to do something for our nation at this time. Since he couldn't be with us to walk in person, he wanted to know if he could at least walk with us in spirit for the day in memory of the disaster of 9/11. We were honored to have him join us in this way.

It was in downtown Sheridan that Waliluke began his furious barking at the unusual creatures along the street. To our amusement, Wali was terrified of the many sculpted figures displayed on the streets. A local artist created some of these sculptures out of barbed wire. Wali kept his distance as best as he could, but if we walked him too close to one, a low growl would emit from his throat before it turned into an angry bark. Perhaps he thought he was protecting us.

The Sheridan Press had done a good job, and that next Sunday several people at Grace Baptist Church recognized that we were the ladies in the paper. It was September 14, and Pastor Anderson introduced us and prayed for us during the prayer time.

## Joni

While we were enjoying the church service the dogs were having some fun of their own. I'm sure Waliluke was the main culprit (not my Cassie!). Looking inside Lady Van Go we saw a bag of candy had been emptied and pieces of wrappers were scattered around. Many other items had been tossed around in a frenzy, probably while they were on a sugar high from all the sweets. We picked things up enough to drive back to the campground. Sam and I decided to do a thorough cleaning of the van.

## Lyn

Our Castle refrigerator had quit working that morning, so I called a repair service to see if there was any possibility of someone coming out today. Roger recognized the brand name of our refrigerator and knew exactly what the problem was. He had read about us in the paper and said he could be out in about half an hour.

He arrived, verified the problem, and replaced the computerized board that had defaulted with many of this particular brand. He then very kindly gave us a reduced rate on his labor. I also asked him about our microwave that we were only able to use if we had our temperamental generator running. He suggested a very simple solution, a heavy-duty extension cord to plug it in to the main electrical supply. Now why didn't we think of that?! It was a great idea and enabled us to use it much more than we had before.

Later, Brad, the principal of Three Peaks Christian School, came looking for the women who were walking and praying across America. Brad had read about us in the paper and was hoping we could come to the school some morning the next week to share in their devotional time. We arranged to be at the school Tuesday morning at 8:15 A.M.

Joni and Sam finished organizing the van and Lyn sorted files. Meredith prepared eggs Benedict. At last we could sit down to eat this great meal. The dogs continued to run about in a frenzy (they had eaten a lot of sweets), and by day's end we were all exhausted!

On Monday we were all glad to get back to the routine of walking after our wild Sunday. We were seeing more and more of the beautiful pronghorn, lots of sheep, deer, cattle, and horses in the pastures. We watched a herd of mountain goats in the distance going down to a pond for water.

Our route took us through Sheridan, heading east on Highway 14 toward Gillette. The hills were still green, but the distant mountains were now coated with a thin veil of snow. For a couple of days we had showers off and on, with a little hail. The weather was definitely changing.

With the beginning of the rainy season we needed to get appropriate rain wear. At the Sport Stop in Sheridan we bought waterproof pants, jackets, gloves and socks. The socks were neoprene and fit over our regular hiking socks. Our purchases were made just in time. The next week they got a good test in freezing rain as we climbed the mountain out of Sheridan. Remember, we chose to wear hiking sandals, even through the winter months. With the neoprene socks even our feet stayed warm and dry.

In Leiter we stopped at the Leiterville Country Club, the one and only building in town. It houses the post office, café, bar and gift shop. We were told the town, population 5, was named for a rancher who had owned the land.

## Sam

Three Peaks Christian School was really fun. Brad took us to the library where they had donuts, tea and coffee waiting. The school of 29 students had grades eight through twelve. We were given a gift from the faculty and student body, and then Brad prayed with us.

Meeting with the students in a large classroom, each of us shared from our experiences. They asked many questions and wrote prayer requests for us. Several asked if they could see our dogs, so we took them outside to pet and play with Waliluke and Cassie.

One class had been studying memorial stones in the Bible, and the teacher got permission to take her students to where we had placed the Sheridan Memorial Stone. We prayed and took pictures at the site, then said good-bye and went our separate ways.

## Lyn

At the town of Spotted Horse, population about 5, we finished our day. When we moved from Sheridan to Gillette, Meredith bid us farewell and began her long drive back to Paso Robles.

It began to rain as I drove the motor home out of the campground, followed by Joni in Lady Van Go. This rain soon turned to a slushy snow. Instead of heat on my feet I was getting an icy draft, so by the time we got to Gillette my feet were freezing. This reminded me that we needed to have the right fluids in the Castle, so checking it in at the Goodyear garage, we went to get a motel. While we were settling in, Dave arrived to be with us for the next week. I was ecstatic! It had been four months since we had seen each other!

## Joni

Waliluke's first experience in a motel had him jumping and running about like crazy. Every so often he stopped in front of the mirror to admire the handsome dog. I was certain that he was hoping the new dog would play with him.

I was delighted to stretch out in a queen-size bed, until both Cassie and Waliluke joined me. Whenever I woke up in the night Waliluke was sitting up looking in the mirror. Then at 4:00 A.M. Wali pooped all over the floor. Since Sam was fast asleep I had the "pleasure" of cleaning up, then taking both dogs for a walk outside in the bushes.

When we got the Castle back the next day we set up camp at the High Plains campground, where Sam and I and the dogs stayed while Dave and Lyn stayed at the motel.

## Lyn

Starting the day at Spotted Horse, Dave walked with us for about a mile-and-a-half, then took over the driving so Joni could walk full-time. During the day we saw several pronghorn. One came quite close to us as we were taking a break at the van, so Joni and I got our cameras ready. I was holding Cassie's leash and was just ready to snap the picture. Without warning Cassie and Waliluke both decided to chase the pronghorn.

I went flying through the air for about twelve feet, then landed abruptly in the grassy area alongside the road. Once everyone was satisfied that I was OK, they had a good laugh at the sight of me flying through the air. Our theme song for the rest of the day was, "She flew through the air with the greatest of ease, the little old lady on the flying trapeze."

Joni and Sam encouraged Dave and me to take a day off from walking to do something special. We decided to visit Crazy Horse and Mount Rushmore in nearby South Dakota. It was sunny and warm, perfect for sightseeing. Of course, we also talked a lot about our experiences during the time we had been separated. Joni and Sam enjoyed the day taking it easy with the dogs.

Heading back through Custer, South Dakota on our way to Gillette, Wyoming we noticed storm clouds gathering. Just before the border it began to rain, then hail! The hailstones, about the size of marbles, came down for about fifteen minutes, then suddenly stopped. We began noticing signs advertising hail repairs for cars. It seems that large hail is not unusual in this area.

Pastor Charles Small welcomed us to Grace Bible Church in Gillette. It was Sunday, September 21. Tragedy had recently struck this small congregation. A young husband and father had been killed in a motorcycle accident, and a week before that another member had died. Still another had just been diagnosed with a terminal illness. Our hearts were heavy for them. For the remainder of our Journey the sight of motorcyclists reminded us to pray for this church.

## Joni

Friends of mine from San Jose, California, Nancy and Ingeborg, arrived to walk with us for a few days. Nancy walked with Sam and Lyn, while Ingeborg and I drove ahead to park the van and walk back.

At Eagle Butte Coal Mine, northwest of Gillette, we stopped at the overlook. Huge trucks, with tires more than twice our height, moved around below us in the coal terraces of this open mine. One was on display at the overlook, along with a shovel bucket that five of us could easily stand inside. A sign told us this impressive bucket could hold twenty-three cubic yards of coal material.

## Lyn

While Joni took a day off to spend with her friends exploring Crazy Horse, Mount Rushmore, and part of the South Dakota Badlands, Dave drove for us. Cassie wasn't too happy about Joni being gone, but we managed to get her to walk. Still she kept stopping to look around hoping that Joni would suddenly appear. Much of the day she rode in the van, perhaps feeling a little closer to "her mama" than when she was walking with us.

East of Gillette we walked past another open coal mine, not quite as large as the Eagle Butte Mine. John was heading home from his shift at the Eagle Butte Mine and stopped to see what we were doing. He showed us some pictures of a stagecoach he runs once a year from Cheyenne, Wyoming to Deadwood, South Dakota.

All too soon Dave had to return home. It would only be three months until we were together again. (Dave includes his brief thoughts about his stay in Wyoming in Appendix 7.)

Trains rolled by with their cargo of coal and other freight. We waved to the crews and they often waved in response. Newcastle's quaint shops, interesting homes and tiny gardens was our Wyoming finale. Sadly many of the shops were closed and boarded up. We prayed and left Memorial Stone number 35, then continued walking.

At the state border we celebrated with yells and hugs. After praying for both states and leaving Memorial Stones under their respective signs we took pictures, then drove back to the Castle. I prepared corned beef hash and fried eggs for a celebration dinner, a meal we usually reserved for Sunday brunch or special occasions, since we all enjoyed it so much. Wyoming was a great state to walk through. Now we looked forward to what South Dakota would hold for us.

Our guests had all left, and now it was time for us to move on to another campground. But before leaving Gillette we stopped at "All God's Creatures" pet store to buy a rain suit for Waliluke. It was brown leather, lined with lambswool. We thought he looked like a World War II flying ace in his new rain gear.

Finally we left Gillette and went to Beaver Lake campground about three miles west of Custer, South Dakota. The owner told Joni he had read about us in the newspaper. It was a beautiful lakeside spot surrounded by pines. There were not many campers. Autumn surrounded us with trees turning yellow and red, and the days getting shorter and colder.

# SOUTH DAKOTA

## *Treasures In Stone*

Entered South Dakota ...................................................... *September 30, 2003*

Finished South Dakota........................................................ *October 7, 2003*

Actual Days in State.................................................................................*8*

Walking Days in State...............................................................................*6*

Total Mileage for South Dakota ..........................................................*98.1*

Total Journey Mileage to Date............................................................*1,464.0*

Capital ...................................................................................... *Pierre*

Admitted to Statehood .............................. *November 2, 1889 ~ the 40th state*

Population..................................................................................*754,844*

Highest Point...........................................................*Harney Peak ~ 7,242 feet*

Lowest Point............................................................*Big Stone Lake ~ 962 feet*

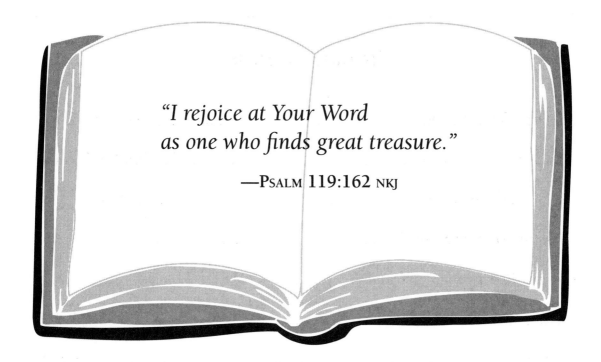

*"I rejoice at Your Word
as one who finds great treasure."*

—Psalm 119:162 NKJ

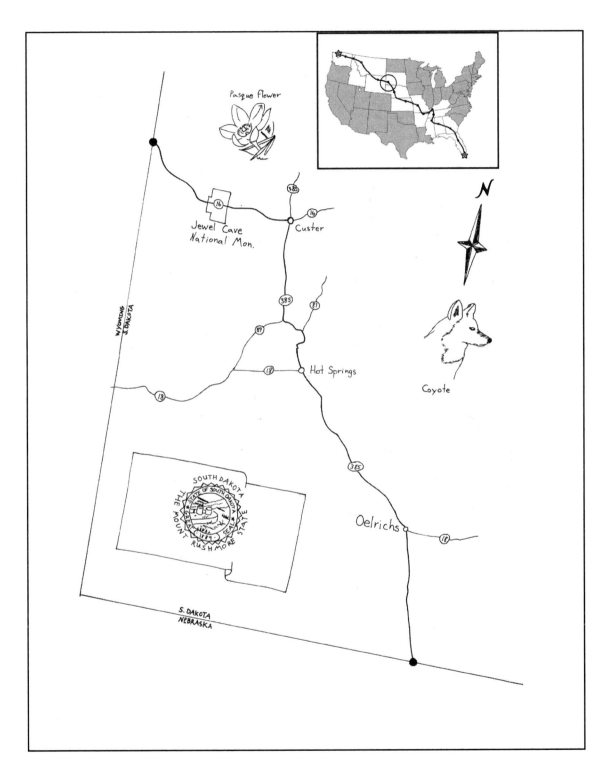

Pasque flower

Jewel Cave
National Mon.

Custer

WYOMING
S. DAKOTA

385

87

89

18

Hot Springs

18

N

Coyote

SOUTH DAKOTA
STATE OF SOUTH DAKOTA
1889
THE MOUNT RUSHMORE STATE

385

Oelrichs

16

16

385

16

S. DAKOTA
NEBRASKA

# Chapter Eleven

# THE TROOPER AND WALILUKE

## *Lyn*

We stood watching quietly as four large buffalo crossed the road about a quarter of a mile ahead of us. Cassie was in the van, but Waliluke was with us on his leash. Thankfully he didn't notice the huge animals—at least he didn't bark. The buffalo were between the van and us. But let's go back to the beginning of this state.

Our entrance into South Dakota was very nice. The first ten or eleven miles were rolling red hills. The road was narrow at times with very little area to step off when cars were coming, especially when trucks were going both directions next to us. We were extra alert and made it through just fine. This section had beautiful rock walls with loose rocks that had fallen close to where we were walking, the perfect place to collect specimens for our rock collections. Joni had asked me to choose a good rock for her while choosing one for myself. I ended up with two special rocks and carried them for the next three miles, shifting them first one way, then another. Though they were small, carrying them while going gradually uphill for three miles made it seem as though they were getting bigger and bigger.

## *Joni*

It was a sunny day though the wind was icy cold. While Lyn and Sam walked on a curvy narrow road, Cassie and I hiked by ourselves. We went into the hills and saw incredible scenery with trees whose foliage was turning beautiful shades of red and yellow. It was nice to be away from the traffic. I was hoping to see some wildlife, but it was peaceful and quiet with the ponderosa pines, blue sky, and rocks. I met up with Lyn and Sam and we finished hiking for the day.

Sunday, September 28 we went to Berean Bible Church in Custer, South Dakota near our camp. Pastor Gary gave a good message on grace. After the service only a few people spoke to us, which was most unusual. Just before we started to walk out one couple introduced themselves to us and began to ask questions. We talked with them for a while, and they asked if we would be able to come to their place for dinner one night that week. Les and Joyce live fairly close to where we were camped, so we arranged for them to call us later with more specifics.

From church we drove to Mount Rushmore so Sam could see the monument. We ate lunch there, and after shopping in the gift shop continued on to Rapid City. There we found a mall where we were able to get some more things for winter and a rain suit for Cassie.

## Lyn

We were walking through the Jasper fire area where a large fire had raged in August of 2000. The results of this fire added to the unique coloring in the Jewel Caves National Monument area. Here we met Randy and Gail, who were curious about what we were doing. They were driving back to their home in Newcastle, Wyoming where they had seen us a few days earlier.

We noticed a definite change in the weather. The nights were getting increasingly cold. One night Joni was up several times because of the cold and unable to stop shivering. At 5:30 I got up and put my sleeping bag over her to help keep some of her body heat in. It was then I realized that the heater wasn't coming on, nor was there any hot water. Then I saw we weren't getting any water at all, cold or hot. Our windows were all covered in frost, and the hose outside was frozen. We did have electricity, so I heated some of our bottled water for tea.

Later I had the bright idea of making hot chocolate shakes. Putting the necessary ingredients in the shaker, I put on the cap and began to shake it. Suddenly the top exploded off and the shake went everywhere, from the ceiling to the cupboard to the floor and everywhere in between. At least it was confined to the kitchen area. We all burst into laughter—it's always better to laugh in this kind of situation. We had learned early on not to let things like this frustrate us too much. The cleanup began, and I was thankful it was so easy to wipe the chocolate off the carpet, clothes and ceiling with nothing more than a damp cloth.

Nearing the town of Custer, Joni had discovered some more beautiful rocks. Many of them were rose quartz, the state mineral. What a treasure for us. We were able to collect several nice pieces to add to our rock collections.

This rocky area had also been the sight of an accident. Two signs had been erected in memory of Adam and Matt: "X marks the spot. THINK! Drive carefully." It always saddened us to see the memorials for people who have been killed along the highways of our country. So many are young children or teenagers.

The day we were to have dinner with Les and Joyce, Joni woke up not feeling well. We called Joyce to see if it would be possible for her to pick us up at the end of our walking day so Joni could stay at the Castle and rest. After the arrangements were worked out, Sam and I drove to Custer and started walking. For a good part of the day we headed south. We had packed extra food and water since Joni would not be meeting us.

Soon after we turned onto Highway 385, we noticed a wide gravel path below us. It seemed to follow the highway so we walked on it away from traffic. It was wonderful and soon we came to a bench beside the trail with the words "Mickelson Trail" embedded in the back. From Pringle we moved to the highway again to turn east.

## Sam

In the afternoon during our lunch stop, Waliluke ate and had a nap. As we began walking again a South Dakota highway patrolman went by. A few minutes later he went past us in the other direction. This time he made a U-turn, then pulled up beside us. He wondered if we were OK, or if there was anything he could do for us. We gave him one of our cards and explained what we were doing. He was quite fascinated and asked a lot of questions.

When Grumman asked if she could take his picture he was happy to oblige. He got out of his car and came around to us, and Waliluke bounded over to give him a good snuggle and get some petting. Trooper Heath loved it and allowed Wali to snuggle all he wanted. We continued talking and looked down to see that Wali had fallen asleep on the trooper's shoe. Finally we said good-bye with promises to pray for each other. We also found out he had only been a state trooper for one-and-a-half months.

## Lyn

Joyce came to pick us up and took us back to Lady Van Go. We then went to the Castle to freshen up and check on Joni before going to Les and Joyce's home. Joni was still not feeling well, so she stayed at the Castle. We had a lovely dinner with Les and Joyce, and were joined by Pastor Gary and his wife Bev.

There had been several frosty nights when our heater had refused to come on. Then one morning we woke up to no frost, and the heater was working. We were beginning to wonder if the heater only worked when it was over a certain temperature—hmmmm, that wasn't a good thought.

We arrived at the entrance to Wind Cave National Park, "Where the buffalo roam, and the deer and the antelope play." This is where we saw the four large buffalo crossing the road. Joni had already joined us, leaving Cassie in the van. We needed to get Waliluke into the van with Cassie so we could walk through the preserve. There was a warning sign to be very cautious around these creatures, as a buffalo had gored one person the previous year.

Much to our relief the buffalo soon moved on and we could get to the van and put Waliluke inside. As we continued walking through the preserve Joni stayed close to us with the van in case we needed to jump in out of harm's way. Over the next six miles we saw several more buffalo, but they were all a good distance away. At the other end of the range we crossed the cattle guard to exit the National Park.

## Joni

The town of Hot Springs had a population of over 4,000 and seemed to stretch on forever. A river ran through the town with a large waterfall, so we followed its course. An old train station with a train and a stone jailhouse were nearby. We enjoyed the architecture of the historic sandstone buildings erected in the 1880s. The hotel reminded me of the sandstone homes in the Cotswolds in England.

The Sioux and the Cheyenne fought over the hot springs because of its healing waters. They came to an agreement that all Indians should be able to come and get the benefits of the hot spring water. Later the white man came and built the town around the springs.

Soon after leaving Hot Springs we found ourselves walking through the rolling prairies. This lasted throughout the rest of the state. We also noticed the temperatures warming up again.

## Lyn

On Sunday, October 5 we attended Living Outreach Church in Custer. Pastor Joel Ziolkowski greeted us as we entered and told us there were refreshments downstairs where we could fellowship with other parishioners. When the service started we were sitting in the second row, as had become our custom. Pastor Joel introduced us and asked us to say a few words about our Journey.

He then gave a very good message on our being uniquely created by God, individually designed to be the person He desires us to be. When we accept Christ we become new creatures, and begin the journey of becoming the very unique individual He has in mind. He told of his own past, and of coming out of alcohol and drugs to be set free from these addictions. We learned that he was one of ten children whose father had begun the sculpting of "Crazy Horse" mountain. His father has since died, and seven of his siblings and his mother are continuing the work.

We went back to the church the next day to take pictures. Noticing the gardener mowing the lawn, we looked closer and saw it was Pastor Joel. He saw us and came over to talk. Before leaving we took time to pray with him, promising to add him to our prayer list.

Seventeen miles north of the border found us walking through the prairies and farmlands. The weather was warm and sunny with blue skies. We stopped and prayed at Oelrichs, a very small town, and left Memorial Stone number 41.

I was not feeling well so we stopped at a roadside park. There was a pond for Cassie and Waliluke to have a swim. We saw an old bedraggled coyote at the pond, but he disappeared almost immediately.

When we reached the border we took photographs, prayed, and left memorial stones. We had now walked through five of our fifteen states!

Our next move was to Chadron, Nebraska. While Sam was packing up, Joni and I drove into Custer to pick up mail and leave the forwarding address. Back at the Castle we each finished our "breaking camp tasks" and were soon ready to head out.

When we drove through Hot Springs we stopped to enjoy a Chinese meal to celebrate 36 years since Dave and I adopted our Korean daughter, Laurie. It has been a tradition in our family that no matter where we are on October 6, we celebrate with an Asian meal. Later I phoned Laurie to let her know I had not forgotten.

While we enjoyed our Asian food, we were soon to discover that Waliluke enjoyed another kind of delicacy.

# NEBRASKA

## *Two Great Ladies*

Entered Nebraska.................................................................. October 8, 2003

Finished Nebraska .............................................................November 7, 2003

Actual Days in State..........................................................................30

Walking Days in State.......................................................................23

Total Mileage for Nebraska...........................................................416.5

Total Journey Mileage to Date...................................................1,880.5

Capital ...................................................................................Lincoln

Admitted to Statehood...................................... March 1, 1867 ~ the 37th state

Population...........................................................................1,711,263

Highest Point.......................................Panorama Point ~ 5,424 feet

Lowest Point................................................Missouri River ~ 480 feet

"In Joppa there was a disciple named Dorcas, who was always doing good and helping the poor . . . All the widows stood around him (Peter), crying and showing him the robes and other clothing that Dorcas had made while she was still with them."

—Acts 9:36, 39

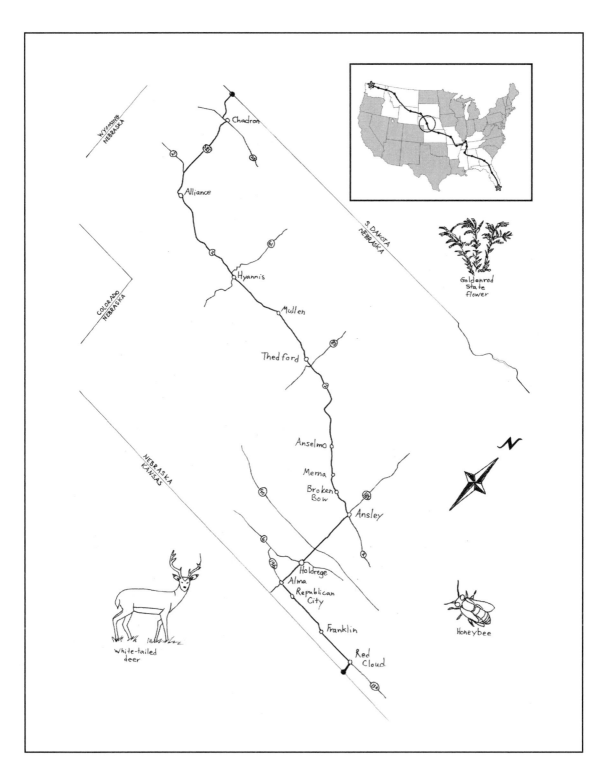

Chadron

WYOMING
NEBRASKA

Alliance

S. DAKOTA
NEBRASKA

COLORADO
NEBRASKA

Hyannis

Mullen

Thedford

NEBRASKA
KANSAS

Anselmo

Merna

Broken
Bow

Ansley

Holdrege

Alma
Republican
City

Franklin

Red
Cloud

Goldenrod
State
flower

N

White-tailed
deer

Honeybee

*Chapter Twelve*

# DELICACIES FOR WALILUKE

### Lyn

In the Bible, Dorcas was a lady held in high esteem by the widows and the poor of her area. She had done much to help them, and they were all so thankful for her many kind deeds.

In Nebraska we met two women that our walking team holds in high esteem. These women did much to encourage us. Their kindness and love blessed us, not just through Nebraska, but also throughout the rest of the walk. Many times when we were feeling down we thought about these two women and thanked God for them. As we tell of our walk through this wonderful state, we'll introduce you to Connie and Georgia. We hope you'll be blessed by the actions of these women just as we were.

We were excited, and looking forward to our first day of walking in Nebraska. What new things would we experience in this state? Finding a list of "do's and don'ts" printed on the internet for Nebraska, we picked our favorite to share with you, our readers:

"In the town of Blue Hill, a female wearing a hat that might frighten a timid person must never be seen eating onions in public." Your guess is as good as mine as to how or why that became a law in Nebraska. And I really don't know when it became a law, or if it is still in their law books. We didn't spend a lot of time pondering this—we had walking to do.

Before walking we stopped by the post office in Chadron. I was expecting a new pair of shoes to come to our general delivery here. My shoe situation was getting desperate and most towns we walked through had very little to offer in the way of walking shoes. My shoes were there!! So were several other packages and letters! The packages contained lots of snack stuff, girl stuff, and CHOCOLATE!!!

### Joni

I drove ahead and parked the van, then began walking back with Cassie to meet Lyn and Sam. I was enjoying the day and looking at the scenery, when suddenly I stepped on something in the grassy shoulder. At the same time I heard an ominous rattling sound and jumped high into the air just as the rattlesnake struck my sandal! After giving my heart time to slow its rapid beating, I circled back around to get a few great pictures of this amazing creature. What a beauty! You may think we're a bit crazy, but we all actually enjoy seeing snakes. While we do have a healthy respect for them, we don't have a lot of fear as long as we know what to expect.

## Lyn

At Mile Marker 173 along U.S. Highway 385 we reached the point where we had walked one third of the way on our Journey across America. We all posed for pictures at "The Spot" before continuing on.

With winter coming we looked for ways to cut mileage and get south faster. Studying our maps, we came up with a change in the route that would cut about 80 or 90 miles from the Journey. With the new route we would stay on Highway 385 all the way to the town of Alliance. From there we would turn onto a country road that was one of the state's Scenic Routes. Had we not made this change, we would not have gone through the areas where we met our two special ladies. Looking back, we see how incredibly God was directing our path.

The first day of our new route took us past some beautiful cottonwood trees with leaves in bright colorful hues. As we were taking pictures of this incredible scene we heard a voice behind us asking if we were photographers. We turned to see a cheerful lady walking toward us on the hill along the road. Pulling out a card to give her, we explained about our Journey of Prayer across the United States. Without hesitation she asked if we had eaten lunch yet, then invited us to come eat with her and her husband. We accepted the invitation and had a delightful meal and visit with Jim and Connie Poitra.

Connie is the first of our two special ladies. While we sat eating sandwiches we learned more about our host and hostess. Jim is a French Chippewa Indian, while the sweet redheaded Connie is of Irish descent. Jim was a delight, and was obviously in love with his beautiful wife.

We learned that Connie was an accomplished artist, well known in the area. After lunch she took us downstairs to see her studio. What a delight. Our eyes were drawn to the bright colors of the trees in the paintings, very similar to what we had been walking past that morning. She paints mainly in watercolors, but also in acrylic/watercolor. Using a watercolor board, she thins the acrylic with water, making the painting much brighter and the colors brilliant. Her work can be found in collections throughout the United States.

I purchased a watercolor titled, "The Old Maytag." Joni chose an acrylic painting of a local pond with the brightly colored trees behind it, while Sam ended up with an oil of "Jackson Hole."

We hated to say good-bye, but knew we should get on with the walk. As we prepared to leave Connie asked us to pray for her. She explained that she had Parkinson's disease and had just recently been diagnosed with the early stages of Alzheimer's. We were stunned as she shared this with us and promised to pray for her. I later entered her name in our book and we have continued to pray for her, not just during the walk, but now in the years to follow as well.

Connie told us she planned to continue painting as long as possible, with the hope of it helping her physically and emotionally. She had begun taking medication that the doctors hoped would slow down the effects of the Alzheimer's. Throughout the Journey we frequently thought of Connie and Jim and prayed for them. They were a real blessing to us that day, and their memory continues to bless us. I hope this story will also be a blessing and an encouragement to all who read it.

One morning at our campground in Chadron, Waliluke slipped out the door of our Castle and ran to a nearby tent to greet the couple staying there. We headed over to get Waliluke and stopped to talk with the campers. They told us their names were John and Margo, they were from Forest Lake, Minnesota. It was refreshing talking with them and we added them to our prayer list.

That evening when we returned from walking we found a small packet on our Castle door with a note and three McDonald's gift certificate booklets. While there was no signature, we were pretty certain it was from our neighboring tent campers who had traveled on while we walked that day. Little did they know how much we appreciated those gift certificates. A McDonald's breakfast or hot fudge sundae was a real treat for us.

With a storm coming, the sunset that evening was great. Wind howled while thunder pounded and lightning flashed between black clouds. The heavens seemed to open in a torrent of rain.

As we prepared to look at some of our pictures on the computer one evening, the power connector slipped from the counter and into the dog's water dish. We grabbed it right away, but it was too late. It had gotten soaked. Without it we couldn't recharge the computer battery, or connect it to the electrical supply.

Continuing toward Alliance we stopped for our lunch break, then we began seeing truck after truck hauling sugar beets. Next we walked past a storage depot where the trucks lined up to dump the sugar beets onto a conveyer belt that carried them to the top of a pile. We watched and took pictures for a while.

Further on we saw a large field of sunflowers ready for harvesting, then several fields of dried corn stalks waiting to be plowed under. It was a fascinating day for us with a variety of classic Nebraska farming experiences.

Alliance is a town of almost 10,000 people. We prayed for the town and left Memorial Stone number 45 at the city sign. This sign declared that Alliance is an oasis in the midst of sand hills. Our prayer for Alliance was that they would be an oasis, sharing the Living Water with others around them.

## Joni

On Sunday, October 12 I felt very tired, so I decided not to go to church. I do not sleep well at night and every two weeks or so, I am so physically tired that all I can do is sleep. Sam and Lyn left for church, and Cassie and I turned over and went back to sleep.

## Sam

Leaving Joni to rest, Grumman and I went to find a church. The service at the First Baptist Church of Chadron had just started when we arrived. After being introduced we shared about our Journey. Pastor Richard Wheatley was fairly new to the church and very missions-minded. The whole service was very enjoyable.

Grumman and I then drove to Rapid City, South Dakota, about 75 miles away to get a replacement for the damaged computer part. It was a long drive, but seemed to be our only choice. In Rapid City we checked out several places. Each sent us to another until finally we arrived at Radio Shack in the big mall. There we met Jeremy, the senior manager. He was very helpful. We had the computer with us, so when he found the part we needed he set it up and tested it for us. He was a Christian young man and we enjoyed talking with him. Soon we were on our way back to Chadron, Nebraska. It was 8 P.M. when we got back to the Castle.

## Lyn

When we returned Joni had finished the laundry and gotten a lot more sleep. She was feeling better for which we were thankful! It had been a successful day for each of us as once again we had the opportunity to experience God at work.

Waliluke, our sweet little adopted puppy, was really into chewing these days. He managed to chew one of Joni's good leather hiking sandals—her favorites, of course. When we left the dogs in the van on Sundays while we were in church, we often came back to see a variety of things destroyed. We tried to cover and hide things and remove what we could before leaving them. Getting to church on Sundays had to include time to dog-proof the van first. Using sheets, we covered everything possible and clipped them with clothespins to whatever we could. Then we put toys and chew bones around and "crossed our fingers."

The gallon jugs that we bought our water in were favorite toys of Waliluke's, not necessarily empty ones. With space in the Castle very tight, our bottles of water were set in every spare corner. We bought twenty to forty bottles at a time, depending how long it would be before we could buy more. Drinking water was something we definitely didn't want to run out of. After Wali chewed through a couple of bottles filled with water, we had to find ways to keep them out of his reach.

We realized that Wali was still a puppy and we tried our best to supply him with all the right chew toys, but in our small quarters we couldn't protect everything from his sharp teeth. One day as we entered the van after a church service we discovered he had chewed through a couple of seat belts. These were in seats we used all the time—ouch! Until we could get these replaced we couldn't use the front passenger seat. We were thankful he hadn't chewed the driver's seat belt.

In Alliance we stopped at the Ford dealer to make an appointment to have the van serviced and the two seat belts replaced. They were able to order them with an overnight delivery promised. The next day was moving day for us, and we planned to spend a little time exploring Alliance while the work was done on Lady Van Go.

## Sam

Before leaving Chadron we did extra Wal-Mart shopping because there would not be another one soon. We stocked up on non-perishable items, including thirty-five gallons of drinking water. With the help of a carryout clerk, we managed to get four full grocery carts and a flatbed cart loaded with water out to the van. Then with me inside the van, the clerk and Grumman passed items from the carts to me while I found places to stow them for the drive back to the Castle. While Grumman and I shopped, Joni prepared the Castle for moving, so we were ready to leave soon after we returned.

On our way to Alliance we saw an interesting "Rest Area." There was a toilet and a recliner sitting on some hay bales. We stopped to take pictures, then continued to a place called

"Carhenge." It was a display of old cars painted gray and arranged to look like England's Stonehenge.

## Lyn

The crew at the Ford Dealer had been great fun to talk with, and after photographing them, we said our good byes and headed out. It was good to have our new seat belts and again ride safely.

Driving to Mullen we set up camp at the Sandhill Motel and RV Park. After getting everything connected, we put together a meal of cubed steaks, mashed potatoes, gravy, and a salad.

For much of Nebraska we walked beside the railroad tracks. We enjoyed waving to the engineers, who usually waved or blew the whistle. For much of our time we walked along State Road 2, designated as a Scenic Byway. The towns here are about eight or nine miles apart, many barely surviving and just about all of them unincorporated.

The town of Antioch used to be a boomtown of about 2,000 people. There are many alkaline lakes in this area. In 1916 factories began extracting potash to make into fertilizer, Epsom salt and soda. After the end of World War I potash was cheaper to import from France and Germany. The Antioch plant closed in 1921, and most of the people left the area.

Memorial stones were impossible to find in these parts of the state. This is the sandhill area and any rocks that were ever around have been reduced to sand. After we used the few stones we had, we resorted to tiny rocks we found along the tracks. These were rough, very difficult to write on, and about the size of an egg. As we neared the town of Ellsworth we noticed some larger rocks by a tree, so we collected some to use through this sandy area.

## Sam

Puncture burrs were a big problem for the dogs through the sandhills. They suffered as they tried to walk in grassy areas. I carried tweezers with me all the time to help pluck the nasty little stickers from their tender paws. For a while we put little booties on their feet, and Wali danced around trying to pull them off. Eventually he ate Cassie's booties, making her very happy. Sometimes it was just too time consuming to remove stickers, so we left the dogs in the van. Waliluke never understood why we wouldn't let him walk with us at those times.

Once again we had a grasshopper plague. Waliluke found this very exciting. He watched them jump from place to place and pounced on them. Frequently we heard a crunching sound as Wali caught one of the unlucky hoppers and ate it for a snack.

The grasshoppers were only two sizes, small and extra large. When Wali caught a small one we heard the crunch, crunch as he devoured it. This was a real delicacy for Waliluke. Gross! When he caught an extra large one he carried it in his mouth like a trophy with its legs hanging out as he marched proudly down the road. Eventually he amputated the legs, dropped the body on the ground and rolled over it

while Cassie looked on in disgust. Unfortunately Waliluke sometimes jumped into the weeds in his rush to capture a grasshopper and came out with his nose full of burrs. It made him absolutely frantic and we had quite a time getting him to hold still while I plucked them out.

## Lyn

Periodically we found portions of old roads to walk on. It was a relief to get off the main road. Sometimes these old roads had piles of sand, dirt and asphalt stored on them, but we could always get by.

Soon after we left Hyannis a truck pulled up beside us, and the men asked if we were "Walking across Nebraska, or something." We told them, "Not just Nebraska, but across the whole United States." With that they got out of the truck to ask questions and we took their pictures. Meanwhile, Joni was walking toward us and some men working on the railroad asked her what we were doing. People were especially curious when they noticed Joni and Cassie walking one direction, Sam, Waliluke and me walking the other way, then the five of us all going the same direction.

One afternoon as we were resting during our lunch break, a car pulled up behind us. A state trooper got out and walked toward the van. When he began to talk Cassie and Waliluke suddenly came to life (they had been asleep) and almost jumped out the window with loud, vicious barks and growls. The poor trooper jumped back and just about had a heart attack.

I got out of the van and went to the back to talk with him. He had just stopped to see if we were OK. We gave him our card and explained about the Journey and that we were on our lunch break. Trooper Mick was very nice, even letting us take his picture after being frightened "half to death" by our dogs. He told us we really got his adrenalin going. At least we knew we were well protected.

# Chapter Thirteen

# A MOTORIZED COVERED WAGON

## Lyn

The weather had turned warm again. A few days earlier we'd been wearing jackets and gloves, and now suddenly found ourselves in temperatures soaring into the low nineties.

At the church we attended on Sunday, October 19 we found a spot to park the van in some partial shade. We had purchased two 25-foot leads. Raising the door in the back of the van we attached one end of the lead inside and the other end to the dogs' collars. They could then choose whether to be outside or inside the van. A donkey in the yard next to the church came our way. He began braying loudly and making such a racket that we decided to find a spot further away. We could just imagine the pastor trying to preach his sermon over the sounds of barking and hee-hawing.

The Sandhills Community Church in Mullen was full of friendly people all very interested in our Journey. We were given a tour of the still unfinished building. This was their first day of using the Sunday School rooms.

Pastor Mark Danielson had us share with the congregation. He used our walk as an example several times in his sermon. Deb took us to lunch at the Cattleman's Café in Seneca, along with her daughter and mother. Pastor Mark, Cindy and their family, as well as their Ecuadorian exchange student, met us at the restaurant. It was a great time of fellowship.

Near Thedford a lady pulled up across the road and asked if we were just out for a walk or if we needed a ride. We crossed the street to tell her our story. She was flabbergasted and asked a lot of questions. We fell in love with this delightful woman. Georgia Finney was the second of our two special ladies in Nebraska. She told us she lived in Broken Bow and was on her way home after visiting a friend who had Lou Gehrig's disease.

We told her our next move would be to Broken Bow, and we would be based there for a week or so. Plans were made to get together after we moved our camp.

## Joni

The same day while I was driving to meet the "girls" I noticed a place called Rainbow Llamas on Llama Lane. While I waited for a train to pass, a truck came up beside me. Monte Dickman introduced himself, told me he owned the llama farm, and invited me to see some baby llamas. I followed him along a dirt road and across the railroad tracks for about a mile and noticed wild turkeys, bulls in a pen and horses in the fields.

He introduced me to his wife, Leslie, and she showed me around the farm. Some of the llamas were for show and some for backpacking. She also showed me two baby llamas just two weeks old. They were so sweet to look at. Leslie asked me to sign her guest book, and I told her all about the Great American Journey. An hour later I joined the "girls" again. I had really enjoyed seeing the llamas.

## Lyn

Walking on we came across a sign telling us about the Nebraska Sandhills. This informative sign certainly explained all the cattle we'd been seeing lately.

---

The Sandhills, Nebraska's most unique physiographic feature, cover about one fourth of the state. The sandy soil acts like a giant sponge, soaking up rain and forming a vast underground reservoir. Hundreds of permanent lakes are found here. However, the same sandy soil makes the area unsuitable for cultivation. Grasses flourish, making the Sandhills ideal for cattle country.

Although the Sandhills were long considered 'an irreclaimable desert,' cattlemen had begun to discover the Sandhills' potential as rangeland by the early 1870s. Huge ranches were established here.

Unsuccessful attempts at farming were made in the Sandhills region in the late 1870s and again around 1890. The Kinkaid Act of 1904 allowed homesteaders to claim a full section of land, rather than the quarter of a section previously allowed. Nearly nine million acres were successfully claimed by 'Kinkaiders' between 1910 and 1917. Some of the Kinkaiders attempted to farm, but most of these attempts failed. Many of the largest ranches broke up about the same time due to regulations against fencing federal land. Today, the Sandhills contain many ranches, but none so large as those of the past.

---

It was moving day again. The Wagon Wheel Motel and RV Park at Broken Bow was our destination. This put us into the Central Time Zone.

There was an interesting article in a magazine that gave this version of how Broken Bow got its name.

*Hewitt in his dugout,*
*Sought a name for his P. O.*
*He suggested several*
*But Uncle Sam said, "No."*
*His two boys went a-hunting*
*An Indian bow brought back,*
*'Twas broken, but they hung it*
*Upon the dugout shack.*
*He shouted when he saw it,*
*"This name will surely go"*
*And Uncle Sam okayed it. . .*
*That's why it's "Broken Bow."*

As I was hooking up the water and electricity, I noticed a metal strip about to fall off the Castle. We joked about the motor home falling apart and having to cover it with canvas, so that by the end we would have a motorized covered wagon. A few minutes later when I opened one of the outside cupboards a piece of the framework fell off and broke into pieces. We all laughed. Maybe our covered wagon days would come sooner than we expected. A sense of humor was a must for this Journey.

Just then Georgia Finney drove up and told us we had been invited to speak at the senior luncheon the next day. Georgia then treated us to dinner at the Tumbleweed Café. This is a very popular restaurant. In fact we hadn't seen one this busy since leaving California.

During dinner we learned a lot about our hostess. Georgia told us she was 83 years young and was married to her first husband for 30 years when he died. She remarried a year-and-a-half later and was married to her second husband for 30 years when he died. We also learned she has two daughters. Her first child was born prematurely at home in the middle of a blizzard 50 miles from the nearest town. Her husband delivered the baby girl who weighed only one pound. Lining a cardboard box with blankets, they put her near the fireplace for warmth, the only heat they had. She survived on cow's milk fed to her from an eyedropper. A few days later we met this daughter, Alberta. Georgia's second daughter, Janeece lives in St. Joseph, Missouri. Georgia also has nine grandchildren, nineteen great-grandchildren, and one great-great-grandchild.

Georgia had some interesting stories of her early life on a ranch. She and a girlfriend rode horses with the cowboys and helped herd the cattle to the nearest railroad station. We encouraged her to get her stories written down, because they're too good to lose. It was obvious she was well known in the area, as many people at the restaurant greeted her.

The next morning Georgia took us out to Adams Land and Cattle Company. There were about 93,000 cattle at this feedlot. The south feedlot had a huge mountain of corn, with conveyor belts continuously pouring more corn on top and tractors spreading it out.

One of the managers of this huge operation, Larry McKey, gave us information on the steers held in the pens. They are fed a diet of corn and alfalfa ground into silage until they are ready to be shipped to market. Three hundred and fifty trucks a day are either bringing cattle into the ranch or transporting them out.

Following our tour of the feedlots we went to the Senior Center for the luncheon of baked chicken and all the fixin's. It was sure good. Then we shared with the group about our walk. They asked many questions and we enjoyed our time with them.

One of the seniors, Lloyd Wells, introduced himself to us showing us a book his wife had written. It was about his experiences during World War II when he was taken prisoner by the Germans. His wife died just before the first copies were printed. We each purchased one of these books and had him autograph them for us.

Lloyd invited us to his home and showed us his collection of plates, china and glassware. There were many handmade patchwork quilts, guns and knives of all types. He showed us a shadowbox with his purple heart and other medals—quite an interesting experience for us.

For the next few days we continued walking along State Route 2 from Halsey, through Dunning, and across the Dismal River. A state patrolman stopped to see if we were OK as we neared Dunning. His name was Sam, so we took a picture of him with our Sam. These patrolmen that we met all seemed so young (at least to Joni and me). Our route went on through Angelo and Myrna, then into Broken Bow where we walked right to our Castle. The last two towns we passed through before turning off of State Route 2 and onto U.S. Route 183 were Berwyn and Ensley.

One day we had stopped at the large Sandhills Cathedral to eat our lunch on their beautiful grounds. The doors to the cathedral were open, so after we ate we went in to look around. It was beautiful. We knelt on a kneeling bench to pray for the area, then took pictures.

Sunday, October 26 as we were getting ready to go to church, there was a knock on the door. Georgia had come to see if we would like to go to church with her. Without hesitation we said, "We'd love to." She attends the First Christian Church in town. It was always our desire that God would lead us to the church He wanted us to go to each week. When someone gave us a special invitation we strongly sensed that was a part of God's leading us. We were able to park our van next to an alfalfa field across the street from the church. This worked as a great place to leash the dogs to their 25-foot lines and gave them some space.

Georgia made sure we met several people before the service. We found them friendly and the pastor gave a good message on controlling the tongue. At the end of the service Pastor Dan told the congregation about us and our Journey. Then he prayed for us and for other requests. He encouraged people to stop and talk with us before they left. Many did come to chat and ask questions.

Joni had been talking to a gal named Lynna. As it turned out, Lynna is a beautician and Joni had been wanting to get her hair cut for a while. She took the dogs back to the Castle, where Lynna met her and led her to the shop where she works. So Joni got her hair cut while Sam and I went with Georgia to the Tumbleweed Café to eat.

Georgia's daughter, Alberta, and her husband, J.B. Morgan, joined us. Another lady, Frieda, also joined us. I wrote in my journal later that "J.B. is an absolute character, a really fun guy and so sincere in his devotion to God." We knew it would be hard for us to leave this very hospitable town.

After lunch Georgia took us to Lynna's shop, where she had just finished cutting Joni's hair—no charge. As we left, Joni thanked Lynna for her generosity. We then went to town to do some shopping and Georgia introduced us to a few more people, including one of her granddaughters.

Another interesting thing we noticed in the Broken Bow area was that gas seemed to be the same price for all grades at most stations. When we got gas, it was just $1.60—well, that was in 2003 in Nebraska!

The day we walked through Merna, Georgia, and Alberta drove out and told us a reporter from the Custer County Chief would be coming to interview us later in the day. The local radio station would also be contacting us for an interview. Carrie, the Chief reporter met us right after lunch. Dale from the radio station met us that evening at the Castle.

## Joni

After the interview, I drove the van ahead and parked it, then quickly jumped out with Cassie to walk back to meet Lyn and Sam. As we all walked to the van together, a sheriff's deputy pulled over to talk with us. He wanted to know if that was our van parked ahead on the side of the road. I said it was, then told him what we were doing.

He told us someone had called in about a green van parked in front of the anhydrous ammonia tanks. They had seen a lady get out with a dog and walk rapidly away. The deputy then explained that they had been having problems with people stealing the gas. He told us it was OK to park there, then took down our license number so he could notify dispatch. They would let other deputies know our van was not parked for illegal purposes. As he left he wished us well.

## Lyn

On our last walking day while based at Broken Bow, we met Georgia at the local McDonald's for breakfast. The manager took our orders. When she learned what we were doing, she told us breakfast was on her. Georgia was standing there ready to pay, so she and the manager had a "friendly discussion" over who got to pay. The manager won. Georgia then introduced us to about a dozen or more of her friends who meet there for breakfast every morning. We had a great time, but finally had to say, "So long" and head out to walk.

Pastor Keith of Broken Bow's Church of God stopped to see if we were OK. He had seen us walking when he drove into town earlier. Seeing us again on his way back to Berwyn, he decided to see if we needed help.

It was starting to get dark as we walked past Ansley on Route 183, and a man stopped to see if we needed help. This was the second time he had seen our van parked along the road and assumed we had engine problems. It was nice to know that people were ready to help ladies in distress, even when they were in a hurry to get back to their cozy homes for the night.

*Chapter Fourteen*

# JONI'S PET MENAGERIE

## Lyn

Moving day again. Shortly before we were ready to leave Broken Bow, Georgia, Alberta and J.B. came to say good-bye. J.B. helped us finish unhooking and even repaired a couple of things. After taking pictures we hugged, shed a few tears and promised to keep in touch. For the rest of the Journey we talked with Georgia most Sunday afternoons.

## Sam

On our way to Alma, where we hoped to find a campsite, we stopped in Holdrege at a veterinarian's office to see about getting a muzzle for Waliluke. We really couldn't afford to replace seat belts too often. In Alma we stopped at the Evangelical Free Church to get directions to the campground. Becky went to get Pastor Glenn Saaman for us. After telling us where the campground was, he asked if we would mind sharing about our walk with their congregation on Sunday. That settled where we would be going to church that week. The Pastor gave us his card and we noticed he had 1 Corinthians 10:31 printed on it: "Do everything for the glory of God." On our Memorial Stones we always wrote, "To God be the glory."

When we got to the campground we found it was closed for the winter. We pulled onto a side street and parked the motor home and van. As we did so a man turned the corner in his car and pulled into the driveway behind us. Jerry came over to see if we needed anything. We told him our problem, asking if he knew of another campground nearby that was open. Though he was unable to find an RV Park for us, Jerry and his wife Barbara invited us to come to their church that Sunday, which happened to be the Evangelical Free Church.

Meanwhile I called my mother to ask her to check out a few places on the internet. Mama phoned back to say she had found a place in Republican City. Patterson Harbor Campground was staying open for the winter. It was six miles off the main road and across the dam, then down a little county road lined with gorgeous trees dressed in their fall colors.

## Lyn

The manager told us we could have any campsite we wanted, since there was no one else in the campground at the time. She also told us the showers were all closed for the winter, but for a small fee we could have a key to one of the kitchenette units and use the bathroom and shower. The camp fee was very low, so we didn't mind paying a little extra.

We spent four walking days on State Route 183. Temperatures were plummeting again and a 20% chance of snow was predicted. The snow didn't come, but we certainly had lots of wind, a sky full of clouds, and a nip in the air.

We layered our clothing as the weather got colder and greatly appreciated the hats and scarves Alyce-Kay, my daughter, had crocheted for us. Here's a list of the clothing we were wearing much of the time on these colder days—two or three layers of shirts, a jacket, vest, scarf, crocheted hat, rain hood, snow gloves, three pair of socks (liners, regular, and waterproof sealskin) and hiking sandals. We looked like snow monsters, but felt so toasty and warm.

This was farming country, with wide-open spaces around us. Miller and Holdrege were the only towns along Route 183 before Alma. Quite a few people stopped along this road to make sure we were OK. With the colder weather people seemed even more concerned for us than before.

Sunday November 2, was our day at the Evangelical Free Church in Alma. I told Joni and Sam that if anyone asked how they could help us, I would tell them we needed to borrow a good vacuum to clean the Castle. Dog hair was a real problem, and our tiny vacuum would not pick it up. We arrived at the church in time to talk with a few people, then get our seats before the service started.

The music was so good this morning. Pastor Glenn asked us to share early in the service, and we had a great response from the congregation. So often we feel like we are doing so little, but time and time again people told us how much they appreciated our prayers for the nation. As Pastor Glenn began his sermon he looked over at us, and out of the blue asked if there was some way they could help us out. I looked at the other two and gulped, remembering what I had said earlier. I had thought the question would come from an individual. But God had taken me at my word, prompting the pastor to ask this question in front of the whole congregation.

After church many responded to our request and some offered other kinds of help as well. That very afternoon Sharon came out to vacuum for us, and Travis came out to do some electrical repairs on the Castle. Sharon also shared several things for us to pray about, both for the area and her family.

Sam and Waliluke walk through the Jasper Fire
- Jewel Caves National Monument area

We saw two open coal mines in Wyoming

Pastor Joel is pastor of the Living Outreach Church in Custer, South Dakota - He is one
of ten siblings whose father was the sculptor of Crazy Horse

Sam and Waliluke really enjoyed Trooper Heath in South Dakota

Hot Springs, South Dakota, a beautiful and unique town

We loved our hiking sandals - very comfortable

Joni stepped on this rattlesnake, and it immediately struck at her and hit her shoe. Note the rattlers shaking.

These men wanted to know if we were walking across Nebraska - They were really surprised to hear we were walking across the whole USA

A special lunch with Jim and Connie Poitra - she told us she had Parkinson's and had just been diagnosed with Alzheimer's as well

Carhenge near Alliance, Nebraska modeled after Stonehenge

We prayed and placed a special memorial stone here at the center of the lower 48 states of America

Lloyd stands beside his truck with its POW license plate.

Saying good-bye to Georgia, Alberta (Bert) and JB as we prepare to move to the next campground

Dave sent flowers to congratulate the team for their accomplishments thus far on their trip - flowers from Dave always had Milky Way Bars included for each team member

Bruce, a truck driver, talks with Sam and Lyn at the diner in Cawker City, Kansas

Can you find the ball of twine in this picture?

Steve plays the organ he had just finished building

Cawker City, Kansas at the Veterans Day Ceremony

Sam, Joan Nothern, Lyn and Brian Spencer near Glasco, Kansas

A Hedge Tree filled with unusual looking hedge balls

Display at the Scott Springs, Kansas Oregon Trail Park

These are some of the great kids at the Kids Club in Miltonvale, Kansas

Lyn with her brother, Ernest, on top of Pike's Peak in Colorado
during our Thanksgiving break

The Miltonvale, Kansas Teens For Christ

Sam and Lyn were excited about a visit by Sam's siblings and mom
at our LaCygne, Kansas campground

Thanksgiving with Lyn's brother and his children and grandchildren

A visit with Santa in Baldwyn City, Kansas

Downtown Lawrence, Kansas is decorated with the Kansas University hawk mascot

We all enjoyed the first big snow at our LaCygne, Kansas campground

Joni's family at San Jose, California Christmas gathering - Beth, Paul, Lori, Joan, Scott and Joni - in front are Ryan and Kyle

Bruce, a Salvation Army bell ringer in Osawatomie, Kansas

Sam and Chip place the Memorial Stone at
El Dorado Springs, Missouri

Joni with the Anacker's and their recently adopted children from Russia
- Joni, Nikolai, Jon, Marilyn - in front are Sergei, Ira, Leana and Marina

Getting together with friends in California - Judi, Dellie, Meredith, Joni and Earline

Lois and Sam enjoy some sisterly time at "Precious Moments" in
Carthage, Missouri on our Christmas break

Dave drove for us the last few walking days before our Christmas break

Some of the remaining devastation from a tornado that struck
Stockton, Missouri in May, 2003

Eva with "Medusa" in Isabella, Missouri

We left a Memorial Stone on this altar

Sam and Joni enjoyed an "icicle fencing match"

Our new signs attracted some attention from passersby shortly
before we finished Missouri

Travis fixed several little things, then went to work on our signal lights (Joni had noticed as she followed the motor home in the van that our rear left-turn signal wasn't working). He came out another afternoon while we were still out walking, then finished after we got back. I was turning the signal on from inside for Travis and he called us out to look at what was happening. With the left turn signal in the "on" position we were surprised to see every outside light on the motor home flashing except the left turn signal. He finally got it fixed, then gave us a prayer request before heading back to his home and wife. We were very grateful for the help Sharon and Travis had given us.

Terry and Debbie Woollen and their daughter, Tana had invited us on Sunday to stop at their farm when we walked by. Monday we arrived at their home at about 1:30 P.M. and they served us a delicious chili soup lunch. It tasted so good, especially in the cold weather. While we were visiting over lunch the family told Joni she had to meet Edith and John, and gave her the address.

Terry left because he was treating a sick calf. In his hand he carried a huge fever thermometer and a giant hypodermic needle. Debbie told us she often drives a semi-truck on their soybean farm.

Before we left, Tana treated us to some beautiful piano music. She is an accomplished pianist. What a delight.

### Joni

After turning onto Route 136 we had only four more days in Nebraska. This road had a few more towns, but most were small. I took Cassie to a veterinarian in Alma while Sam and Lyn walked. Cass' had an ear infection from an allergic reaction to the grasses in the area. I got the necessary medication and the vet offered me another dog, a lab/heeler mix. Lyn and Sam were thankful that I said, "No."

The vet also told me about an auction in town where they were auctioning off bulls. I went to see what it was like and took a few pictures. The cowboys drove a bull into a pen and the auctioneer began the bidding. It was very interesting and I was tempted to add a young bull to our menagerie. Sam and Lyn were grateful I didn't.

After the auction I went into town to find Edith and John. Locating their house, I told them that the Woollen family had said I had to meet them because they were also from England. They were originally from Manchester, England and had been in the States since 1946. I told them about our Journey, then left to find Sam and Lyn. I really enjoyed talking to this delightful couple.

## Lyn

One "young" couple, Jess and Bernice (Jess told me he was 87 years young!) stopped and talked with Sam and me. They were delightful. Later they came by again with a "younger" couple in the car with them. They saw Joni walking toward us and stopped to talk with her first. Joni asked if they had gotten one of our cards and they said they had gotten one from the tall thin lady. When I heard that, I was elated that they thought I was thin, even with all the layers of clothes on!

There were a lot of creeks and rivers to cross as we continued. One town we passed through was Franklin, population about 1,200. This seemed like a real city to us. The town had a nice little Memorial Park with tributes to various wars and those who had given their lives for our freedom.

Just outside of Franklin we met a young man as he was coming out of a farm. His name was Steve and he and his brother farmed this land with their father. He told us their crops were soybeans, milo and corn, plus some cattle. This seemed to be pretty typical of the farms in this area.

Meanwhile Joni met Mike and a couple of hunters. She said that Mike was especially excited about what we were doing. A few minutes later a woman pulled in ahead of us and stopped. She walked back and told us she was Yvonne with the Franklin County Chronicle. She had received a call from a lady telling her that her son Mike had met some women walking across America. Thinking it might be something worth reporting about, she called the newspaper. Yvonne interviewed us and took our picture (we were so wrapped up, we looked like chubby little snowmen).

Moving day came with just a few miles left to walk in Nebraska. We packed up our stuff and headed for Kansas to find a new campsite. When we checked out of Patterson Harbor Campground we asked about the cost since we hadn't yet paid. Dee looked at us and asked, "How about $50.00?" Wow! Were we surprised. This was for eight days of full hook-ups, plus the use of the shower in the little cabin.

On our way to Glen Elder State Park on U.S. Route 24 in Kansas we passed through Cawker City. We saw a tiny RV Park behind a little diner and tucked that information into our minds—just in case. Arriving at the state park, we found it did not have sewer hook-ups, just a dump station. That just didn't work in our situation, so we decided to go back to Cawker City to check out the place behind the diner. It was a good choice. They had only six or seven spots with full hook-ups. Most of the campsites were reserved for the weekend, but we could have site number three. The place was Jaybird's Chicken and RV Park. We thought that was an interesting name and we'll tell you more about it in the Kansas chapter.

It was our last day of walking in Nebraska. Red Cloud was our final town in this state. A sign in front of one house had a cutout of a cowboy hat on top and the words proclaimed, "Grandma and Grandpa's—Open daily—Kids spoiled here—Cookies, swings, hugs, piggyback rides." As we went up to take a picture, a lady and her grandson stepped out and he got onto the school bus that had just stopped out front. After seeing him off we told the grandmother what we were doing. Her name was Mary. She and her husband owned a store downtown, Shades West, and they invited us to stop in on our way by. When we arrived at the store we met her husband, Doug and daughter, Tara. There were several life size cutouts of famous cowboys around the store and a variety of great merchandise.

On the edge of town a historical marker told us about Red Cloud:

---

Red Cloud, named for the Oglala Sioux chief, was founded early in 1871 on homestead land filed upon by Silas Garber and Company July 17, 1870, at Beatrice, the nearest land office. It is one of the oldest communities in the Republican Valley. When Webster County was organized, Red Cloud was voted the county seat at the first county election, April 19, 1871. The election was held in the dugout of Silas Garber, Nebraska's governor, 1875–1879.

The mainline of the Burlington and Missouri River Railway reached here in 1879, accelerating immigration from the East and abroad, bringing together a colorful variety of cultural heritages. During the 1880s Red Cloud served as a division center for the railroad. The architectural design of Webster Street was established during that prosperous time when many of the first frame and log structures were replaced by more elaborate buildings of brick and stone.

Red Cloud was the childhood home of Willa Cather and it is known throughout the world as the setting for her six Nebraska novels and numerous short stories. The pioneers she knew in the town and on the nearby farms live on in her writings.

---

We soon came to the state line for Nebraska and Kansas. In the bitter cold weather we stopped and prayed and left our Memorial Stones for the two states. Nebraska's state song is titled, "Beautiful Nebraska." Some of the words read:

*Beautiful Nebraska, peaceful prairieland,*
*Laced with many rivers, and the hills of sand;*
*Dark green valleys cradled in the earth,*
*Rain and sunshine bring abundant birth.*
*Beautiful Nebraska, as you look around,*
*You will find a rainbow reaching to the ground;*
*All these wonders by the Master's hand;*
*Beautiful Nebraska land.*

And so, we finished this beautiful state with much joy, and in great anticipation of what we might find in our days of walking through Kansas.

# KANSAS

## *The Heart Of America*

Entered Kansas......................................................*November 7, 2003*

Finished Kansas .................................................. *December 12, 2003*

Actual Days in State.................................................................36

Walking Days in State.............................................................20

Total Mileage for Kansas.....................................................324.8

Total Journey Mileage to Date............................................2,205.3

Capital ..............................................................................*Topeka*

Admitted to Statehood.................................*January 29, 1861 ~ the 34th state*

Population.....................................................................2,688,418

Highest Point..............................................*Mount Sunflower ~ 4,039 feet*

Lowest Point.................................................. *Verdigris River ~ 680 feet*

*"I urge then, first of all, that requests, prayers, intercession and thanksgiving be made for everyone—for kings, and all those in authority, that we may live peaceful and quiet lives in all godliness and holiness. This is good and pleases God our Savior, who wants all men to be saved and to come to a knowledge of the truth."*

—1 TIMOTHY 2:1–4

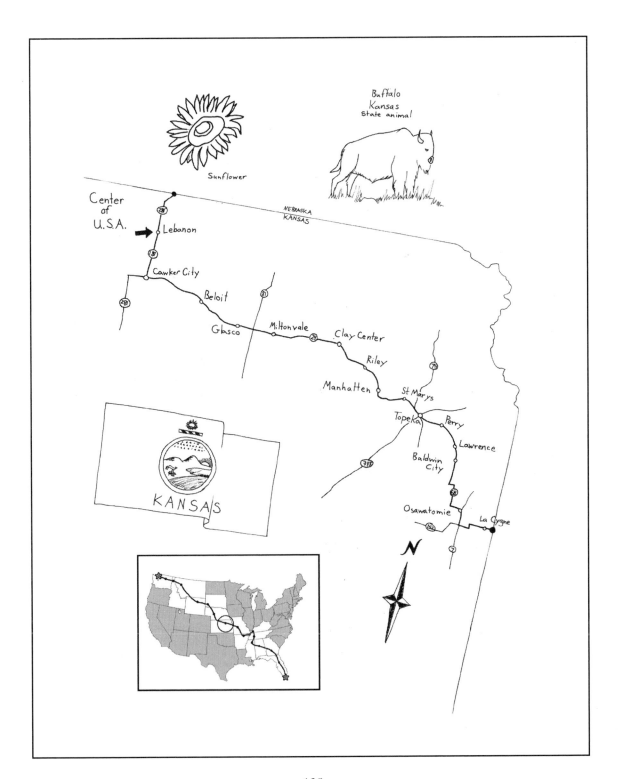

Sunflower

Buffalo
Kansas
state animal

Center
of
U.S.A.

NEBRASKA
KANSAS

Lebanon

Cawker City

Beloit

Glasco

Miltonvale

Clay Center

Riley

Manhatten

St Marys

Topeka

Perry

Lawrence

Baldwin
City

Osawatomie

La Cygne

KANSAS

N

*Chapter Fifteen*

# A CASTLE FULL OF PHEASANTS

**Lyn**

As we entered the seventh state of our long Journey, we felt a sense of accomplishment, hope and excitement. We were making headway; our bodies were responding nicely to all the exercise, and best of all we continued to meet wonderful people. Many people told us they would pray for us, and we had plenty of opportunities to pray for others.

Our entrance into the state was along U.S. Highway 281. Eight of our 20.5 miles that day were in the state of Kansas late in the afternoon and evening. Scenery was great, and we enjoyed our usual "conversations" with the cows in the pastures along the highway. We always complimented them on their beautiful earrings (you know, the colorful tags the cows had dangling from their ears). Generally they stopped to stare at us as we passed.

Speaking of cows, did you know that the Cow Chip Capital of Kansas is located in Russell Springs in Logan County, in the northwest part of the state? This was another of those interesting tidbits we got off the internet.

Some pheasant hunters stopped to ask if we were OK (they had gone past us and decided to come back to check on us). It's nice to know that if we actually had car trouble along some of these roads, there would be people concerned enough to stop and help. When they heard what we were doing they were quite amazed, and pulled out some money, which they gave to us with instructions to enjoy a meal on them, and a thank you for praying. This sort of thing happened from time to time and we really appreciated it. It was never easy to accept money from people, but we were learning that they often wanted a tangible way to thank us for praying for our country, and to refuse their gift would be insulting to them.

With nighttime closing in on us, Joni drove ahead to find a spot where she, Cassie and Waliluke could wait comfortably, while Sam and I continued walking. There were no streetlights on these country roads, so when darkness came it was pitch black.

We suddenly found ourselves on a very busy two-lane highway. A lot of this was commute traffic—yes folks, they do have commuters in states other than California.

The commute hour was over almost as quickly as it had begun, but now we found it replaced by very heavy nighttime trucking.

We noticed a parked truck on the other side of the road with lights on and flashers going. As we got directly across from the truck the driver jumped out and came across to ask what on earth we were doing. He had seen us earlier in the day as he was heading north. Returning hours later, he saw us still walking, and he had to know what was going on. We told him our story, and he asked a lot of questions. He told us he was heading to Cawker City for the night—in fact he grew up there. When he found out we were staying at Jaybird's RV Park, he asked if we would meet him at the diner for a meal. We agreed and went directly there when we finished walking.

Arriving at the diner Bruce introduced us to Jay, the owner. Over dinner Bruce told us about himself and the town. He shared that the town got its name when a group of men agreed that the winner of a poker game would have the town named after him. A few days later we saw a sign in town that gave more details:

---

Four men, E. Harrison Cawker, his step-father James Peyton Rice, R.G.F. Kshinka, each from Milwaukee, and John J. Huckle from Towanda, Pennsylvania founded this town with each owning one quarter section, which formed the four wards of the town. The four men played poker to decide which of the men the town would be named after. Cawker City was incorporated June 2, 1874.

---

Bruce also told us about the famous ball of twine which had started many years earlier when he was a kid. He and other boys often spent time with a local farmer and rolled leftover pieces of twine into a ball as they talked (the farmer couldn't bear to throw the pieces away). Over the years the ball grew and grew until finally someone suggested they contact the Guinness Book of World Records. Sure enough, it was the biggest in the world, and it became an official record. Now, once a year, the locals gather for "Twine-A-Thon" to add more twine that they've saved throughout the year. Every few years they have to build a bigger shelter for the ball. But, we're getting ahead of ourselves since we still hadn't actually walked to the twine—that would be a few days yet.

Saturday, November 8, was opening day of pheasant hunting and it seemed we were the only ones in the RV Park who weren't pheasant hunters. As we drove out to our start point we noticed orange-vested, orange-capped people throughout most of the fields stalking their prey. Joni wanted to round up all the pheasants and hide them in our Castle until after hunting season, along with the deer and any other creatures that were open game at this time.

All day we walked between fields of hunters and stopped to talk with many of them. They weren't allowed to shoot toward the roads at any time, so our only danger was when we needed to make pit stops. Of course, the only danger in that was simply that one of them might be looking for a place to make a pit stop also.

Scott had already bagged two pheasants when we talked with him (the limit is four per day). We talked with a father and son named Bill and Bill. Also J.W. and David, who we met the day before, stopped to say "hi" again.

While we were talking with Scott, another man, Kent, drove up to see if we were OK. He had seen us the night before as he drove his big tractor down the highway. Sam's and my eyes popped open as he mentioned this fact. We remembered seeing a big single light very high up, coming toward us on the road well after dark. It looked like a train engine heading our way. Only when he got right beside us could we see it was a huge tractor.

## Joni

As I sat in the van that night waiting for Lyn and Sam, I saw a strange light floating back and forth in the field across the street. In my imagination I was sure it was aliens playing in the field. I got my camera and took several pictures (all that can be seen in the pictures are lines of light across a dark background). Suddenly the funniest looking tractor I had ever seen came toward me.

The next day I walked up as Lyn and Sam were talking with Scott and Kent. Lyn introduced me to my alien. Kent the tractor driver raised his eyebrows and slowly shook his head as we talked about our UFO story. He told me he had been spraying the field the night before.

We hated to say good-bye to such fun people, but it was time to move on. There was a lot more to see and experience in this state.

## Lyn

A short time later we came to a sign announcing that the geographic center of the continental United States was just one mile west of our route. We opted to drive there and take time to pray in the very center of our nation. Much to our delight a small chapel stood there, and we went inside to pray. As the verse at the start of this chapter suggests, we prayed for all those in authority and for every person living in this great land. We asked that God would take our prayers in every direction from this central point of the United States and bless this nation: "Bless this nation with Your love and with a longing in the hearts of all men and women for truth. May many turn to You in repentance and receive Your salvation. For only in You can any of us experience true peace." Our Memorial Stone number 74 was a white stone that we had chosen especially for this central spot in our land.

During our time at the Center of the United States we made a few phone calls to let people know where we were. The longer we stayed, the colder it got, and as we started walking again we noticed a few snow flurries. None of it was sticking and we weren't too far from our campground, so we just enjoyed it.

When we finally got back to the Castle, a lady was waiting with a floral arrangement for us. It was from Dave, for "The three ladies walking across America." Dave typically included Milky Way bars in bouquets to me when I was on long-distance walks. We were not disappointed—the candy bars were there. The florist had included her own special touch when Dave told her what we were doing. With each candy bar she included a small silver shoe charm, and placed a few pheasant feathers in with the flowers.

Sunday came around again, and we had already picked out our church. I'll have Joni tell you this story.

## Joni

Earlier in the week I visited the United Methodist church of Cawker City and saw their ornate Victorian organ built in 1886. Because I love organ music so much, I told Lyn and Sam, "This is where we will go to church this Sunday!"

On Sunday, November 9, Steve Richardson was playing the organ in church, and it was absolutely fantastic!! Pastor Ross Olson warmly greeted us and invited us to share about the walk during the service.

They had a patriotic theme that morning because of Veterans Day coming up. The congregation sang, "America the Beautiful," "My Country 'Tis of Thee," and "Battle Hymn of the Republic." They also played a recording of "Some Gave All," by Billy Ray Cyrus.

The pastor's sermon was titled, "Some Gave All." He used Mark 12:42–44 about Jesus sitting at the Temple treasury. As he sat there, many wealthy people put large amounts of money into the treasury. A poor widow came and gave her last two mites, equal to a quarter of a penny—all she had. Jesus told his disciples that the poor widow had put more into the treasury than all the rich people had put in all day. He said, "For all they did was cast in of their abundance; but she cast in all that she had." The widow was one who gave all. Our veterans "all gave some," but "some gave all," just as the widow had given her all.

The church, and the entire service, reminded me so much of the Episcopalian services I had been used to in England. Following the message Pastor Ross asked the ushers to place an offering plate in back for people to put money into for our Journey. That really took us by surprise and touched our hearts.

I talked with Steve, the organist, about my love for organ music, and he invited me to come to his shop that week. I went to Downs the following day, where he had converted an old church into a workshop for making organs by hand. He showed me one he had just finished building, and played it for me—beautifully!! He also showed me another organ he was in the process of building, demonstrating the intricacies of the keys and pedals. On a nearby table was a book of photos taken in Vienna and Germany, where he had learned his craft.

Steve also showed me where he was renovating the old church. He was slowly removing paint inside the building and had been able to identify different layers and date them back to the 1800 wallpaper. An impressive and fascinating project.

## Lyn

Meanwhile, as Sam and I walked through Downs, Scott, the pheasant hunter we had seen on Saturday, drove up. He was heading home to North Carolina and wanted to wish us well on the rest of our Journey. When we asked him how many pheasant he had caught, he told us nine.

Walking between Downs and Cawker City we noticed a tree with a strange "fruit" hanging from it. They were large yellow balls. The skin was thick and wrinkled into ridges, looking like a yellow brain. We eventually found that these were hedge balls growing on a hedge tree.

And since we're talking about "strange fruit," here's another "strange" law that was once on the books in Kansas. "It was once illegal to serve ice cream on cherry pie in Kansas." Why? We have no idea, and probably most Kansans have no idea either, but now you know.

We walked into Cawker City and stopped at the famous "Ball of Twine" to take pictures. A man from the church we had attended Sunday stopped and took pictures of the three of us in front of it. Here are some of the statistics of this famous twine ball: It was started in 1953 by Frank Stoeber, gained Guinness Book status in 1973, and now measures forty feet and five inches in circumference. Standing over ten feet high, it has almost outgrown its fourth building. As of August 15, 2003, it weighed 17,552 pounds, and its twine, if unwound, would stretch out to 7,009,942 feet. Wow! Frank Stoeber died in 1974, just a year after the Guinness Book gave his ball of twine special recognition.

Throughout Cawker City we noticed the store and office windows all had paintings hanging in them. In each picture was a ball of twine somewhere for the onlooker to find. For instance, in one picture a ball of twine is the center of an eye. In another it sits outside the door of a brick building, and still another the farmer stands with his famous pitchfork while his wife holds the twine. Lady Liberty holds a twine ball up high in place of the usual flame, and the Mona Lisa holds it in her lap. This is only a small portion of them, but you get the idea. A local artist, Sher Olson, who is also Pastor Ron's wife, painted the pictures.

# Chapter Sixteen

# "DO YOU SWEAT A LOT?"

*Lyn*

On Veterans Day we walked as far as Beloit (over 18 miles) and quit at 2:30 P.M. in order to get back to Cawker City in time for their Second Annual Veterans Day program at the City Park. Many of the people that we had seen at church on Sunday were there. Pastor Ross Olson was the master of ceremonies, and Steve Richardson played a small portable organ for the program.

Members of the American Legion, as well as servicemen who had returned from Iraq, were present. At the end of the service two men folded a large flag while a lady explained the meaning of the folding procedure. Near the end of the program Pastor Olson introduced us. Many people came to talk with us, including Linda, the official keeper of the Ball of Twine.

During the Veterans Day program both Cassie and Waliluke sat with us (it was all outdoors). They behaved quite well, sleeping through most of it. Whenever we stood, Waliluke always stood up. He watched with fascination when the men retired the flags—we were afraid he was going to start barking at them, but he didn't. Whew!

When planning this Journey in California, we had sent letters to Chambers of Commerce across America that we expected to be on our route. The first reply came from a lady by the name of Joan Nothern. We had kept contact with Joan and planned to get together when we walked through her area of Glasco, Kansas.

Just two miles out of town we phoned Joan at her work at the local school. Soon she and Brian Spencer, the superintendent of schools for the area, came out to meet us. They walked with us for a short distance, then Brian asked if we would be willing to come that evening to share at a Kids Club, and a Teens for Christ Club in Miltonvale. Arrangements were made to meet later.

We finished our walking for the day, then drove back to Glasco to meet Joan and her 92 year-old mother, Rhea, for dinner at the local diner. With this dinner we celebrated our first six months on the road, and we had a delightful time with our two new friends.

Meeting Brian in Miltonvale, he led us to the church where about 50 children in the Kids Club were waiting for us. These boys and girls were all very attentive as we shared some of our experiences and showed them our United States map with our route highlighted. When we opened it up for questions one little boy, about six years old, put his hand up and asked, "Do you sweat a lot?" These kids were great, and we could have easily spent an hour or two with them, but it was time to move on across town to the Teens For Christ Club.

There were about 30 teens at the meeting. Brian told us about eighty percent of the kids in town attend these two groups. The teens seemed to be very committed to God and listened intently, then asked some great questions. One of the leaders had the teens set out three chairs for us to sit on, they then put their hands on us and prayed for our Journey. It was very touching to hear these teens pray for us. Many of them gave us prayer requests, which we later entered into our book. We have faithfully prayed for both of these clubs and their leaders.

We learned so much about rural America. Many of these small towns didn't even have a grocery store. People often had to travel 25 to 50 miles to buy groceries. Sam and I laughed as we thought about our hometowns of about 20–30,000 in California. We had considered these to be small towns until this walk. Joni lives in the big city of San Jose, so the towns of rural America were kind of a shock to all of us. Many towns, like Cawker City, had populations of 500 or less. When we came to a town of more than 1,000, it seemed like we were in a city. In most of these places the economy was very poor, yet over and over we were blessed by the loving generosity of the people. We were often asked to pray for these poor rural communities. We did—and still continue to do so.

Campgrounds this time of year were a unique experience. Winter schedules began when the first snows and frosts hit. Almost all RV Parks on the back roads were closed, so we had to resort to finding camping spots near freeways, usually miles away from our walk route. Often we called Dave and Alyce-Kay and had them look for campgrounds on the internet. We really appreciated the help they both gave us in finding some great spots.

For our next move Alyce-Kay located a campground that was open just off of Interstate 70 in the little community of Paxico, Kansas. Although quite a distance from our walk route, it was about the only full service campground still open. The owners, Dan and Judy, were very kind to us, and we became instant friends.

After stopping at Miltonvale to pray and leave Memorial Stone number 81, we met Duane and his wife, Cathy. Their daughter was a Teens For Christ leader and had shared with them about our Journey. Duane invited us to come to a dinner at their church that evening in Clay Center.

Duane and Cathy own the "Bear Bottom" place where Duane is a cabinetmaker. He showed us his shop, and also Cathy's special breed of cats that she was raising. These cats looked quite unique and Joni fell in love with them. She jokingly (at least we think she was joking) asked if she could bring a kitten along to add to our menagerie. Besides the cats, Duane and Cathy also had a donkey, goats, a dog named Bear, and other critters. Several carved bears were scattered around the yard. The beautiful pond in front of their place was actually a swimming pool.

Finishing our walk for the day we went to the Clay Center Christian Church where the dinner was being held. We were welcomed with corsages and treated like honored guests. During the program the pastor had us share about our walk. It was a wonderful evening, and we were peppered with many questions. The pastor's wife, Lisa, had grown up in Bakersfield, California, so she knew about the area we were from. These wonderful people blessed us with an unexpected "love offering." On November 15 we walked our 2,000th mile, just after passing through Clay Center.

Paxico, where our campground was located, was a small town of 211 people. We found a charming wooden church in town, the United Methodist. Brian Timmons, a nearby seminary student, was the pastor. On November 16 we attended their service.

Back at our Castle we ate lunch, then Joni did laundry. Sam and I drove about twenty miles into Topeka to do the shopping at Wal-Mart.

Since Cawker City, we had been walking along U. S. Highway 24. Our route took us past the Fort Riley Military Reservation, where General Custer had formed his famed Seventh Cavalry in 1866.

Manhattan was a good-sized town, and we made an appointment to get our van serviced later in the day. Then we drove on north of Manhattan, where our walking would begin. As we were getting out of the van, both dogs began to bark. Turning to see what they were barking about, we saw Joan Nothern, our friend from Glasco. After a hug and greetings, we found out she was on her way to Topeka for some meetings and had been watching for us. What a delight to see her, though only for a few minutes since she had to hurry on. However, she told us she would be watching for us on her return trip.

We finally walked into Manhattan and Joni took the van in to be serviced. Sam and I continued walking and saw a restaurant advertising pumpkin pies. Now that sounded mighty good to us, so we stopped to get some. We ate ours right away, and got a piece to go for Joni since we figured she would be along soon. Because of unexpected brake work it took longer than usual. It was well after dark before Joni got back to us. She finally got to enjoy her pie when we got back to the Castle.

Before setting out from the campground in Paxico to walk we met Judy and her mother, Betty, in the office. They invited us to attend church with them the next Sunday. Betty was quite excited about meeting us and asked if she could pray for us. After praying for each of us individually, she sent us on our way.

Because of an accident on Highway 24, we were re-routed through St. Marys to Westmoreland. The detour took us an extra two hours, but we figured this was all part of the journey God had planned for us. We also realized that if Betty hadn't asked to pray for each of us, we might very well have been involved in the accident that was blocking the road. Prayer works in many ways.

Our lengthy detour took us through some interesting territory, including the Scott Springs Oregon Trail Park. There was an outstanding display of a covered wagon and team sculpted by Ernest White in 1993. We stopped for pictures and read the signs that told some of the interesting facts and stories. One of the signs told us:

---

Historians have estimated that between 250,000 and 300,000 emigrants used the Oregon Trail between 1840 and 1869. At least 30,000 emigrants died along the Oregon Trail, leaving an average of 15 graves for every mile of the trail. Disease, especially cholera, accidents and hardships took their toll; very few were killed by Indians. Most trailside gravesites are unknown but road construction occasionally uncovers lonely emigrant graves. A monument nearby marks the grave of a child at the Scott Spring Oregon Trail campsite. Other graves have been found in the timbers.

---

Finishing up at Scott Springs we continued on to Wamego. After 1:00 P.M. we finally started walking. Joan Nothern spotted us on her return trip from Topeka, and we prayed together for Wamego and left Memorial Stone number 86. We walked the mile or two to McDonald's and enjoyed hot fudge sundaes together. Joan then continued on her way home.

It was dark by the time we walked through Belvue to the east side of town. We had been walking with flashlights for about an hour when we decided to call it a day. Though we'd started very late, we still managed to walk 16.5 miles.

Joni's twin brother, John, phoned from England to say that he had become the grandfather of twins. The girls, Louise and Hannah, born prematurely weighed about one pound each. (At the time of this writing the twins have matured into healthy toddlers.)

## Sam

Each evening when we returned from a day of walking, we formed a brigade from the van to the Castle handing things in from the van. After getting settled inside the RV this evening, Waliluke, who had just finished walking 15 to 20 miles, decided it was time to play. He coerced Cassie into playing with him by running the full length of the Castle, then literally bounced off the wall to turn around and pounce on Cassie. Then they rolled and ran (mostly Waliluke) and jumped on everything and everyone until suddenly Waliluke plopped down and fell instantly to sleep.

Waliluke had a crazy game he and Joni played each day when she dropped us off to walk. He liked to crouch down until she was even with him in the van. Then Joni honked the horn (a very funny sounding horn, by the way), and Waliluke took off racing with Lady Van Go, dragging me along as I held his leash. Of course, Waliluke never won a race, but he sure tried. He always kept us laughing and wondering, "Where does he get his energy?"

## Lyn

St. Marys was a small town with lots of nice shops, and people to visit with. A highlight of St. Marys was the college. A marker placed by the Kansas Historical Society told us:

---

This city and college take their name from St. Mary's Catholic Mission founded here by the Jesuits in 1848 for the Pottawatomie Indians. These missionaries, who had lived with the tribe in eastern Kansas from 1839, accompanied the removal to this area. A manual labor school was operated at the mission until 1871. From it developed St. Mary's College, chartered in 1869. In 1931 the college became a Jesuit seminary. A boulder on the campus marks the site of the first cathedral between the Missouri river and the Rocky Mountains. Built of logs in 1849, it became the See of Bishop Miege, "Bishop of the Indians." Vice President Charles Curtis, part Kaw Indian, was baptized in this parish on April 15, 1860. The mission was an important stopping point on the Oregon trail. Here also was the U.S. Pottawatomie agency. This building still stands 600 feet northwest of this marker.

---

(Did you know that Charles Curtis was U.S. Vice President under Herbert Hoover from 1929 to 1933? Now you do.)

Then we walked on through Rossville, Silver Lake, and Kiro. From Kiro our route took us along the north end of Topeka and out to a large fruit stand where we enjoyed hot apple cider. We walked as far as Perry, then stopped to wait for Janell, a friend of my family's, who was passing through the area on her way to her home in Omaha, Nebraska. She had been a missionary in Africa the last few years, and would soon be going with a mission team to Poland.

Rocks that we could use for Memorial Stones were often hard to find. As we walked toward Lawrence we found a nice supply of them in a dry creek bed, plus a great brick that I claimed for my own. Stamped on this brick were the words, "Lawrence, KS."

We stopped at the Visitors Center in Lawrence to find out about the area. It was very cold when we arrived and we heard that there might be snow flurries that evening. Not wanting to drive back to our camp in the dark with snow coming down, we called it a day after only 13.7 miles. It was a long drive back to our campground and we were very tired.

We woke up to a very cold Sunday morning, November 23. Dan came from the office to see if we had water. It was only a trickle, so he got his torch and thawed the frozen hoses. He also filled our onboard water tank and disconnected our water hoses to keep them from freezing.

Our morning routine finished, we met Judy and Betty and followed them to church at Skyline Heights Christian Faith Center in Maple Hill. This was a small, very loving and open church. It was a special day for the people of this congregation. They were celebrating Pastor Galen Schutter's 40th birthday with a special service. We were asked to share and answer questions about our walk.

Pastor Galen asked the people to give an offering for us as they felt led. We never ceased to be amazed by these acts of generosity, especially since we made it a point never to ask for money. Yet time after time people gave to help us on our way. God always provided.

That morning the congregation had a time of thanksgiving as people stood to verbally give thanks to God for the things He had done for them. A special meal was given in honor of the pastor's birthday. We ate hearty soups and cake. All were delicious! Finally we said good-bye to these wonderful people.

# Chapter Seventeen

# POLICE ON THE HUNT FOR JONI

## Lyn

On Tuesday we prepared to take a trip to Woodland Park, Colorado to spend Thanksgiving with my brother and his family. That morning we moved the Castle to another part of the park, where Judy and Dan told us we could leave it for our time away. We drove as far as Goodland, Kansas to spend the night. Late the next afternoon we finally arrived in Woodland Park.

Our Thanksgiving break was wonderful as we enjoyed a festive dinner with Ernest and Bernice, two of their children and seven grandchildren, followed by a couple of days of visiting and sightseeing. There were many things to see in this part of Colorado—Pike's Peak, Garden of the Gods, the Cripple Creek gold mining area, and the quaint town of Cripple Creek all lit up for the Christmas season.

That Sunday we attended the New Covenant Christian Fellowship with Ernest and Bernice. Pastor Chris Austin asked us to share about our Journey. Many came to us after the service to ask questions or to say, "Thank you." After church we went to lunch with Ernest and Bernice at a Chinese restaurant, then headed back to Kansas to continue our walk.

We arrived back at the Castle after dinner on December 1, but didn't bother to hook up since we were moving to a new campsite the next day. Linn County Park near La Cygne, Kansas was our next stop. It was a beautiful park off the main road.

## Sam

As we were settling into our new campground, my mom, Alyce-Kay, and three of my siblings as well as two dogs and a number of cats and kittens arrived in nearby Butler, Missouri. This was about 25 miles from our RV Park.

They would be staying in a motel there for a couple of nights, so I would be able to spend time visiting with them. They were heading to eastern Tennessee to our new home. I began this walk as a Californian, but would end it as a Tennessean. Joni, Grumman, and the two dogs had the Castle to themselves while we had some family time.

Mama brought paper snowflakes to hang in our Castle. She had arranged for people to send us gifts throughout the Advent season. Many sent their packages with Mama, each marked with a specific date for opening. From then until Christmas we decorated our Castle with lights, stockings and ornaments sent by many wonderful friends and family members. It was all such a nice surprise. Money was even sent for us to buy a small tree.

When Mama left she took Joni's and Grumman's collections of rocks to store in the basement of our new home. Grumman and Poppy (Dave) would stop by after the walk's finish to pick them up and take them to California. This gave Joni and Grumman room to continue collecting rocks from the remaining states of our Journey, much to my dismay. After my family left to continue their journey to Sweetwater, Tennessee, we continued our walk.

### Lyn

It was great to start walking again! We enjoyed the shops as we walked through the college town of Lawrence. Replicas of the college mascot, large multi-colored birds, lined the streets. A sign under one said, "Gogh Hawks Gogh." Further on was an area of Victorian homes, many either renovated or soon to be.

Temperatures these days and nights were in the low twenties and teens so we were really beginning to experience a mid-west winter. We needed to buy propane for our Castle soon, or we'd be left in the cold with no possibility of heat.

I checked at a store about having propane delivered:

> Lyn: *"Do you deliver propane?"*
> Man: *"We ain't got no truck."*
> Lyn: *"Can I bring my RV here to fill it?"*
> Man: *"We ain't got no truck."*
> Lyn: *"Do you know if you'll have a delivery soon?"*
> Man: *"It might be."*
> Lyn: *"Would you come out and deliver it to us?"*
> Man: *"Might do."*

We left there totally uncertain as to whether or not we would be getting propane soon, but it was certainly an interesting conversation.

During the next few days we walked through Vinland, Baldwin City, Le Loup and Rantoul. Between towns we walked through farmlands and enjoyed watching the animals grazing in the pastures.

As we walked by one small farm, a gal asked us where we were from. We told her, and explained what we were doing. Chrissy was pretty excited about this information and invited us in for some tea. We met her husband and two daughters, her dog, Montana, her potbellied pig and many goats. Some of the goats were "fainting goats." She explained that this particular breed plays dead at the first sign of danger, thus the name, "fainting goats."

In Baldwin City we saw Santa Claus standing outside McDonald's ready to have his photo taken with children. Since there were no children around at the moment, we stopped to chat with him. We all had our Santa hats on (furnished by some of our friends from California), and had a little fun with the "jolly old man." The photographer and Santa were both members of the Knights of Columbus. He took photographs of the three of us with Santa for the local newspaper. What a blast!

It was Sunday, December 7, and we left the RV Park in time to look for a church. Pastor Mike Allen greeted us at the La Cygne Christian Church and asked us to share with the congregation.

We really enjoyed the service. Pastor Mike was preaching parts six and seven of a series titled, "My Journey to the Big Dream." Part six was called "Am I ready for the Giants?" He talked about obstacles to overcome to bring our dreams to reality. Part seven was called, "Do I realize that this is just the beginning?" The whole message really fit our Great American Journey. The rest of Sunday was spent doing our regular chores and relaxing.

Getting desperate for propane (we still hadn't heard from the "Ain't got no truck" man), we unhooked the RV and drove it into town where we left it. The clerk at the store assured us it would be filled during the day. At the end of our walk that day we were happy to return to find that the tank had indeed been filled.

Another evening, as we finished walking in the town of Osawatomie, Sam and I waited by a bridge. Here's Joni to tell the rest of the story.

## Joni

I had gone to see the John Brown Museum, then proceeded through the town to meet Lyn and Sam by "the bridge." Dismayed to find out there was more than one bridge leading out of town, I went first to one then another. Finally, feeling very frustrated but relieved when I saw them at the "Old bridge," I parked there. As I stopped, a policeman pulled up behind me. He explained that someone had called in to say that two people were out walking near the bridge. Since they'd had problems at this bridge before, they didn't want to take chances when things looked a bit suspicious. (We always knew we were suspicious looking characters.)

We explained what we were doing, and he assured us we had done nothing wrong. In fact, he seemed quite pleased that we were praying for the nation and told us to keep up the good work. The officer then noted that I had parked the van on the wrong side of the road. (Oh dear, I thought, now I'm in for it.) He and his partner stopped traffic for us to get back out where we belonged. Sam said, "That's the way she always drives—she comes from England." These policemen were really delightful people.

## Lyn

Osawatomie—a name that tickles the tongue. Our previous day had finished in this town, so it naturally started there the next. It was raining and cold, with thunder and lightning. We decided to stop at a local café for a hot drink and also to see what we could find out about the weather predictions for the day.

Bruce greeted us at the door of the restaurant, as he rang the bell while collecting donations for the Salvation Army. He was thrilled with our story and proceeded to tell us about his son having bicycled across the states. He went on to tell us that his son had wandered away from God for years, then had finally come back and was now a missionary in Taiwan. Stories like this always encouraged us. As we sat warming ourselves with cups of hot cocoa, Bruce came to our table to pray for us. Wow! How special.

The thunderstorm continued, so we decided to have a second breakfast while waiting for a break in the weather. As we sat there looking out the window a car parked next to ours. Three impeccably dressed people, two perhaps in their seventies, and the third about twenty years younger. The older woman took a piece of gum from her mouth, leaned over, and stuck it to the bottom of our tire! We were shocked that such an elegant looking woman would do such a thing, and laughed hysterically. In fact, thinking about it now makes us laugh again.

The thunder and lightning stopped, the rain slowed, and we began walking. Going through the town of Beagle, we placed a Memorial Stone by the old church. Somewhere after Beagle, a large white dog joined us and followed until we turned onto Highway 391.

It was soon time to call it quits, as we needed to drive to Butler, Missouri. JoAn Thomas had flown from Canada to Kansas City, and had then taken a bus to Butler. We had not seen her since she left us in Washington. Driving back to camp with JoAn we noticed the rain had changed to snow. Fortunately we didn't have far to go. The roads were getting slick and we drove very carefully.

The next morning we woke up to a beautiful snowy scene. We chose not to walk that day, mostly because of the drive out to the main road. While the snow plows kept the main roads cleared, the little back roads were left with snow and ice. Neither Joni nor I was ready to drive on roads in these conditions. Waliluke and Cassie had a blast in the snow, romping, playing and rolling. The low temperature for the day was 19 degrees, with a high of 32.

JoAn put on her Santa hat later in the day and came out with a bag of gifts swung over her shoulder. When Waliluke saw her he barked furiously. JoAn had to remove her hat before Waliluke would allow her to give us our gifts. She proceeded to give us each face masks to replace our "grasshopper kerchiefs." These would come in handy when the bugs became plentiful again in the spring. Next she handed us each a certificate stating that we had walked across the center of the conterminous (yes, that is a word—includes all the states except Hawaii and Alaska) United States. There were also thick socks and chocolates. It was a fun day and evening, even though we had not been able to walk.

That night the temperatures plummeted to nine degrees! We woke up to no water—even our pump didn't work—but at least we had heat. We hauled tap water from the restrooms for some of our needs, and used our bottled water for others. It took us longer to get ready, but we finally drove away from camp after 11:00 A.M. to begin walking.

It was a fun day of walking in the snowdrifts alongside the road. Waliluke especially enjoyed the snow as he romped and dove headfirst into snow banks, then slid down a hill or bounded from place to place. Cassie ran in circles and ate the snow, then chased a small herd of deer down into a ravine.

When we reached the La Cygne High School we prayed and left Memorial Stone number 100 by the town sign. Walking back to the road from the sign, I suddenly found myself up to my knees in snow. We all laughed so hard that I could barely get out.

The snow in La Cygne was partially melted, leaving a mixture of mud and slush for us to walk through. We finally got through the town and back to easier areas for walking. There was only about ten miles left in Kansas when we quit for the day. We could hardly wait to begin a new state!

That evening Sam and I drove to Ottawa, Kansas to meet Sam's boyfriend, Chip Gruver. He'd taken the bus from Sweetwater, Tennessee to visit Sam and walk with us for a week-and-a-half. They were very happy to see each other (understatement)! For the next few nights we would have five people and two dogs in the Castle. Joni and JoAn slept on the bunks at the back of the RV. Chip was on an upper bunk at the front of the RV. Sam slept on the couch, and I was on a cot squeezed between twenty bottles of water and the couch. Tight, but manageable.

As we walked the last part of Kansas the next day, Roger of the Osawatomie Graphic came to interview us. Not wanting to delay us, he interviewed us while we walked.

He left us when we turned from Highway 69 onto Highway 52. By mid-afternoon we reached the Kansas/Missouri border. There we stopped to pray for the two states and leave Memorial Stones numbers 101 and 102. We also took our ten-mile "manna break" (lunch) at this point.

We walked a little over four miles in Missouri before calling it quits for the day. The date was December 12, seven months after we began our Great American Journey.

Joni stepped out of the Castle the next day and slipped on the ice, hitting her head hard. After she got up she began packing to go home!

# MISSOURI

## *Winter Delight*

Entered Missouri .......................................................... December 12, 2003

Finished Missouri ........................................................... January 26, 2004

Actual Days in State ........................................................................ 46

Walking Days in State ...................................................................... 18

Total Mileage for Missouri ........................................................... 253.5

Total Journey Mileage to Date ................................................... 2,458.8

Capital ...................................................................... Jefferson City

Admitted to Statehood ................................. August 10, 1821 ~ the 24th state

Population ................................................................... 5,595,211

Highest Point ............................................. Taum Sauk Mountain ~ 1,772 feet

Lowest Point .................................................. Saint Francis River ~ 230 feet

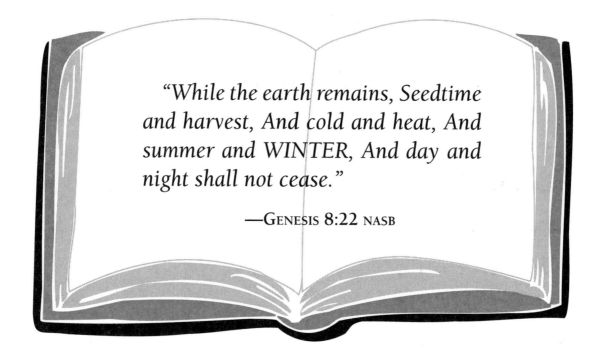

"*While the earth remains, Seedtime and harvest, And cold and heat, And summer and WINTER, And day and night shall not cease.*"

—GENESIS 8:22 NASB

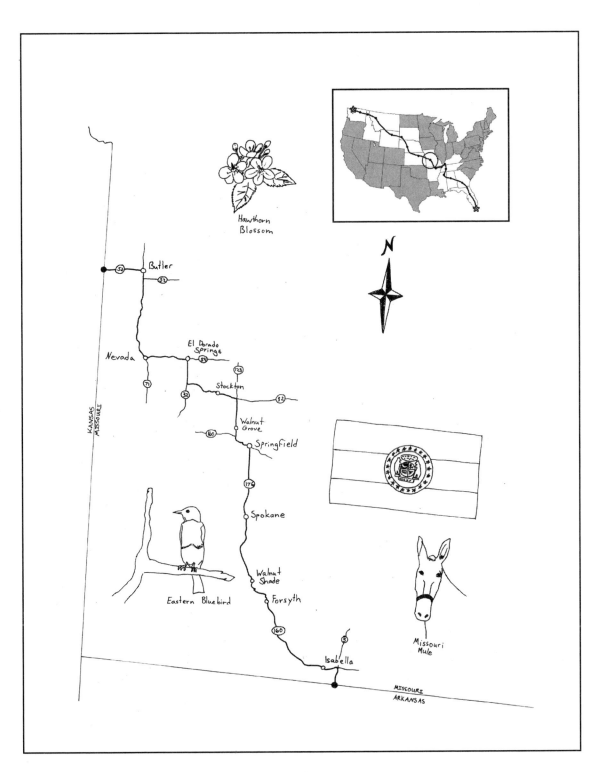

Hawthorn Blossom

Butler

52

53

El Dorado Springs

Nevada

54

123

71

32

Stockton

32

Walnut Grove

160

Springfield

17

Spokane

Walnut Shade

Eastern Bluebird

Forsyth

160

5

Isabella

KANSAS

MISSOURI

MISSOURI

ARKANSAS

Missouri Mule

157

*Chapter Eighteen*

# THE EARTH SHOOK OUR HOME

---

**Lyn**

The day after we began walking in Missouri it began to snow again—enough that we took a day off to work on laundry and paperwork. Under a dark gray sky, frost glistened on the bare branches of the hedge trees, and snow-laden pine branches graced the campground.

We discussed our next Castle move, since we were now facing more potential bad weather. The next day was Sunday, a day we would never choose as a moving day. However, we needed Joni to drive the van for our move, but she would be going home for Christmas break in a couple of days. With another storm on the way, it seemed wise to make our move that Sunday.

It was here that Joni stepped out of the Castle, slipped on the ice, and fell, hitting her head really hard. Getting herself up she moaned, "I'm going to pack my suitcase to go home to sunny California!"

Fortunately the weather was good on Sunday, December 14 (Dave's birthday). We packed up the Castle and headed out for our next campsite at Arrowhead Point near El Dorado Springs, Missouri. Very cautiously we drove the two miles of unplowed side roads from our campground to the main road.

The 100 miles to El Dorado Springs crossed through picturesque farmland and woods. Everything was covered in deep snow, but it did not seem to bother the cows and horses.

The camp road at the new place was very icy, so we drove slowly and gingerly. The showers were already closed for the winter, but we did have the full hook-ups. After we got all settled in we sat around and sang carols and shared our thoughts about "what Christmas means to me." It was a good evening.

We decided it would be best to take Joni and JoAn to the airport in Kansas City on Monday to spend the night before their flights out the next day. JoAn was returning to her home in Canada, and Joni was going home to California.

Monday morning we were all up fairly early, and set out in Lady Van Go at a little after 10 A.M. We had to stop at the post office and Wal-Mart in Butler, and Cassie had to be seen by a veterinarian. With tranquilizers and a kennel, Cassie was finally prepared for her first flight to California.

Somehow while we were getting in and out of the van, the sliding door got knocked off the track. We drove to the Ford dealer in town to see about getting it fixed. Though they told us it couldn't be done, they finally managed to get it back on the track when we insisted we had to get to Kansas City that day. They told us we should not open the sliding door until it could be repaired. So, for the rest of the day whoever was sitting in the back seat, including the dogs, had to climb over the front seat.

In Kansas City we got JoAn, Joni and Cassie settled into a motel, ate a meal together, then said good-bye, and headed back to our Castle. (JoAn includes her thoughts about her time with us in this state in Appendix 9.)

## Joni

After a 7 A.M. wake-up call Tuesday, I said my good-byes to JoAn. Cassie and I took the shuttle to the airport. They allowed me to keep Cassie until boarding time. I then gave her a tranquilizer and the baggage man allowed me to take her into the hold on the underside of the plane. There she got into her crate and settled down. I went upstairs to the cabin and got my seat. We had an uneventful flight home, with incredible views of the Rockies, including Pike's Peak.

## Lyn

After we returned from seeing Joni and JoAn off, we continued walking for another five days before we quit for our Christmas break. During this time Chip took the responsibility of driving, while Sam and I walked. Like Joni, he usually parked ahead and walked back to meet us. He told us about a pecan place that we would soon be passing, so we all stopped in and watched as they sorted, hulled and prepared the pecans.

The road we planned to walk on through Butler came to a dead end, so we decided to do some exploring in the van. We found a detour that would take us south of our originally planned route.

Walking along Highway 71 toward Rich Hill and Nevada (this is pronounced Ne-vay-da), we found a side road away from traffic, but parallel to the main road. It had been dark for a while now and we were using flashlights. A state trooper drove up beside us to see if we were OK. They had received several calls from people reporting lights on the side road, so the trooper came to investigate. He was glad we weren't having car trouble and wished us well.

When we arrived back at the Castle we were delighted to see Dave and our granddaughter, Lois. They had arrived about an hour earlier. After getting everyone settled in the Castle, we fixed some dinner and headed to bed.

Frank and Kevin of the Baxter Bulletin interviewed us at the city limit sign for Mountain Home, Arkansas

The crew at Wendy's Restaurant in Mountain Home, Arkansas
- Ken, Josh, Steven, Nathan, Thea and Christina

A special heart from Lyn to Dave on our 44th wedding anniversary near Salem, Arkansas

An evening with our camp hostess, Nancy and her three friends
- Norma, Kay and another Nancy

Eddie of Hedges Portable Toilets had our sewage pumped in no time
- Walnut Ridge, Arkansas

Cassie chased these donkeys injuring herself and Joni in the process

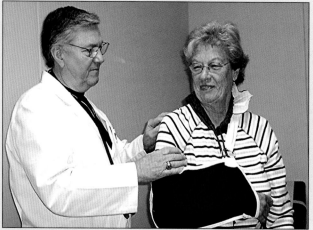
Dr. Lancaster put Joni on "restriction" for driving until her shoulder healed
- Walnut Ridge, Arkansas

Placing the Memorial Stone at Glencoe, Arkansas on Sam and
Waliluke's last walking day with us

Elnora Free Will Baptist Church between Walnut Ridge and Pocahontas, Arkansas where we enjoyed some of that good southern gospel music

Joni hugs the giant raven at Ravenden, Arkansas

The congregation at Clear Lake Free Will Baptist Church - Relton and Loyse, Robert and Marilea with Kendall

Lyn with her new flag trying hard to smile after Sam and Waliluke left the team in Arkansas

Lyn with Mayor Raymond Gunter of Campbell, Missouri

Torrey and Larry wait to board the Mississippi ferry with the seeder they were delivering to someone in Tennessee

In Hickman, Kentucky we had Sunday dinner at the Langford home
- Tim, Karen, Andrea, MaryEvelyn and Amy

Minnie at her gift shop in Hickman, Kentucky

Officers Danny H. and Danny S. tell Joni the best places to park the van

Chris, a reporter with the Messenger of Union City, Tennessee

Joe and his "friend" of Warren's Bonwood Exxon in Jackson,
Tennessee where we had more repairs done on the Castle

Clark Shaw, owner of The Old Country Store and Restaurant with two employees, Pam and Paige

Michael interviewed us for Channel 7 ABC News in Jackson, Tennessee

Cody, Jim, Cara and Justin of Indiana met Russ at a campground and followed him to Jackson to meet the "women walking across America"

Ken of Uncle Bubba's Antique Store in Pinson, Tennessee

Jennifer gave this lei to Lyn as a reminder to pray for her husband, Jimmy stationed in Hawaii

Becky, Peggy, Judy, Katrina and Richard of Selmer, Tennessee

Janice and Donald at "Garden of Eden" gave us these scarves and pins

Russ with Bekka and her father, Pastor Morris at the Senior luncheon

Janice, Tess, Greg and Paula after a family reunion

That's Lyn hanging out with 13-year old Elvis Presley

Russ was busy on the computer in the ditch beside the road at the Mississippi/Alabama border

Jeannine and her dog - she was camp manager at Barnes Crossing Campground in Mississippi

Crystal, Roberta, Olivia and Maxine at McDonald's in Vernon, Alabama

Lyn and Joni place a special Memorial Stone at this fire hydrant to mark the 3,000th mile spot on the 333rd day of the walk

Patricia and Martha, wife and mother to Jeff with National Guard Troop 877 in Alabama

We attended Easter services at the Trucker's Chapel in Cottondale, Alabama

Katey's daughter, Alex was born with Spina-Bifida

Dottie, Jim and grandson, Jake, stopped to get a picture taken with us

Michelle interviewed us on "Good Day Tuscaloosa"

Mary, 82 years young, was working in her garden near Vance, Alabama

During the next two walking days we were able to use Dave's rental van while Lady Van Go was at the Ford dealer being serviced and having the sliding door repaired. We walked to Nevada then turned east onto Highway 54. Here we saw many gravel trucks going back and forth all day. One driver's curiosity got the best of him. He pulled over to find out what on earth we were doing. He had seen us smiling and waving at everyone and wondered what was going on. We laughed with Jay as we shared about our Journey and took his picture.

After Jay got off work, he pulled up ahead of us in his car and waited. Then he asked if he could interview us for the local paper. He was a free-lance reporter as well as a gravel truck driver. He did a beautiful story about our Journey.

After walking through El Dorado Springs we turned south on Highway 32. This took us through a tiny town named Filley, and to a few miles before Stockton, where we finished walking. Our Christmas break officially began at this time. We wouldn't walk any further until Joni and Cassie returned on January 5, 2004.

On the 21st of December we attended Park Street Christian Church in El Dorado Springs. The pastor, though still a student, preached an excellent sermon. We felt very welcomed in this small church.

Dave and I did some scouting in Branson on Sunday afternoon, looking for a good campground for our Castle for the Christmas break. Many were closed for the season, or their showers had been shut down for the winter. We would be camped here for about three weeks so we needed a place with full facilities. We found the perfect place at Oak Grove RV Park.

Driving from Arrowhead Point on December 22 to Oak Grove Park we found a very nice site close to the restrooms. The manager asked for two of our Great American Journey cards so that she could put both sides up on the bulletin board for other campers to read.

This moving day turned out to be a rather significant day in several ways. Chip helped with the move, then we gave him and Sam some time alone. That evening we went to the bus depot in Springfield and waited until Chip was on his bus and headed back to Tennessee.

Earlier that day we had been shocked to hear that a 6.5 earthquake had hit our hometown of Paso Robles that morning. It was about six-and-a-half hours after the quake before we were able to reach Russ, our son, by phone. He assured us he and the house were fine, but the downtown area had been hit pretty hard, and two women had been killed. A major town landmark, the Acorn building, had fallen. We added Paso Robles to our prayer list, as well as the families of the two who were killed.

Our Christmas break was filled with writing and mailing Christmas letters and exploring the town of Branson. We took our granddaughters, Sam and Lois, to the Dixie Stampede and the Precious Moments Inspiration Park. We were able to sleep in and relax, read, and watch videos. We also drove to Springfield, and to Lake of the Ozarks to visit friends and family.

Christmas Day came and we enjoyed a wonderful Christmas dinner at the Country Grand Buffet. The choices of food were incredible, and the aromas tantalizingly inviting as we filled our plates with turkey and ham, cranberry sauce, biscuits, candied yams, mashed potatoes and gravy, stuffing, a variety of vegetables, and even a little catfish. Then, of course, there was pumpkin pie, apple pie and a variety of other desserts to choose from. It was a wonderful Christmas Day for all of us, even though we were far from our homes.

On December 28 we attended church at the First Presbyterian Church of Branson. We enjoyed the singing of Christmas songs, and were introduced by the pastor, then greeted quite warmly by the congregation.

January 2, 2004 Dave and I went for a walk to have a few last minutes alone before he took Lois home to Tennessee. Sam had enjoyed some great "sister time" with Lois during the few weeks she was with us. (For Dave's brief thoughts on his time with us in Missouri see Appendix 7.)

January 3, 4, and 5 were travel days for Sam and me. We left the Castle at Oak Grove RV Park in Branson and drove the van to Lee's Summit, Missouri near Kansas City. We checked into a motel for the night. On Sunday we woke up to ice everywhere. Sam was able to scrape enough ice off of the van windows so we could see, and I drove very carefully to the Lee's Summit Presbyterian Church. Pastor Dave Moore greeted us and introduced us during the service.

Pastor Moore's sermon from Jeremiah 29 and 31 was very fitting for the Great American Journey. He talked of how a book starts with a dream, how that dream is often lost or shattered, then comes back and takes hold, and how the actual writing has a cost and a reward. He compared this to the church and to individuals.

The Great American Journey began with a dream in 1953, faded away over the years, came to life again, and now was actually happening. As I look back on our Journey I realize it was the most difficult experience I have ever had, but also the most rewarding. I was so thankful that God brought us to this church for this particular message.

At 4:00 P.M. Sam and I headed out for the Kansas City airport to meet Joni and Cassie as they returned from California. The drive was harrowing, as a slushy snow had begun to fall. The roads were slippery, the windshield was impossible to clear completely, and it was dark.

At the turnoff to the airport there had been an accident. No traffic was allowed into that particular entrance. With Sam's excellent navigation we were able to find our way to another entrance and to an underground parking lot. It was now 5:30 P.M. Joni's plane was due in at 7:30, but all air traffic was running late because of the weather. The garage was well lit so we could read, talk, and walk Wali around in a small sheltered grassy area.

Finally I went in to meet Joni and Cassie, while Sam stayed outside with Waliluke. It was so good to see each other after such a long time—well it seemed like a long time. We retrieved Joni's luggage, then rescued Cassie from her kennel. Cassie had suffered a traumatic flight to Kansas City, messing her kennel and having to ride in it for however far that had been. Cass was still somewhat in a drugged state, and obviously not feeling herself. We got her and the kennel cleaned up enough to put into the van.

We headed to our motel in Lee's Summit, where Joni gave Cassie a complete bath. The trip back went much better, since the slushy snow had stopped and it was much easier to see. We were happy to be safely in our room again.

The next morning we left our motel about 11 A.M. with some snow coming down, but not the icy slush. Our drive back to Branson went well, and we just enjoyed listening as Joni told us about her time in San Jose.

### Joni

It was so great to see Lyn, Sam and Waliluke at the Kansas City airport. I was eager to tell them about my trip.

My son, Paul met me at San Jose airport and drove me to my friend Joan's house, where Cassie and I would stay. All the family was there to greet me: my daughter Beth, daughter-in-law Lori, and three grandsons Scott, Ryan and Kyle. It was so great to be surrounded by my noisy happy family, all asking questions. Beth had kept in touch by e-mail with my family in England about my progress across the states. I appreciated my son and daughter's encouragement so much on this Journey. Cassie and I slept for about 12 hours that night!

Scott's 14th birthday was on December 18th, and we all went out for dinner to celebrate. Then on Saturday the 20th Beth had arranged an open house so I could visit with friends and catch up on all the news.

A special friend of Lyn's and mine, Marilyn and her husband Jon, had adopted five siblings from Russia in September 2003 while I was away. She and Jon introduced us all to Nikolai, Ira, Leana, Sergei and Marina.

Kymberli, a reporter from the Almaden Times came and interviewed me about the Journey. (She wrote continuing updates throughout the rest of the walk and a final one after we finished.)

On Monday the 22nd at 11:15 A.M., we heard on the news there had been a 6.5 earthquake in Lyn's home town. I immediately phoned her son Russ to see if he was OK. Then I phoned Paul and Beth in Morgan Hill where we have our family business. They felt the quake even there, 140 miles north of Paso Robles.

Christmas arrived and we all spent a beautiful time together. Then for the New Year I prayed for good health, peace and tranquility for my family; for God's grace to help Lyn, Sam and me finish this walk in love and peace, and that we will make a difference by our prayers. To God be the glory.

All too soon my vacation was over and I had to say good-bye. Beth drove Cassie and me to the airport. Cass was very reluctant to get into her kennel, and I was not allowed to accompany her into the hold. We did arrive safely in Kansas, tired and messy, but it was great to be back with the team once more.

## Lyn

January 6 was indeed cold—a mere nine degrees Fahrenheit. We decided to go ahead, hoping it would get warmer before we got started. It did warm up some, but still by the end of the day, it had only reached 25 degrees. We walked just six miles that day through the town of Stockton, but at least it was a start after such a long break.

Stockton, a small town of less than 2,000 people, was hit by a tornado in May 2003, and the devastation was still very evident: trees were uprooted, homes collapsed and businesses destroyed. We found many homes and shops had already been rebuilt, and others were in the process. Back at the Castle in the evening, the temperature had already dropped to 16 degrees.

I wrote a letter to President Bush telling him about our Journey of Prayer and letting him know we were praying for him. The next morning we mailed it at the post office, then went to return a rented DVD.

Back in the van, the engine refused to start. It didn't take us long to figure out that our anti-theft alarm system was the problem. Even after trying to disconnect it, the engine wouldn't start. Finally we called for help from AAA. They towed Lady Van Go to a specialist that could help with the problem. The owners of the "Rolling Stones," Jason and Michael, explained that the whole system could be replaced for about $150, or they could simply remove the old system for $22.50. It seemed pointless to replace it, so we just had the system removed. By now it was too late to walk.

Another day lost! We tried to remind ourselves that this was God's Journey, and not get upset by the delay. But it was hard, and we wanted so much to be out walking.

*Chapter Nineteen*

# THE BROKEN PIPE MIRACLE

## Lyn

**W**e walked 15.5 miles from Stockton to Fair Play. Arriving at the Castle, we discovered a water pipe had burst. We called a repairman, Randy, who told us it would be a fairly expensive repair project. We needed time to think, talk, and pray about this before deciding how we would handle it. We phoned Dave to get his input as well.

The three of us struggled and prayed for the next few days. Temperatures were very cold, and we were all tired. Our opinions differed greatly as to what should be done about the water pipes.

On Sunday, January 11, we attended the Grand Old Gospel Hour service at the Chateau by the Lake Hotel. The service was wonderful, and just what we needed. An associate pastor, Ginger, gave the message. She talked about keeping our focus on what God has called us to do, and not getting sidetracked by the enemy. Ginger said that as Christians, we have no right to be offended by others, but we do have the right to forgive each other.

As we on the team struggled with issues, we knew we had to get back on track. For the rest of the week we were able to get in some good walking mileage, but were still not sure what we were going to do about the water pipes. We just kept praying.

In order not to let the enemy sidetrack us, we needed to keep our focus totally on Christ and the purpose of this Journey. An old hymn says, "Turn your eyes upon Jesus; Look full in His wonderful face; And the things of earth will grow strangely dim in the light of His glory and grace."

Along State Highway 123 we had no shoulder to walk on. Fortunately there was also little traffic. Our route took us through the towns of Aldrich, Eudora, and Walnut Grove.

Joni had a funny thing happen one evening. While waiting for us in a bank parking lot in Walnut Grove, suddenly cars came from out of nowhere and filled the lot. The people just sat in their cars, and Joni wondered if there was going to be a drug raid or something. A few minutes later a Bookmobile drove up and parked, and everyone jumped out of their cars and lined up to check out books. Walnut Grove is obviously a town of readers.

From Walnut Grove we were blessed with a trail for one whole day of walking. This was the Frisco Highline Trail, a part of the Rails to Trails system. Joni drove to Springfield and walked back with Cassie to meet us. The day was filled with watching rabbits, squirrels and a variety of birds. Signs were posted along the trail, telling of a mixture of wildlife that could be expected in the area, and of the permanent wetlands along the path. We ate our lunch on one of the many benches along this trail.

Springfield is a sizeable city, so we walked through on small side streets. For a short distance we walked on an unfinished trail, where we spotted a beautiful red fox running out of some bushes and across a field. He was too quick for us to get a picture, but what an exciting sight.

In a school parking lot we saw a large United States map, including the outline of each state, painted on the asphalt. We took a video of each of us walking across the states to our final goal of Florida. Now that we had walked through all 15 states of our planned route, we figured we could pack up and head home. The idea gave us a good laugh as we continued walking through Springfield.

We walked only about 7.5 miles in Springfield, then quit early to go visit my nephew and his family. While visiting with David and Melissa and their two children, Tahlia and Sylvie, we learned they were expecting another baby later that year. We rejoiced with them and their exciting news, and at the end of a delightful afternoon we left for camp.

Another day of walking in the rain, yet with all our rain gear on we were warm and dry, leaving Springfield on U.S. Route 160. This was a divided highway with wide shoulders—what a blessing. It was also a much busier highway, but that just meant more people to wave to. It was good to see some enthusiastic return waves as well.

While walking after dark one evening with our flashlights, a policeman stopped to make sure we were OK. He was quite excited when he heard about our walk and the book we would be writing about it. Matt gave us his card and asked us to please send him a copy.

Mail was always sent to us care of general delivery in whatever town we were staying. Most postal clerks were quite friendly and helpful. In fact, when we walked in they often had our mail waiting for us. In Branson we got to know three of the clerks quite well, since we were there for over a month. Two clerks were really helpful, but we had some difficulties with a third. We'd tell her ahead of time that Joni was staying in the van with the dogs, but was willing to come in if she had mail. Still the clerk lectured us and refused to give us Joni's mail until she came in. We figured this gal needed a little extra prayer. Fortunately most of our experiences were positive.

## Joni

Walking south one morning on Highway 160, and later on 176, we found ourselves on a country road. It was really very quiet, with no traffic. The farms and fields looked eerie with low-lying fog through the trees.

## Lyn

Sunday, January 18, we decided to attend the Cowboy Church in Branson. Some ladies in a store had recommended it. We met Pastor Al and Norma Jean as we went in. They later introduced us to the rest of the congregation. The band consisted of three guitars, a mouth organ and a bass. Each member of the band sang or played individually, as well as together. Most of the service was good ol' country gospel songs sung by some very talented country singers, including Mary Lou Turner, Rhinestone Tina McKinney and Johnny Long. Johnny sang "The Old Rugged Cross" and "How Great Thou Art," some of our favorites. It was good foot-tapping music, and we enjoyed it.

Early the next week we walked along a road with elegant icicles hanging from the table rock, sparkling in the sunshine. We passed through Walnut Shade and Merriam Woods. Joni parked Lady Van Go in the Ozark Mountain Christian Church parking lot. In front of the church was an altar with several stones on it. Carved on the front of the altar were the words, "What mean these stones?"

Throughout Israel's early history they left stones at various places to commemorate ways in which God had worked on their behalf. God told the Israelites that when their children asked what these stones meant, they could explain the event that had taken place there and how God had worked in the situation. You can read about one such incident in Joshua, chapter four.

This altar intrigued us, and since we were preparing to leave a memorial stone of our own in Merriam Woods, we decided this would be the perfect place for it. We prayed and left our stone on the altar. Then, finding there was no one in the church office, we left a note and our card in the door. Later we heard from them that they printed our story in their church newsletter.

Continuing on to Forsyth we passed beautiful lakes, rivers, hills and woods as we walked through the Ozark region of Missouri. The day was cloudy and very cold. Joni said it reminded her of Kent in England in the winter.

We were still without plumbing in the Castle, but were again thankful for the campground with such wonderful facilities we could use in the meantime. One evening while sitting in the Castle, I began putting together some sandwich-board-style signs printed in large black letters. These were simple, easy-to-read signs slipped over our heads and fastened together with Velcro. Mine read "Walking to Florida," while Sam's stated, "Started in Washington," and Joni's told people we were "Praying for America." After this, quite a few people slowed down to read them, and several stopped to see if the signs were really true, giving us some great opportunities to talk with people.

We enjoyed towns like Kissee Mills, Hilda, Reuter, and part of the Mark Twain National Forest. We arrived back at our Castle on January 20 in time to turn on the radio and hear President Bush's State of the Union address. Since we seldom have time to listen to news, it was good to hear the President's speech.

For several days we enjoyed huge icicles hanging from the table rock along the highways. Once we stopped to break some off, and Joni and Sam had a mock fencing match with the spears of ice. Waliluke thought the ice was great to eat and chomped on several pieces.

One morning I had prayed specifically for an opportunity to minister to someone that day. Within a few minutes I met Karen, and she told me about some struggles she was going through in her life. I was able to talk and pray with her. Telling me she did not enjoy reading Scripture, I was able to share some simple techniques and encourage her to read just small portions each day, starting with the book of John. Karen then showed me her mother's Bible and her own very first childhood Bible. That was pretty special.

Randy, Justin and Kevin saw us one day and tried to read our signs. Reading that we were walking to Florida, they really wanted to find out more, so when they saw us again they made a quick U-turn to talk with us. We spent several fascinating min-

utes with them, as they told us to watch out for leeches and other bugs when we went into the woods. We were thrilled to meet these real down home country people near Ocie. The town of Theodosia came soon, and we continued across Bull Shoals Lake on a large, beautiful bridge to the town of Sundown.

168

During the week since the water pipes had burst, two checks came in from unexpected sources, totaling $700. These came from friends who knew nothing of our need for new water pipes, or the tune-up and repairs needed on the van. We phoned Randy and set a time for him to make the repairs, and scheduled the van work also.

On the morning of January 22 I took Lady Van Go to the garage and waited while they did the work. I paid the bill, then returned to the Castle. In the afternoon Randy came to put in the new water pipes. When he presented the bill, I looked at it, did some figuring, and realized the total for this and the van came to exactly $700. God had brought those two checks to us at precisely the right time. For us, it was the miracle we needed to lift our spirits. Of course we shared the story with Randy, of how God had worked in this instance, as we gave him a check for the repairs he had done.

Later I called the two friends to thank them for their checks and explained how they were used. One of the ladies told me she had originally sent her check several weeks earlier, but it had been returned because we had moved on from that address. Then just the week before it occurred to her that she needed to mail it again. We believe this was no coincidence—rather it was truly a God-incidence. "Indoor plumbing" once again! We were ecstatic! Thank God for this wonderful campground.

The next day we were able to move out of Branson (we had been there just over a month) to the White Buffalo Resort RV Park, just outside of Mountain Home and Buffalo City, Arkansas. We still had a little walking in Missouri, but in a few days we would be walking in Arkansas!

Our final two walking days in Missouri took us through the town of Isabella and the outskirts of Gainesville. Going through Isabella, we noticed a large, intriguing piece of driftwood in front of a house. A lady was on her porch talking on the phone. We heard her say, "There are some people walking in front of my house with dogs. I have to go see what this is all about."

Eva told us that the driftwood piece we were admiring was named "Medusa." We took pictures of Eva with "Medusa." Eva then invited us to come in for tea, and we sat in an enclosed porch where we could watch the dogs—there were a lot of things that Waliluke would love to chew. Her husband, Robert, and his 92 year-old mother, joined us as Eva served a delicious tea. This family had come from Hungary many years ago, and Robert worked in the movie industry. Eventually they chose to retire in Isabella, Missouri because, "We like it here."

We had only six miles to walk in Missouri for our final day in this state. As we headed south on State Route 5 toward Arkansas, a man stopped to tell us we were walking right into a snow and ice storm. It was getting colder! We kept the van fairly close and walked in short spurts in between weather reports on the radio. We heard there was a

60 percent chance of snow that night. A few times we did see snowflakes and ice pellets.

Bill stopped to talk with us, and was very interested in what we were doing—especially when he found out we were praying for those in the military. He then told us, with tears in his eyes, that his grandson had been killed in Iraq just ten days earlier. We left promising to pray for him and his family. We have continued to pray for them to this day.

After crossing the border into Arkansas, we began walking in our ninth state! There would be lessons to learn in Arkansas, where 24 of our 38 days would be non-walking. There would be pain and heartache, but we would keep going.

# ARKANSAS

## Delays and Loss

Entered Arkansas ................................................................... *January 26, 2004*

Finished Arkansas .................................................................... *March 3, 2004*

Actual Days in State .............................................................................. *38*

Walking Days in State ........................................................................... *14*

Total Mileage for Arkansas ............................................................... *182.2*

Total Journey Mileage to Date ......................................................... *2,641.0*

Capital ................................................................................. *Little Rock*

Admitted to Statehood ..................................... *June 15, 1836 ~ the 25th state*

Population ...................................................................... *2,673,400*

Highest Point ................................................ *Magazine Mountain ~ 2,753 feet*

Lowest Point ....................................................... *Ouachita River ~ 55 feet*

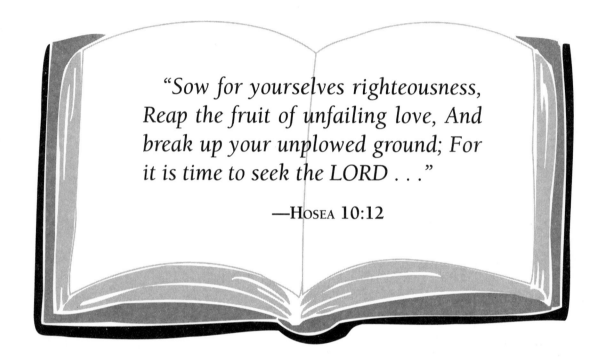

*"Sow for yourselves righteousness, Reap the fruit of unfailing love, And break up your unplowed ground; For it is time to seek the LORD . . ."*

—HOSEA 10:12

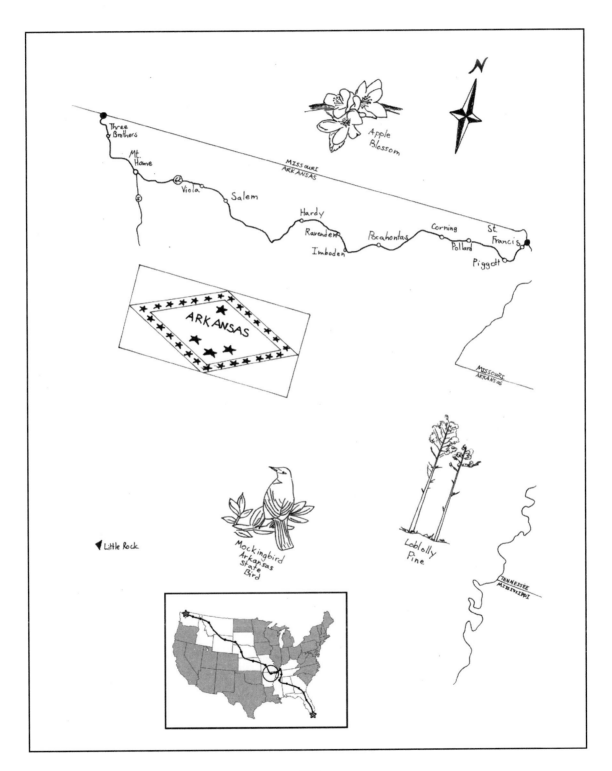

Three
Brothers

Mt.
Home

Viola

Salem

Hardy

Ravenden

Imboden

Pocahontas

Corning

Pollard

Piggott

St.
Francis

MISSOURI
ARKANSAS

Apple
Blossom

ARKANSAS

MISSOURI
ARKANSAS

Little Rock

Mockingbird
Arkansas
State
Bird

Loblolly
Pine

TENNESSEE
MISSISSIPPI

173

# Chapter Twenty

# A TEMPER LOST

*Lyn*

Arkansas at last . . . but if you noticed on the state page, we were in the state for a full thirty-eight days, and only walked fourteen of them. You may also have noticed that the title we've given this state is, "Delays and Loss." While physically this state was not difficult, emotionally and spiritually it was excruciating. We were doing our best to "break up unplowed ground" with our prayers, but the enemy (Satan) never likes it when work is being done for God, and he does his best to stop it. We were hit pretty hard by the enemy in the state of Arkansas. It was indeed time to seek the LORD.

Join us now as we journey through Arkansas and share with you some of our struggles and joys. Let's begin with a Sunday. It was January 25, and we still had a few miles left to walk in Missouri, but we had already moved our camp to Arkansas and attended the First Christian Church of Mountain Home on this particular day. We were staying at the White Buffalo Resort, where Nancy was co-owner along with her brother.

Nancy was a delightful person, and we felt really blessed to be around her. She invited us to visit her church that first Sunday in her state. We were greeted by many people, and sat with Nancy for the service. She introduced us to the congregation during the special time for visitors, and we were asked to share what we were doing.

Pastor Lee Nirschl gave a message on Matthew 21:28–32. During the service Bill sang a solo, "Holy Ground." This is a beautiful song, with wonderful words, that we hadn't heard in years.

Joni reminded us later that we had sung this hymn on the "Colorado Prayer Adventure" in 1996. Our team for that trip had a church service on top of a mountain. The sun broke through a cloud and shone around us as we were singing this song.

As Bill sang ". . . we are standing in His presence on holy ground," our hearts were blessed and we were overwhelmed by God's love. The song talks of angels being all around as we stand on this holy ground. Little did we know how much we would need God's presence and the encouragement of His angels around us in the weeks ahead here in Arkansas.

We began walking in Arkansas in freezing cold, with icy slush raining down on us. The first town in Arkansas was Three Brothers. A lady told us she thought it could have been named for the nearby mountains. She pointed out an old building that was once a grocery store/post office. Apart from a small wooden church and a cemetery, that was the extent of Three Brothers.

I'd had some phone calls early that day that, along with the cold, had disturbed me and made it hard for me to concentrate on the walk. It was a very frustrating day, and we ended up walking only ten miles. We had no cell phone service at our campground, so I had to find a place in town where I could get reception. Gloom and depression filled me, as I knew I had a deadline to make this phone call. During the conversation I lost my temper and hung up quickly. Heading back to camp, I was feeling very low.

One morning while working on this part of the book and thinking about the events of the day, I picked up my Bible to read my daily portion. I was at Exodus 32, reading in The New Century Version. As I read about Moses being up on the mountain with God, and the people below wondering what had happened to him, I suddenly noticed something in this very familiar section that I hadn't really thought about before.

The Israelites became restless. They had no idea what had happened to Moses. He had been gone a long time and they wanted to get moving. They approached Aaron and told him to make gods to lead them. So Aaron collected gold from the people, melted it down, and with a tool shaped it into a calf! Then he told the people, "This is the god that brought you out of Egypt." The next day the people sacrificed to this golden calf, sang and danced, and acted in ways that God had specifically told them not to. Only a few days earlier they had stated, "We will do everything He (God) has said" (Ex. 19:8). Now here they were ready to forget about Moses and his God.

Moses came down from the mountain as the people were in the midst of their wild orgies, saw what was going on, and threw down the stone tablets with the ten commandments God Himself had given him. Confronting Aaron he said, "What on earth have you done?" (my paraphrase). Aaron told him, "The people wanted me to make them gods to lead them out of Egypt, because you didn't come back like you were supposed to" (my paraphrase). "So I collected gold from them, threw it into the fire and out came this calf" (Ex. 32: 24).

Now here's the thing that struck me as I was reading this. No one took responsibility for their own actions—neither the people nor Aaron. Believe me, they were not the first ones to slip up like this. We could begin with Adam in the Garden of Eden: "You know that woman You gave me, God? She gave me some of the fruit . . ." And Eve: "The snake tricked me . . ." I could go on and on, but I think you get the idea. It is in our human nature to make excuses for ourselves when we do wrong.

Right here in America today, we see and hear about people not taking responsibility for themselves. We eat too much and get overweight, so we sue the fast food chains, because they make food taste so good "we have to eat it." A person trips and hurts himself and sues several people, because he didn't see the object he tripped over. Another has a car accident and sues the maker of the vehicle as well as the one he hit, because, "Surely, it's not my fault?!" A person commits a crime and says, "I did it because my mother—or father—was abusive. I can't help the way I turned out." The point is that we each need to look at ourselves and take responsibility for what we do, beginning with me. We all have a choice in any situation.

I'd like to blame my loss of temper on the cold, my fatigue, the person whose call I was responding to, anything or anyone but myself. But, quite frankly, I had a choice. I could choose to remain calm and work my way through the problem at hand, or I could say, "forget it," and yell. I chose the latter. Granted, that choice was made in a split second, but it was still my choice.

It is my prayer that we in America will wake up and begin to choose to recognize right from wrong, my responsibility versus blaming another. There were other incidents throughout our Journey where I had to choose between accepting responsibility, or placing blame on something or someone else. I certainly didn't always make the right choice, and often didn't even recognize when I made a poor choice until much later. Because I was the leader, I needed to set an example and take responsibility for all my actions. I'm hoping and praying that you, dear reader, will take time to stop and think about your own actions.

How will I choose next time? How will you choose next time?

### Joni

The next day we woke up to a temperature of eight degrees, with a wind chill factor of zero. We decided not to walk because it hurt to breathe in the cold air. I had learned that my grandson, Scott, was in the hospital in San Jose with pneumonia. This concerned me a great deal, and that, along with the dreary weather, made me feel quite low.

## Sam

I was feeling low because I was not able to talk with my boyfriend, Chip, on my cell phone. There was a phone booth near the camp restroom, so we could talk when he was off work. But I would get extremely cold while talking, then have to hang up for a while and sit in the restroom next to the heater. After warming up, I'd return to the booth and talk some more. All this was very inconvenient, and I was tired and cold. Things like this contributed to my emotional frustration. Similar things for each of us added to the burdens we struggled with and drove us all into varying degrees of depression.

## Lyn

By Wednesday, the 28th of January, we were ready to get out and walk. Fortunately the weather cooperated. It turned out to be a wonderful day, though our early morning temperature was a mere twelve degrees. This steadily rose, and sunshine warmed the day, and our bodies. We took our time getting ready, spent time sharing from our Scripture reading, and a little more time with our morning prayers than usual. We began walking at noon, much later than usual, and entered Mountain Home, a town of 11,000. Throughout the day people stopped to talk with us and marveled about our Journey.

As we began to pray at the Mountain Home city limit sign, two men walked up. They were Frank and Kevin from the Baxter Bulletin, the local newspaper. Someone had called to let them know that "some women were out on the road walking to Florida, and they should get out there and interview them." They asked some good questions and took pictures as we prayed and left our Memorial Stone number 136 for Mountain Home.

As we entered town, Christina stopped on her way to work to see if we needed a ride. At an auto shop we passed, Dean and his father wanted to know what we were doing.

Roxie stopped and asked us to pray for her 20 month-old grandson, who was in the hospital with seizures. If Roxie reads this she will know that we are still praying for her and her grandson, Cameron.

A young man came running out of a Wendy's restaurant, calling to us. His manager had sent him to invite us to come and eat our dinner there—on the house. While ordering dinner we realized that the manager was Christine, who had offered us a ride earlier. Christine asked if it would be all right for her staff to come sit with us when they weren't busy and ask us questions about the Journey. We were delighted.

Because of the ice cold weather they weren't very busy, so we were kept busy answering questions. In fact, the few customers that were in the restaurant joined in on the question and answer time. Some of the customers pulled up chairs to talk more, like John and his daughter, Alyssa, and another gentleman, Charles. It was a beautiful time.

These people asked thoughtful questions:

Q: "Why walk across the nation to pray for our country when you could pray while sitting at home?"

A: "Praying at home is fine and very good, but we felt called for this period of time to pray step by step across the nation—to pray with insight for the people and places where we walked."

Q: "Why do you think America needs prayer?"

A: "Our country has gone through a lot since 9/11, and needs continuous prayer. Every country, every person needs prayer. We have found that the Americans we have met have been grateful to hear that someone is praying for them and their country, and we also appreciate hearing that people are praying for us,"

Q: "Do you have significant others at home, and why aren't they with you?"

A: (I was the only team member with a husband.) "My husband is incredibly supportive and has encouraged me from the very beginning to step out on this Journey. He is at home working to help support our efforts, also keeping up our web site, and sending updates to people who are praying for us around the world. He does fly out to join us from time to time, and we talk on the phone almost every night."

As we prepared to leave Wendy's, we asked if we could get a picture of the whole staff. There was a lull in business right then, so they all came out and lined up. After getting a few pictures we said good bye to Ken, Josh, Steven, Nathan, Thea, and Christina. Thank you, Christina, for the dinner and the opportunity to share with your wonderful crew.

# Chapter Twenty-One

# THE SEWAGE DILEMMA

### Joni

After dropping off Lyn and Sam to finish walking through Mountain Home the next day, I was looking for a place to park the van and listening to the local radio station. The DJ was reading from the Baxter Bulletin about three women walking across America. Then he said, "I can see two of them walking along on Highway 62 past our radio station right now." I really had a big smile on my face when I heard this.

### Lyn

We had noticed the radio station as we walked by earlier. And now, people began to honk and wave to us as we continued walking. One lady came out of her store when she saw us and gave us each a bottle of water.

That evening we had dinner at the home of our camp hostess, Nancy, and three of her friends, Norma, Kay, and another Nancy. They fed us a delicious dinner, and we enjoyed a wonderful evening of getting to know each other.

Moving day came, and we said good-bye to Nancy. As we were unhooking the Castle we discovered the valve for the black water (bathroom sewage) was frozen (the temperature was 14 degrees) and wouldn't open. We decided to wait and dump when we got to our new camp.

As usual, I drove the RV with Sam along as navigator, while Joni followed in Lady Van Go. From Mountain Home we drove through all the little towns that we had walked through the previous week including Henderson, Gepp, and Viola.

We stopped in Salem at a Dairy Queen and felt the urge to have hot dogs. Eating our chili cheese dogs and drinking hot chocolate—ummmmm, good!

We arrived at the town where we expected to camp, only to find the campground pretty run down, the restrooms intolerable, and flooding over the campground a very high possibility. Homes near the campground were all on stilts (not a very good sign), and heavy rains were predicted.

We began phoning other campgrounds. At last we found one in Walnut Ridge and were given directions to 2-J RV Park. It was just after dark when we pulled in and Jewel came out to guide us to our spot. Once we got parked, he told us we could check in the next morning before he and his wife, Jean, left for church. I asked him where they went to church, and made arrangements to join them for the 11 A.M. service.

It was cold and dark, and I began hooking up the Castle water, electricity, and sewage using a flashlight to see. Joni and Sam were busy setting up the inside and preparing dinner. Electricity and water hookups went fine, but trying to hook up "Slinky" and "Slunky" for the sewage didn't go so well. I couldn't find the "Y" pipe to hook them up to. I had done this dozens of times and knew exactly what to do, but something was wrong.

Going inside I had a strange look on my face as I said, "Our sewage drain pipes are gone. I've looked and looked and can't find them." We were again without indoor plumbing, but how good of God to bring us to this place where we were right next to a clean, warm bath house.

The next morning, February 1, we headed off to White Oak Baptist Church where the pastor, Brother Sam Stewart, came over and introduced himself. During the service he interviewed us, and gave his congregation a chance to ask questions.

After church we went to lunch, then drove around the town of Walnut Ridge where we were staying. Back at camp I went to talk with Jewel and Jean about propane and a repairman. He was very helpful with names and phone numbers.

Monday we began the process of finding a repairman. It was 4:30 P.M. before someone could come to look at the Castle. He informed us that it would be necessary to dump our sewage before anyone would even consider doing repairs. Now that presented a real problem. How could we dump if we couldn't hook up our dump hose? That was a question no one had an answer for. It was suggested we drive out to a dirt road and dump the sewage. That didn't sound like a reasonable solution to me.

The next morning we drove in the van to Kelly's RV Repair in nearby Paragould. We talked with James, explaining what we were doing and what our problem was. Joni asked if a porta-potty place would be able to pump our sewage out. James thought that might work and called Roto Rooter and lined up a time for them to come to our Castle.

Sam and the dogs had stayed at the RV Park, while Joni and I went to find help for our problems. While we were gone she had hauled water from the bath house into the Castle and washed all the dirty dishes that had piled up. As we returned she was washing the mold from our windows. Sam and Joni were both susceptible to bronchial infections, and mold could really aggravate this kind of problem, so it was good to see it come off.

The next morning Eddie showed up from Hedges Portable Toilets in a pumping truck and set to work. We were amazed how quickly he finished, and were grateful to pay the $60 fee.

Then we called Kelly's and made arrangements to bring the Castle in, so the repairs could be done as soon as possible. On the way we stopped to get propane. Surprisingly it took 22 gallons, when 17 gallons was the most it had ever taken before. We figured we must have used a lot more than usual.

At the RV Repair Shop in Paragould James told Kelly about our problem, and what he proposed to do. We watched as Kelly put his head in his hands and just sat there—that was a bit frightening. He came to tell us that several repair jobs were already scheduled and they might not get ours done until the next day. That was OK—we could get a motel for one night.

We called 2-J's to hold our spot at the camp, and went into the town of Paragould. After walking the dogs we drove to Sonic for lunch. We had the laptop computer with us, and a DVD, so we sat in the car eating and watching our own "drive-in movie."

Kelly's phoned to say we had another problem, a bad gas leak. They moved our Castle from inside their garage to the outside because of the strong smell of gas. They discovered that the propane tank had been overfilled, so gas was escaping through the overflow valve. It was suggested that the thermostat be set at 68 degrees for the night to use up some of the propane. It would also keep our water pipes from freezing—snow and ice were predicted for the night.

In Paragould we got a room at the Ramada Inn, one of the few places where dogs were allowed, and were very thankful for a nice place to stay for the night. The next morning Joni and I took Cassie and Waliluke out for a walk through icy pools of melted snow and slush, while Sam enjoyed a swim in the indoor pool.

In town I went to a florist to order flowers to be sent to Dave on the 6th of February. This would be the first time we would be apart for our anniversary in 44 years of marriage.

Kelly called to say that our Castle was ready, so we went to pick it up. The bill wasn't nearly as bad as we expected—whew! Indoor plumbing again! After getting pictures of Kelly and the whole crew we were on our way back to 2-J's. There was a lot more snow on the ground at the campsite than there had been in Paragould. Hooking up was a mess, since much of the snow was now melted slush.

## Sam

Friday, February 6, our first day of walking in a week, and it was Grumman and Poppy's anniversary! At 9:30 a lady from Kay's Enchanted Florist delivered a large floral arrangement. We all knew this had to be for Grumman. The beautiful basket of flowers had the usual Milky Way bars in it for each of us.

In a field of snow Grumman drew a big heart, and wrote in its center, "D & L—44." I took pictures of her standing beside the heart, and we ended the recorded memo by calling out, "Happy Anniversary!" It was so neat to see the love that my grandparents have for each other stretch across the miles that now separated them.

## Lyn

As we walked I called Jim and Betsy Hawkins in Paso Robles to ask them to do me a favor. They happily agreed to my request that they go to our house and sing "Dream, Dream, Dream" to Dave, from Lyn. Popularized by the Everly Brothers in the 1950s when we were dating, this was our special song.

Later Dave called me and began singing "Dream, Dream, Dream." Jim and Betsy had just left after delivering my "gift" of the song. He told me his eyes filled with tears as they began to sing—he's very romantic and tenderhearted. We thanked each other for the floral arrangements, and Dave told me that our good friends, Charlie and Earline Ferrell, had invited him for dinner that night. Though it was hard for Dave and me to be apart on this special day, friends, family, and the day's experiences helped to bring us close together in spirit.

God was so good to give us the one-day of reprieve on the 6th, even giving Joni the good news that her grandson was out of the hospital and making good progress.

# Chapter Twenty-Two

# EMERGENCY ROOM VISIT

## Lyn

The morning of the 7th was a winter delight, but all would not remain so. Walking through snow flurries, with deep snow banks hugging either side of the plowed road, was really quite enjoyable. Snowflakes landed on us in such a way that we could actually see their delicate designs—beautiful! Waliluke loved the dry, fluffy snow.

In Salem we were invited into the Dairy Queen to eat whatever we wanted "on the house." Jamie and Mary graciously waited on us.

## Joni

I drove ahead to park the van and walk back with Cassie. Seeing four or five donkeys in a snow covered field, I stopped to take a photo. Cassie suddenly took off with her leash still wrapped around my wrist, pulling me over and down a snow covered bank, dragging me until I could free myself from the leash. I picked myself up and found my camera in the snow, hoping the lens was not damaged. First Cassie chased the donkeys, then the donkeys turned and chased her, kicking and showing their teeth. After this process was repeated several times I managed to grab Cassie's leash again and hold her. The donkeys had either bitten or kicked Cassie, catching her ear, and it was now bleeding badly. My shoulders were hurting, and I felt quite shook up. Lyn and Sam came and helped me to the van, then we went to look for a veterinarian. Dr. Kathy Mills was very nice, and cleaned the blood from Cassie's ear before putting in a few stitches. Lyn drove us back to the RV, where I took some pain pills and lay down on my bed.

The next morning was Sunday and we planned to go to church, but my shoulders were giving me such pain that Lyn and Sam insisted on taking me to the emergency room at the hospital in Walnut Ridge. Jewel gave us directions to the hospital, and would let his church know what had happened so they could be praying for me.

As Lyn drove she sang "Count Your Blessings," and Sam read to us the last verse of this beautiful hymn.

> *So amid the conflict, whether great or small,*
> *Do not be discouraged, God is over all,*

*Count your many blessings, Angels will attend,*
*Help and comfort give you to your journey's end . . .*

Certainly angels have been in attendance—my injuries could have been a lot worse. Truly God is giving us "help and comfort to our Great American Journey's end . . ."

## Lyn

The Admissions Clerk at the hospital emergency room was a young fellow who had been at the church the previous Sunday, and he recognized us. Michael, Erica, Polly and Dr. Cranford were a wonderful health care team. The X-rays showed no fractures, but the doctor wanted a radiologist to look at them in case there was something he couldn't see. We left the hospital with instructions to see another doctor the next morning.

Before leaving for the hospital I had called Earline and Charlie to have people praying in my home church. Dave told me later that by the time the request got through the prayer chain, I was the injured one. Remember that old game of "Telephone Gossip"?

Sam called her mom so their church could also be praying. Alyce-Kay said she started to ask the pastor to pray for Joni, when Kitty raised her hand and asked prayer for Cassie. So he prayed for Cassie and the whole team. How sweet of Kitty to think of Cassie (Kitty was Sam's eight-year old sister).

Monday morning we took Joni to see Doctor Ted Lancaster. Going to the doctor is not usually considered a "fun thing," but this time it was. The nurse, Joyce, had Joni weigh in as Sam and I looked on in anticipation. We knew we were all losing weight, but we had no way of telling how much. When Dr. Lancaster came in, he was a delight! He was very interested in our Journey and joked and laughed with us throughout our visit.

He checked Joni over very thoroughly, and she asked him if it would be OK for her to drive. He looked at me and I shook my head, "No." He proceeded to put Joni's arm in various positions and ask if it hurt. We all laughed as Joni screamed and screwed up her face in pain!! He then told her she would have a real problem in an emergency since it hurt so much to lift her arm. She felt really bad about not being able to drive, but we'd rather miss walking than have her in an accident.

Doctor Lancaster wanted Joni to see an orthopedic surgeon the next day. So on Tuesday, we saw Dr. Woloszyn at the outpatient clinic. He said there were no breaks or torn ligaments, but that an inflamed bursa in each shoulder was causing the extreme pain, and he proceeded to give her a cortisone injection. Sam and I took pictures of this whole process. Even in pain we see humor.

We decided that the forced time off would be a good time to get my leg and foot checked, as it had been giving me a lot of pain. I saw Doctor Peyton, who was Dr. Lancaster's daughter. She was delightful, just like her father. She X-rayed my foot—no fracture, but some arthritis. She prescribed a few days of rest with some special exercises for my foot, then a return visit the next week.

The doctors and nurses we saw were wonderful. They all asked lots of questions about the walk, and frequently expressed amazement at what we were doing. We three agreed that we could never go to the doctor alone again, but must always get together to make our doctor visits—it was just a lot more fun this way. Of course, we knew this would never happen, but it was fun to imagine.

The Nakamura's, friends of Sam's, were passing through Walnut Ridge and came by to see her. After giving them the "Castle tour," we had a nice visit. Then they continued on to Tennessee.

Instead of just sitting around for these forced days of rest, we decided to drive to Little Rock. Letting Jewel and Jean know we were leaving the RV there for a couple of days, we took off for the big city. We went directly to the Visitor Center, picked up maps, then drove to the State Capital. Once inside we noticed the Governor's Reception Room standing open, and no one around. We walked in and decided to pray for Little Rock right there. Though we never left a Memorial Stone in Little Rock, we did pray in a most memorable place.

We got a room at a Day's Inn. Alyce-Kay met us in Little Rock to take Sam and Waliluke home for a few days' rest, while Joni and I continued our "R and R." We sure missed Sam and Waliluke the next few days.

The next day Joni and I drove around Little Rock, and toured the Old State House (a very interesting place) and the Peabody Hotel. We had heard about the ducks of the Peabody Hotel, and now we actually got to see them swimming in the pond. Then we had to drive back to Walnut Ridge and our Castle.

For the next ten days, we still couldn't continue our Journey. In between doctor appointments, and waiting for Sam and Waliluke to return, we did some sightseeing.

## Joni

We visited Hardy, with its boardwalks and antique shops. Over in Pocahontas we went to see St. Paul's Catholic Church, an old stone building. Going inside we viewed the many glorious stained glass windows.

In the town square we saw the old Randolph County Courthouse, which is now the Visitors Center. We talked with Wayne Gearhart, the Executive Director of the Chamber of Commerce. I asked how Pocahontas got its name. No one really knew. I told Wayne about St. George's Church in Graves End, Kent, England where Pocahontas is buried. He showed me some old black and white photographs of Graves End and Pocahontas' statue—small world.

## Lyn

On Sunday, February 15, we attended the Elnora Free Will Baptist Church between Walnut Ridge and Pocahontas. It was a great service with lots of good old southern gospel music—real toe-tapping music. Pastor Jaral Dean and his brother Jerry led the music.

Dewrell and Oneta took us to a nice little restaurant in Pocahontas where her 84-year old father, Ralph Jarrett joined us for lunch. He had lived in Pocahontas all his life.

That evening we decided to return to Elnora Free Will Baptist Church, as we had been invited for a special sing-along. We were more than ready for some more of that good old southern gospel, toe-tapping music. Throughout the evening they kept saying things like, "Now here's a good song for those California girls." They also asked us to share about our Journey. What a wonderful time. In the midst of setbacks and struggles, God always had something special to brighten our day.

We called Sam to let her know we would be ready to walk again by Thursday if she could get back on Wednesday. Alyce-Kay called to let us know that Sam would not be able to return before the following Monday, but would not explain why. After much discussion we agreed to wait before walking again. It had already been 11 days since we had last walked, and we were struggling with having to wait longer, especially not knowing what the situation was. We prayed about it and tried to give it to God, but it was difficult.

Joni and I were getting "Castle fever," so we decided to do something special during our forced time off. Looking at our maps, we decided to go to Saint Louis, Missouri and visit the famous Arch.

*Thoughts from Lyn's journal: "As I read my Bible this morning before we left, I came across the passage in Joshua 14 where Caleb talks about being as fit at 85 as he was at 40. He asked permission to go to battle against the people of Hebron to get the land he had been promised. I compared this to God calling two 'old women and one young girl' to walk across America—the 'old' women still as fit in their 60s as they were at 40." We laughed at the thought. God always gave us something to laugh about when we needed it.*

We were in good spirits as we headed for Saint Louis. Across the border in Fairfield, Illinois we were able to get a motel room for the two of us and Cassie. Dinner that night was at Carlos O'Kelly's Mexican Restaurant. Isn't that an interesting name for a Mexican Restaurant?

The next morning we drove to Saint Louis and parked at the Riverfront parking garage, then walked to the Arch. The Gateway Arch is 630 feet, the tallest National Monument in the United States. From leg to leg at ground level is also 630 feet.

## Joni

The tram carrying us to the top went up inside the curve of the arch. The capsule was really small, with a doorway about four feet high. We had to bend down to squeeze through the door into the capsule that held five people. It takes four and a half minutes to ascend to the top, and three minutes to descend. Getting out of the tram we walked into a corridor at the top of the Arch. This corridor was approximately 8 by 50 feet. Through small windows, 7 by 27 inches, we could view all the downtown area of St. Louis. The Mississippi River could be seen below us. The Missouri River meets the Mississippi about 15 miles north of the Gateway Arch. A strong wind was blowing, and it was kind of scary feeling the sway of the Arch. Actually, in a 150 mile wind, it will only sway 18 inches from side to side.

Descending in the tram to the visitor center and bookstore, we made our way to the Odyssey Theatre and saw "The Great American West" on the giant screen. This was a historical film of the westward movement in the States. It also included parts from the Lewis and Clark Adventure.

Then we walked through the Missouri History Museum, one of the most informative, interesting museums I have ever seen. It tells the story of Lewis and Clark, as well as the history of the west. An imposing statue of Thomas Jefferson commands the entrance to the museum, which then opens into a half circle. Along the ceiling is a time line, beginning in the early 1800s, expanding by decades toward the back of the museum, and ending in the 1900s. We then went back to the van to give Cassie a walk.

## Lyn

Saturday was the big Saint Louis Mardi Gras' parade, which we eagerly anticipated. Being the naive ladies that we are, Joni and I headed out for the parade. There we joined hundreds of others trying to catch the bead necklaces being thrown out to the crowd. Only later did we find out what that represented. Sometimes it's better to just remain ignorant. Between us we caught about ninety bead necklaces.

Sunday, February 22, we looked for a church as we drove back to Walnut Ridge, Arkansas. In the outskirts of Saint Louis we found a small church called Victory Independent Baptist Church and went inside. We heard a real "fire and brimstone" type message. They were preparing for a church revival, and we made a note to add them to our prayer list.

# Chapter Twenty-Three

# HEAVY HEARTS LEARNING TO COPE

*Lyn*

Sam was coming back Monday evening. We could hardly wait. During the day I filled out my absentee ballot for the California Primary. We did letter writing and laundry. Sam called from Memphis to let us know where they were—about two hours away by car, a little longer by foot.

When they arrived, we sat and chatted for a while. Then we got into a lengthy and difficult discussion, and most of us ended up in tears. Some very harsh things were said, and we were emotionally drained when we finally settled into bed. Perhaps none of us slept too well that night. We all had a lot to think and pray about.

The next morning we were up early and prepared to head out for a day of walking. Alyce-Kay decided to stay and drive for us that day. She also wanted to make sure that Sam was up to walking and ready to do the remaining months with us. None of us felt really good, but we thought we would feel better if we got back to our walking.

At first Alyce-Kay met us every two miles, then she stretched it out to every four miles, which suited us fine. Sometime during the morning, a reporter showed up from the local Salem newspaper. Seeing him approach, I asked Joni to do the talking as I was not feeling up to it. She answered his questions beautifully, and I later commented that she could really become a professional speaker. Joni laughed at this idea.

Other than the reporter, it was a pretty uneventful day. When we got back to the Castle, Alyce-Kay prepared and served our dinner. We very much appreciated Alyce-Kay driving and fixing our dinner.

The next day Sam wasn't feeling good, but really wanted to walk. However, as we drove toward the start of our day's route, she and Alyce-Kay realized it wasn't going to work. Sam was emotionally exhausted and did not feel she had the strength or the will to go on.

With heavy hearts we turned around and went back to the Castle. Sam packed her belongings and we agreed it would be best for her to take Waliluke. With hugs and tears we said good-bye, and Alyce-Kay, Sam and Waliluke headed out. As they backed out Waliluke looked frantically out the window at us, wondering why they were going off without us again. He even barked at us to get into the car. It was very sad.

Once they had gone, Joni and I drove out to start walking. We knew we had to go. It would be much better than sitting around and allowing the depression to overwhelm us, yet it was very difficult to start our walking without Sam and Waliluke.

Joni dropped me off, then drove ahead to park the van and walk back with Cassie. I found it very hard to look at the cars coming by. I didn't feel like waving or smiling, yet after a few minutes of walking and praying I forced myself to do both. As I did I began to feel better, and it became easier to keep the smiles and waves going. Still, it was a sad day, and we would miss Sam and Waliluke a great deal throughout the rest of the Journey.

February 26, 2004—my 62nd birthday. A McDonald's breakfast was at the top of the list to start the birthday right. The weather was sunny and beautiful, helping to lift our spirits. At the town of Ravenden we stopped to take pictures of the giant raven set in front of the shops.

When Joni walked back toward me she spotted a small American flag along the road. It looked new, and had obviously fallen from a passing car. Joni picked it up and brought it to me as a birthday gift. We decided to duct tape it onto my walking stick, which I was using full time now to help alleviate the pain in my leg and foot. The flag was quite noticeable, and from then on people began to wave to us differently—definitely with more enthusiasm.

At the end of the day Joni treated me to a pizza for my birthday dinner in Pocahontas. Our waitresses, Barbara and Amy, were interested in our walk, then asked if they could have our autographs. It was a delightful evening of focusing on something other than the heaviness in our hearts.

As the days passed since Sam's departure, the aches and hurts began to heal, though a bit of a scar would always remain. Daily we continued walking, getting into a good workable routine with just the two of us. At last we walked into Pocahontas, where we had been going for much of our shopping and eating during our time off. It was exciting to finally walk through this town, where we had made friends with several people and had been treated so kindly. Brinkley's Auto Service had serviced our van and rotated our tires for free as a way of saying, "Thanks for praying for our community." Wayne, at the Chamber of Commerce, and his daughter, Malinda, had shown us much kindness as well. Then there was Nancy, the very helpful clerk at Wal-Mart. God was certainly helping us to overcome our sadness.

The American flag that I now carried all the time attracted attention to our Journey, as more and more people began to notice us. Though it was still February, we sometimes found temperatures soaring into the eighties. There would still be some drizzly, rainy weather ahead, but for now the sunshine really helped wipe away our dismal feelings.

Patricia and Trina in the post office in Omaha, Georgia

Officer Cliff and Assistant Police Chief, Ralph "ordered" us into their police car in West Blocton, Alabama

Russ and Joni greet Ronni - center - at the Birmingham airport

Ronni with some friends near Florence, Georgia

Johnnie, Wes, and John in Verbena, Alabama

Providence Canyon State Park

Ranger Pat Patterson at Providence Canyon State Park
out of Lumpkin, Georgia

Eddie and Dianne from Richland, Georgia - she is the pastor of the church here

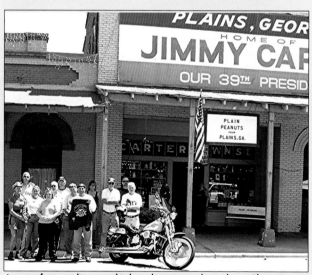

A group of motorcyclists wanted to have their picture taken with us in Plains, Georgia

Joni and Lyn with Mayor Boze Godwin of Plains, Georgia

One of many beautiful bayous we walked past

Joni, President Carter, Rosalynn, Dave, Lyn and Ronni at the President's church

Jacky McCorkle with the Albany Fire Department called the local news and got things rolling. He is also Lee County Commissioner

Kathryn Simmons, and the crew that filmed us for the TV news of WALB-TV news of Albany, Georgia

English, Kathy, Patricia - the children are Savannah and Jacob

Lyn, Ronni and Joni with Albany, Georgia Chief of Police and Juvenile Court Judge

Joyce and Ernie also saw us on WALB-TV and stopped to take pictures and pray with us

Lyn with Officer Reggie at the Emergency Services Cook-off

Lyn gives the keys to the Castle to the new owners, Scott and Pam
- this would be their home

We enjoyed talking with Lieutenant Burnett of the Doerun Police Department

Hansel and Imogene waited and watched for us for several days
after the WALB-TV airing of our walk. We sat and talked with them
at their house, then they prayed with us

Carol and Jackie with the Green Oaks Center for the Developmentally Disabled asked us to share with some of the disabled people in their group

Roy and Leon, two brothers stopped to talk with us as they were passing by - delightful!

Norma and Evelyn at the Ramada Ltd in Valdosta, Georgia - God's special provision for us

It was exciting to visit with Stephanie and James with Ethan and Christopher near Valdosta, Georgia. She gave us each a feather rose she had made.

This is the Suwannee River about which Stephen Foster wrote "Way Down Upon the Swanee River"

We were fascinated by the Mount Zion Slaves Cemetary near Lake City, Florida

We met Ray at the First Christian Church in Lake City, Florida - I really liked his tie

Joni and Cassie are crossing the bridge over the St. John's River out of Palatka, Florida

Grace and Pastor Hoover celebrating their 56th wedding anniversary at the Ormond Beach Alliance Church - their niece, Deborah is with them. Deborah was the pianist for the church service that morning

Lyn can "hear again" thanks to Dr. Darwin Caraballo and his nurse in Ormond Beach, Florida

Ronni was responsible for us meeting this delightful couple,
Wally and Dorothy of San Mateo, Florida

Our new friends in Korona Beach, Florida

Chuck, Rick and Leo were a delight to us

We enjoyed putting our feet into the Atlantic Ocean - finally!

Riley showed us through the African Methodist Episcopalian Church
in Ormond Beach, Florida

Ronni and Lyn getting ready to drive Lady Van Go on the white sands of Daytona Beach, Florida

Joni's twin brother, John, arrived from England to walk with us for a week in Florida

Tony welcomed us into his tire shop until the electrical storm had passed.

A live armadillo "poses" for pictures for us

We left a special Memorial Stone at Suntree United Methodist Church in Viera, Florida

At the eastern edge of Pocahontas we stopped to look at The Century Wall:

---

The Century Wall includes a few presidents, a few poets, a few inventors, scientists, and artists. It includes those who challenged us to do more than we ever thought we could, and admonished us when we did less than we should. The Wall will help us remember those who, with their special gifts, made us smile when we didn't think there was much to smile about, or who helped us see with eyes we didn't know we had. It depicts those who, with their extraordinary vision, gave us glimpses of worlds we hadn't dreamed even existed. The Wall portrays those who walked where we walked at the best and at the worst of times, and those who ventured where we never could. The Wall introduces us to Americans whose footprints went largely unnoticed, but not unfelt, and to those who have made us consider whether the ways in which we are different are really more important than the ways in which we are alike. It places before us men and women who, in all the rich and beautiful tapestry that is America, helped to shape this nation in the 20th Century.

---

There are actually three walls here—the first with pictures of men and women from 1900 to 1940; the second from 1941 to 1965; and the third with pictures from 1966 to 2000. The Century Wall was unveiled on July 4, 2000.

We were able to get several good pictures of this impressive Wall to study later. As you read this book we encourage any who pass near Pocahontas, Arkansas to go through the town, and take time to look around. Visit the Town Square, the Chamber of Commerce, and the beautiful St. Paul's Catholic Church. Then spend some time at The Century Wall. We left Memorial Stone number 148 when we prayed for this wonderful community.

Continuing on, we began to see beautiful bayous with their strangely shaped trees. Over the next few days we passed by or through towns such as Biggers, Reyno, Datto, Corning, and McDougal. People frequently waved, and quite a number stopped to talk with us. There were also newspaper interviews at two or three places.

Our final Sunday in Arkansas was February 29. We chose to attend the Clear Lake Free Will Baptist Church on a dirt road not far from our campground. Arriving right behind another car, we were assured that a church did indeed still meet there. The small congregation welcomed us, and we boosted their usual number from five to seven. A family of three, Robert, Marilea, and their son, Kendall; and another couple,

Relton and Loyse, made up this tiny congregation. Robert, Marilea and Relton took us out to a meal afterwards in Pocahontas.

Heading east at Corning on Highway 67, we continued to McDougal, where we met Kathy. Her son, Trey, was in the military serving in Iraq. We put his name in our book and promised to pray for him.

In the town of Pollard, we noticed that at one end of the town was Hope Baptist Church, and at the other end was Harmony Baptist Church. It seemed to us that these two churches stood as sentinels to watch over the town of Pollard and to protect it from evil. Our prayer for Pollard was that it would be a town that would honor God.

In Pollard we also noticed a nice memorial for a Doctor John Howell, a chiropractor in Piggott and Pollard who had died very tragically at the age of thirty on March 7, 2003. A few citizens in Pollard greeted and talked with us.

Piggot, Arkansas, with a population of close to 4,000 was our last major town in this state. We had rain much of the day. Joni and I met at the town square, then took some time to look in several of the shops. We met Judy and Sheila in an adorable little shop called "Feather Your Nest." They told us we must stop next door at the Chamber of Commerce to find out more about this Delta area. It seems the Mississippi River used to flow on the other side of the mountain, west of Piggott. As a result there is delta soil on both sides of this town—a phenomenon found only here, and someplace in Siberia.

At the Chamber of Commerce we met Theresa, a sister to the doctor whose memorial we had seen earlier. She attended the New Hope Church in Pollard. Her excitement grew when we told her about our prayers for Pollard, and the Memorial Stone we'd left there. She was going to a service at her church that evening and could hardly wait to tell them about our prayers and the Memorial Stone. Theresa asked us to stop at the Piggott Times for an interview. She called ahead and told them we were coming. When we arrived, Carla interviewed us and took photos. She met us again shortly before we reached the Arkansas/Missouri border to take a picture of us walking.

At 5:30 P.M. on March 3 we crossed the border from Arkansas to what is called the Boot Heel of Missouri. The state line was at the east end of the small town of St. Francis, and the border is actually at the middle of the St. Francis River. We prayed for the town and the two states, and left our Memorial Stones.

On March 4, we moved from 2-J RV Park in Walnut Ridge, where we had camped for so long. Our next site was at the Portageville/Hayti KOA in Missouri. This was our first move without Sam. She had always enjoyed doing most of the inside packing, while Joni and I ran last minute errands, unhooked all the outside hoses and cords, and packed them all away. We worked out a system of our own, and made a checklist so that nothing would be left undone, making it a point to go over this checklist every time. This also meant I did not have someone riding with me in the RV as navigator. Sam had also been our main dinner chef, so now Joni and I shared this task. We were learning to fill Sam's shoes, but we still missed her very much.

We left the state of Arkansas with a deeper yearning in our hearts to "Seek the LORD." Many struggles had come and gone, and now we must move on, but we would continue to "Seek the LORD" daily in whatever state we were in.

# MISSOURI'S BOOT HEEL AND KENTUCKY

## *Mississippi River Crossing*

Entered Missouri's Boot Heel ..................................................March 4, 2004

Finished Missouri's Boot Heel..................................................March 9, 2004

Actual Days in State...........................................................................6

Walking Days in State........................................................................4

Total Mileage for Missouri Boot Heel .......................................62.5
  *(Missouri Boot Heel facts in the Missouri State section)*

Entered Kentucky ....................................................................March 9, 2005

Finished Kentucky....................................................................March 13, 2004

Actual Days in State...........................................................................5

Walking Days in State........................................................................2

Total Mileage for Kentucky .............................................................9.1

Total Journey Mileage to Date...................................................2,712.6

Capital ..................................................................................... Frankfort

Admitted to Statehood......................................... June 1, 1792 ~ the 15th state

Population..................................................................................4,041,769

Highest Point..........................................Black Mountain ~ 4,145 feet

Lowest Point...........................Mississippi River in Fulton County ~ 257 feet

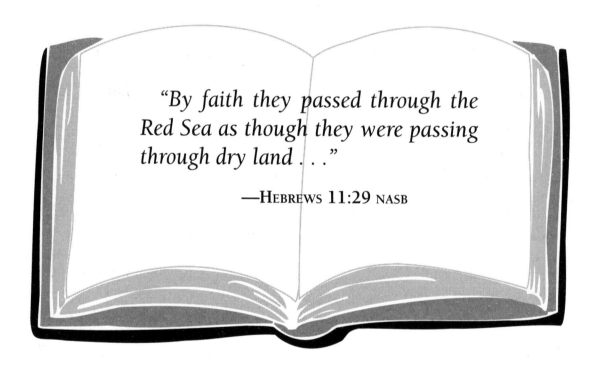

"By faith they passed through the Red Sea as though they were passing through dry land . . ."

—HEBREWS 11:29 NASB

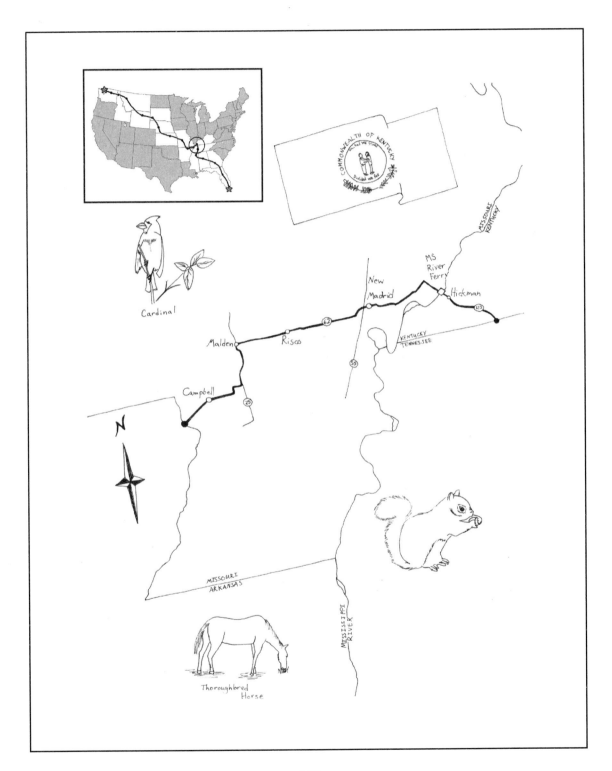

Cardinal

COMMONWEALTH OF KENTUCKY

MISSOURI
KENTUCKY

MS
River
Ferry

New
Madrid

Hickman

Malden

Risco

KENTUCKY
TENNESSEE

Campbell

N

MISSOURI
ARKANSAS

MISSISSIPPI
RIVER

Thoroughbred
Horse

# Chapter Twenty-Four

# MISSISSIPPI CROSSING AT FLOOD STAGE

## Lyn

It was cloudy and rainy most of that first day back in Missouri. The first town we came to in the Missouri Boot Heel was Campbell. Since I previously lived in Campbell, California, we thought this might be a connection to explore. Stopping at City Hall we met Mayor Raymond Gunter and his office staff. We gave Mayor Gunter our greetings from Paso Robles Mayor Frank Mecham. Then we took pictures of the Mayor as well as Frankie Tomason, the Collector, Kay Vinson, Deputy Clerk, and Randy Meadows, Street Department.

The Mayor called Brian Allen of the Campbell Courier, who came to interview us. In fact we found out that he had actually gone out looking for us earlier, when someone had called to tell him that two ladies were out walking on the highway carrying a flag. He is also owner and chef of the La Bella Italian Restaurant.

Campbell is a small town of 2,165 people, and we enjoyed taking pictures of the downtown area. One man stopped to ask what we were doing, and when Joni told him we were walking across America praying for the nation, all he could say was, "Golly, gee!"

Heading towards Risco we saw a sign on the side of a restaurant that read, "Cotton Pickin' Café—Open only when harvesting."

One day a cute little black lab puppy came running out to play. I just walked on, but he kept following me. Seeing him playing with rocks, I tried tossing a rock into his yard, hoping he would go after it and stay there. Further and further from his house he continued to follow. Finally in desperation I called Joni to ask her to bring Lady Van Go so we could take this puppy home. When Joni arrived a few minutes later with the van, the puppy and I got in and I told Joni where the pup lived. Joni burst out laughing. She had thought I wanted to keep the puppy to walk with us. It was a sweet dog, but no way did we need another animal to care for. The couple and their little boy were only too happy to have their puppy returned.

A man called to us one day as we walked past his farm. Bill told us he had just celebrated his 75th birthday. He had lived in this area all his life except while he served in the military many years before. He and his son still raise soy beans, wheat, corn and hay. Philip arrived a few minutes later and we were able to take pictures of father and son together.

Walking along, we met Jeannie and Mike Reed from Clarkston, and later Jim and Marian Bidwell from Portageville. Gary from Gideon also stopped. With each delightful visit we gained more insights into life in their part of the country.

Walking the last couple of miles of the day, a car stopped with two men and their wives—Kenny and Nancy Carlisle and Arthur and Juanita Duncan. Kenny, "Big Daddy," had seen us earlier and was very curious about Joni and Cassie going first one way, then turning around and going the other way! We stopped to take photographs of the sun setting and the new moon rising. Driving back to our campsite we stopped to chat with the camp owners, Dan and Joyce Webb.

On Sunday, March 7, we attended the Dry Bayou Baptist Church of Portageville. Arriving at 9:45 A.M. for the church service, we were just in time for Sunday School. We attended a women's class, then stayed for the church service. Both were very enjoyable.

Pastor Stan Smith and his wife Hazel shared some of the local history with us. A dry bayou, for which the church was named, ran beside the church and had been created by the 1811 earthquake. (We'll share more about this phenomenal earthquake a bit later.) At this time the "dry bayou" had become a "wet bayou," filled by the rains. By summer it would, no doubt, be a "dry bayou" again. In the back of the church we found a list of military from the area who were presently serving in Iraq. We took a copy to add to our prayer list.

Leaving the church we drove to New Madrid to have lunch and do some scouting. We found a nice buffet where we could choose from a variety of wonderful southern dishes. The candied yams prepared in the southern way had become one of our favorites. Our meal was delicious, and the waitress was friendly and informative. She gave us some ideas for our route to the Mississippi River crossing.

Leaving the restaurant we drove our potential route to the ferry. The weather was beautiful and we prayed it would hold for the week. Dave had heard that the Mississippi River was expected to flood later in the week. At this time everything looked fine, and no one in the area seemed to be at all concerned. If all went well we would cross the Mississippi River on Tuesday, March 9.

### Joni

Walking through New Madrid we took the time to stop at the museum to find out more about the big earthquakes of 1811 and 1812. The Richter Scale had not yet been invented, but the biggest shock had been estimated at about 8.8. A series of shock waves continued through this area for over a year. The bigger shocks were felt as far as 1,100 miles away, and actually caused the Mississippi River to run in reverse for a while. The course of the river was changed at this time. Fortunately there was little loss of life because it was a sparsely populated area. When things finally calmed down, they rebuilt the town.

We walked on the levee road most of the way from New Madrid to the Mississippi. On the walk toward the river, the weather began to turn very cold and windy. We didn't see another woman all day in this "neck of the woods," but several men stopped to see what we were doing, or if we needed help. Two of these men were heading home after a day of fishing. They had a large catfish in the back of their truck and let us take a picture of it.

We enjoyed the views from the levee road, with the bayou on one side and the rich delta farmland on the other. Mike Bryant from East Prairie stopped to ask what we were doing, then said, "I think you are doing a great thing walking across the States representing our Lord and Savior." He supplied us with names of trees and birds of this area. On either side of the levee were bald cypress, cottonwood, maples, Shumard red oaks, and pecans. There were bald eagles, least terns, Mississippi kites, herons and hawks. Cassie reveled in the day, since she could run and play without her leash.

## Lyn

At the Mississippi River we saw the ferry pulling out with a full load. This gave us time to take pictures, pray and place our Memorial Stone number 162 at the Missouri sign. Torrey Gunn and Leonard were waiting with their truck, carrying a large seed planter to deliver to a farm in Tennessee. There were four smaller vehicles (ours included) waiting with this truck. When the ferry docked again the smaller vehicles got on first, then the truck with the planter. The truck took up one whole side of the ferry.

The Mississippi was rising rapidly and was expected to flood that evening. The ferry workers were rushing to get as many people across as possible before they had to close. They expected to be able to do only two or three more crossings after us, so we were very thankful to have made it that day. Then it would be several days before the ferry would be able to run again.

During the river crossing we noticed the reading on the depth gauge at the deepest point was 52.0 feet. Logs and branches bobbed in the swift, turbulent waters. When crossing from the Kentucky side, the ferry took about thirty minutes going against the current, but our crossing with the current took only fifteen minutes.

Once on the other side we found a place to park the van and walk back to pray and leave Memorial Stone number 163 for the state of Kentucky. Then we walked to the top of a small hill and quit walking for the day. Since we were only walking nine miles in Kentucky we wanted to do most of it in one day.

We drove through the town of Hickman, Kentucky, then a corner of Tennessee, and crossed a bridge over the Mississippi back into Caruthersville, Missouri to return to our campground at Portageville.

March 10 was our moving day from the Missouri Boot Heel to Tennessee. We ordered breakfast at the camp to celebrate our move to the east side of the Mississippi. Joyce prepared a great breakfast. Joni had ordered the pancake breakfast (all you can eat) while I ordered the bacon, eggs, hash browns and toast.

Finally we packed up the Castle and headed out, stopping for gas in Hayti. We had never had engine problems in the motor home, so it was a great surprise when it refused to start after getting gas. We tried several times, then waited awhile and tried again. Nothing! Finally I gave in and called for roadside assistance. At last James came to our aid, but after trying several things he had to tow our Castle to his shop in Kennett, Missouri. We followed in Lady Van Go.

We spent the afternoon in the waiting room while James worked on finding a solution to our problem. By late afternoon they had pinned it down to the ignition switch—they thought. But it would not be finished until the next day.

During the afternoon James' wife, Kim, came in with her two girls. As we talked they invited us to join them for the weekly church dinner that night. It was a full spaghetti dinner, and a great opportunity to meet a lot of new faces.

We found a motel in Kennett that allowed Cassie in the room. It was good to settle in for the night, but oh, so frustrating that we would have yet another day of no walking. Still people continued to encourage us not to give up.

The next morning we wandered around Kennett, then went back to the shop to see how our Castle was doing, and James told us the bad news. Because of the age of our beloved Castle they were having a hard time getting a new ignition switch, so we still had another day of waiting. We spent more time roaming around town, making phone calls and trying to relax. The hardest part was just feeling so helpless.

Another morning and another day of waiting! As soon as possible we were at the shop checking on the Castle. They had the ignition switch in, but still it wouldn't start. We made a quick decision to get some necessities out of the Castle, and leave it there to be worked on. Then, driving on to Tennessee, we would get a motel and continue our walking. We told them we would call back early next week to find out what was happening.

In Union City, Tennessee we got a room with a refrigerator and microwave. Then we could fix our dinners there rather than eating out all the time. We also went to the post office in Humboldt, Tennessee where we had mail waiting for us. This was one bright spot in the midst of our troubles. Finally we went to bed with plans to get out and walk the next day!

Excerpts from my journal for Saturday, March 13:

*Today I got up at about 5:30 and opened my Bible to 1 Corinthians 13 in The Message version. "Love never gives up. Love cares more for others than for self. . . trusts God always, . . . always looks for the best, never looks back, but keeps going to the end . . . Trust steadily in God . . . hope unswervingly, love extravagantly. And the best of the three is love.*

*I found this Scripture very moving for me this morning. It touched me in so many areas of this Great American Journey. There have been many times when we briefly considered giving up. We've learned to give God the glory as we've seen things happen that never could have been done in our strength. It has been very humbling to have people like Norma Jean in Branson tell us how honored she is to meet us, then give us a hug. Congregations in churches have applauded us and prayed for us and urged us on. We've had to learn to get along with each other when we have so many differences. Certainly we have learned to trust God in many situations. We've learned to look for the best in each other and in people we meet on the road. We are still learning not to look back, and we are determined to keep going to the end. We will trust steadily in God. We will hope unswervingly. And we will love those around us extravagantly.*

We talked about these thoughts as we drove to Hickman, Kentucky to begin our walking.

It had been four days since we had walked off the ferry and up the hill. It was shocking to see that the area where we had walked from the ferry was under water from the flooding of that night. It would be several days yet before the waters would recede enough for the ferry to run again. Wow! What a relief that we got across when we did.

Cassie romped and splashed in the water covering the road. She was surprised at times to find the water deeper than she expected. We entered the Port of Hickman by the sea wall built to protect the town, laughingly referring to this as "The Great Wall of Hickman."

Minnie's Shoppe was a delight, as was Minnie, herself. She had lived in Hickman all of her 76 years, and had witnessed its demise from a bustling town of yesteryear to the quiet, somewhat forsaken town of today. Hopefully this town will yet make a comeback.

There were a surprising number of people to wave to as we walked on through the town. We collected our Kentucky rocks, and I even scooped up some Kentucky soil to take back home from my ancestral state.

Nearing the Kentucky/Tennessee border we were greeted by William, who wanted to know if we needed a ride. Two more cars stopped close to the border to ask what we were doing. Joy and Allen in one, and Roger and Cory in the other, were most congenial and interesting.

At last we reached the border. We took several pictures, prayed for the two states, and left the Memorial Stones at the state signs.

We had not done anything so dramatic as passing through the Red Sea on dry ground as the Israelites had done, but we had at last made it across the Mississippi River, just before the water flooded over the banks. We wondered if God had perhaps held the flooding back a little longer for us. We'll probably never know, but it is an interesting thought. We do know that God was with us as we walked through these two small sections, the Missouri Boot Heel and Kentucky.

We looked forward to Tennessee, and wondered what magical scenes we would see in this state. Would we see spring flowers begin to bloom, or would we have to wait for yet another state? How about our beloved Castle? Would they be able to get her running so we could have our cozy little home again, or would we have to find other modes of shelter? For now we were happy to see the start of a new state. The rest would come as we kept moving ahead. We had faith that God was providing for us and we didn't have to worry about the future. He would open the "seas" of our trials and testings so that we could continue to walk through on "dry ground."

# TENNESSEE

## *Warmer Weather*

*Entered Tennessee*....................................................*March 13, 2004*

*Finished Tennessee* ...............................................*March 26, 2004*

*Actual Days in State*........................................................................*14*

*Walking Days in State*.......................................................................*9*

*Total Mileage for Tennessee*.................................................*134.6*

*Total Journey Mileage to Date*..........................................*2,847.2*

*Capital* ..........................................................................*Nashville*

*Admitted to Statehood* .........................................*June 1, 1796 ~ the 16th state*

*Population*.................................................................*5,689,283*

*Highest Point*.....................................*Clingmans Dome ~ 6,643 feet*

*Lowest Point*......................................*Mississippi River ~ 182 feet*

*"If there is any encouragement in Christ, if there is any consolation of love, if there is any fellowship of the Spirit, if any affection and compassion, make my joy complete by being of the same mind, maintaining the same love, united in spirit, intent on one purpose."*

—PHILIPPIANS 2:1, 2 NASB

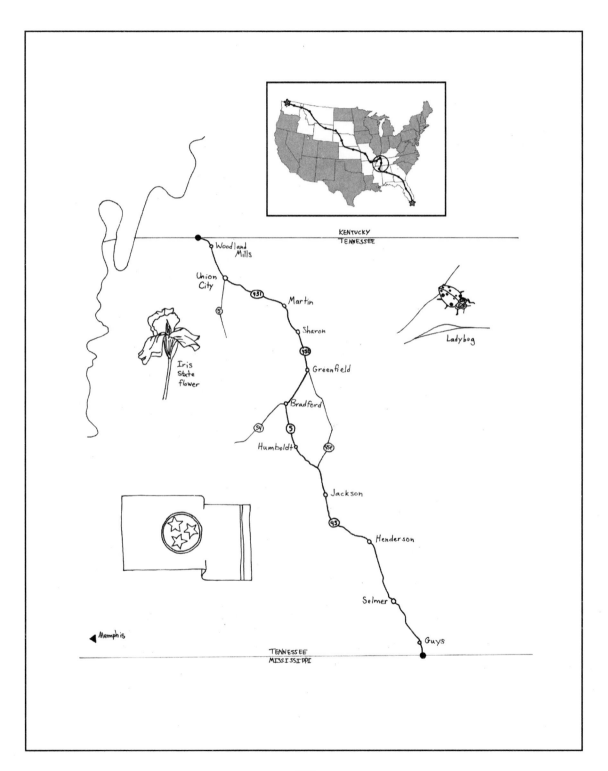

KENTUCKY
TENNESSEE

Woodland Mills

Union City

431 Martin

Sharon

45E Greenfield

Bradford

54 5 45E

Humboldt

Jackson

45 Henderson

Iris State flower

Ladybug

Selmer

Memphis

Guys

TENNESSEE
MISSISSIPPI

209

*Chapter Twenty-Five*

# A BIRTHDAY CAKE FOR CASSIE

*Lyn*

As we left Kentucky and entered Tennessee we were greeted by "Ant-I-Litterbug," who encourages us with "Don't be a pest, clean up your mess!" At Woodland Mills we met Rhonda in front of her house. She shared how grateful she was to have her home, built by "Habitat for Humanity." Truly a gift from God! How blessed we are to live in this country where so many people have been helped by the generosity of wonderful organizations like this.

A young man named Eric drove up beside us. He had seen us walking and was curious. Just three weeks earlier he had returned from serving in Iraq with the United States Army. We shared with him what we were doing, and that we were praying daily for those serving in the military. His name would be added to our book of prayer requests.

As he left he said, "Keep up the good work," and told us we were doing something he couldn't do. However, we knew he had done something we could never have done in his service to our country, and we were quick to let him know. His was a truly touching story, and the pain he experienced from the things he saw in Iraq was very real. No doubt it will be something he will always remember. Eric, if you read this, be assured we are continuing to pray for you.

The variety of churches we were privileged to attend across the United States was incredible, and always there were some that were extra special. The church on Sunday, March 14, was one of those. I wanted to attend a church in Kentucky, so we headed back to Hickman. God lead us to the West Hickman Baptist Church. We arrived ten minutes before the service began and were immediately met by the official morning greeters.

Tim Langford sat down with us to ask a few questions about our Journey. He was in charge of the "welcome and announcements" part of the service and wanted to get as much information as possible about what we were doing. Tim did an excellent job of sharing with the congregation about our trek, and during the greeting time many came to welcome us. Several told us they had seen us walking the day before. When Pastor Brent Lee got up to speak, we were immediately captivated by his speech and mannerisms. He spoke with great fervor from Jeremiah 2, barely looking at his notes. We were blessed with his powerful message.

Tim Langford and his wife, Karen, invited us to their home for a Sunday meal. What a treat to spend more time with these wonderful Kentuckians. The Langfords have three daughters. Andrea, the eldest, rode in our van to direct us to their home.

On the way she introduced us to "Kudzu," a plant that literally takes over everything in its path. At this time it was a barren brown vine spread wildly over ground and plants on some land near their home. Andrea told us it had been brought to this area from Asia to help control erosion. Little did they know how thoroughly it would take over. We learned that they often burned whole fields of the stuff to get rid of it, only to have it grow back with a vengeance. This was our first "Kudzu" experience, but certainly not our last.

Arriving at the Langford home we found a long driveway lined with a dramatic display of bright yellow daffodils. Never had we dreamed how happy we would be to see flowers blooming and trees budding. So incredible!

Once in the Langford home, MaryEvelyn and Amy, Andrea's sisters, greeted us. This family made us feel so much at home. Karen served a delicious dinner of grilled pork chops, sweet corn, green beans, potato patties, and rolls. Then we finished off with apple pie. What a feast! The food and the fellowship with this loving family were wonderful. Someday we hope to come back to see them again.

That evening we celebrated Cassie's fifth birthday. A plain hamburger patty served as her special birthday cake. She didn't share even a bite with us.

Monday morning we began walking right from the motel—well, I did while Joni drove ahead to park the van and walk back to meet me. Walking past a church I read the sign in front, "God sent a repair crew for this broken world—and we're it!" On the other side were these words, "With the promise of eternity, who needs Happy Hour?"

We took a break and did a little scouting in the van. When we started walking again it began to rain, so on went the rain gear. I realized I had left my rain pants in the motel, but wet legs aren't too uncomfortable unless it's freezing cold. We went through Martin and continued on to the town of Sharon. There we decided to call it a day after walking 21.5 miles. The next day we walked 18.5 miles, with about 13 of them on a very busy highway.

## Joni

As Lyn walked, I parked on a side road in Greenfield. A police car stopped, and Officers Danny Harris and Danny Smith got out. They asked me what I was doing parked there. After sharing my usual story and giving them a card, I was allowed to take their photo. They told me the locals are very suspicious of strangers parking on their side streets—especially out of state vehicles. They assured me it was legal to park where I was, but strongly suggested I park on the highway shoulder. Fortunately the highway shoulders are wide in this area, so I felt comfortable parking there. When I met up with Lyn, I told her that two policeman had handcuffed and searched me and accused me of being a spy—again. Then I laughed. (Actually I've never been handcuffed or searched, but it sounded good.) It always is interesting to know that we are "suspicious looking characters."

## Lyn

In Greenfield there just happened to be a Baskin Robbins. We bought ice cream, and walked away satisfied and happy with our taste buds savoring the flavors of our favorite ice cream delights.

We called the place where the Castle was being worked on to see what was happening with it. No one could answer our question, and we were told to call back in half an hour. This time they said they still hadn't been able to find the source of the problem. Anxious to get the Castle moved ahead to another area, I told them I would be calling a towing company to move it to another town where they had better diagnostic equipment. About half an hour later, they called us back to say they had found the problem and we could pick it up. We told them we'd be there the next day to get it.

Outside the town of Bradford we prayed and left Memorial Stone number 171. We finished the day on Highway 54, heading southwest.

Back in Union City we ate at Arby's, where we had a fun conversation with the assistant manager, Lori. Being a dog lover, she gave Cassie a plain roast beef sandwich. Cassie grabbed it and gobbled it down.

At our motel that evening we had a call from Chris, a reporter for the local "Messenger" newspaper. She interviewed us over the phone and made arrangements to meet us the next morning for photos.

The next morning Chris met us at the motel. We went together to the Union City sign, where she took pictures of us placing the Memorial Stone. Then driving from Union City, Tennessee we went back to Kennett, Missouri to pick up the Castle.

When we arrived, the garage was closed for lunch, so we waited. When they opened up they brought the RV around to the front while I paid the bill. It was an expensive repair job, but we had no choice. This was a big setback for us financially, especially after having to pay for a motel that week. Then we also lost two full walking days, and that added stress.

Finally we drove the Castle and the van back to Tennessee, with our sights set on the city of Jackson. Arriving there we stopped to get gas, only to find that the engine would not start—again.

We called our emergency road service, but were told we didn't have coverage for the RV. We knew better than that, and asked them to check with our Southern California office, which they did, and then reported back that we did indeed have coverage! Thinking that in a town the size of Jackson there would be no problem getting a tow truck, we were surprised to hear that the closest truck was three and a half hours away. We explained we were blocking pumps at the gas station, so they suggested we call the local police to see if they could at least get us towed away from the pumps. How very frustrating—could anything more go wrong?

About this time we noticed that our owner's manual for the RV was not in the glove compartment, so we called the repair place in Kennett, Missouri to see if they had it. Sure enough they had been using it while working on our motor home and had forgotten to replace it. We asked them to mail it to Dave, knowing it would be easier to have him mail it to us.

While I waited with the Castle, Joni went to see if she could find an RV Park. She secured a spot for the night in one nearby. When Joni returned we prayed, then tried turning the key in the RV again. This time it started and Joni led the way to the RV Park. We were so tired and dismayed that we did very minimal set-up, and went right to bed.

I woke up during the night, unable to go back to sleep, so I decided at 1:00 A.M. to read my Bible. I had been praying that God would just give us an answer to this dilemma with the Castle. I read from Judges 2 and sensed that God was saying we needed to prepare to rid ourselves of any encumbrances and get on with the Journey. After my Bible time, I felt such relief in my spirit. I lay back down, went right to sleep, and slept until almost 7:00 A.M. What a good feeling!

The next morning at breakfast, we talked and decided if we needed any more big repairs, we could get a good tent, put the RV in storage, and tent camp the rest of the way.

Twelve miles west of Jackson we found JOY-O campground. Then we went back to get the motor home. The RV started up immediately. Then, about ten miles from Jackson the RV began slowing down, and it was obvious the engine was stopping. It backfired loudly, and Joni said later she thought the Castle was blowing up as she heard the loud bang and saw thick black smoke belching from both sides of the RV.

Fortunately there were wide shoulders to pull off onto. I thought to myself, "Here I go again, calling the emergency road service." But this time they were out in less than an hour.

Barry came with the tow truck and towed us back into Jackson to Warren's Bonwood Exxon garage. Joe Warren and Ray Meeler looked it over. After explaining about our

Journey we told them we didn't want to spend too much, and we asked them to give us an estimate before they did any work. He offered to buy it from us for $200. Looking back at this offer later, we wondered if we should have taken him up on it.

The two of us went to get some lunch while the men checked our engine. Then seeing a Wal-Mart, we went to look at tents. There was a very nice one that we could stand up in, with plenty of room for Cassie plus a few other things. The price was right, so we made the purchase.

Back at the repair shop Warren told us they had found the problem. It would not be too costly, so we went ahead with it. But with our new tent, we were now ready to get rid of our "encumbrances" whenever necessary.

Finally we got our Castle to the JOY-O campground, and settled in for the night. It had been rough the last couple of weeks, having to get so much work done on the Castle, but we had met some truly wonderful people through the experience. We had laughed a lot during this time as well, mainly because if we hadn't laughed, we would have cried. God was so good to us through all of this.

The next day we were able to get back on the road walking. It was a beautiful sunshiny day, nice and warm, with very little breeze. Trees were starting to bud, and the grass was a lush green. As we walked along the street we saw a life-size metal sculpture of Christ on a cross, with a cowboy kneeling down and his horse beside him. It was a very moving piece of art.

Wendy, from the Jackson Sun, called and interviewed us over the phone. She checked out our web site and found it quite interesting.

Several people stopped to talk to us today. They were always curious, especially about Joni as they often saw her walking toward me, then walking with me the other direction. When we stopped walking for the day, we were only eight miles from Jackson.

# Chapter Twenty-Six

# HAPPY HOUR

***

**Lyn**

The next morning we began walking at the edge of Humboldt toward Jackson. Wendy's article about us was to be in the Jackson Sun that morning, and she encouraged people to watch for us and wave. So as we walked we had all kinds of people waving and honking at us. It was great. We spotted Jimmy raising flags in front of the VFW building and stopped to talk with him. He was very friendly and told us what each flag was. The first was the American flag, of course. Then there was the Tennessee state flag, and their VFW Post flag, and finally the POW/MIA flag. Naturally we took several pictures.

A couple stopped to ask if they hadn't seen me a few days earlier walking in Martin. They remembered it had been raining. I told them, "Yes, I had indeed been walking there, and explained our Journey. I thanked them for stopping to talk, but the couple countered with, "No, don't thank us—we thank you for what you're doing." We found this kind of response very touching.

I saw a car pull onto the shoulder ahead. As the man got out of his car, I could see the insignia on the door of a TV News station. Michael Ellis was with Channel 7 ABC News. He wanted to interview me and tape some footage.

As he taped I kept hoping Joni would come along, but she didn't. For quite a while he taped me as I walked along the road. Then I saw Joni on the other side of a high barbed-wire fence. After parking she had taken a short cut, only to find herself stuck with no way out. The newsman filmed her where she was. It was to be on the 6:00 o'clock news.

Clouds were building up above us, reminding us that the newsman had told us a storm watch had just been put out for a lightning storm that could drop two or three inches of hail.

Just then I got a phone call from my son, Russ. We knew he was on his way from California to be our driver for about a month, so that both Joni and I could walk full time together. Since it was already starting to rain, we decided to meet him in a fast food restaurant where we could eat lunch. A few minutes later we were all together, and Russ introduced us to Cody, Jim, Cara, and Justin—college students from Indiana whom he had met at a campground the evening before. We all had some great conversation.

While Russ and his dog, Loki drove back to the Castle to sit and relax, Joni and I took advantage of the afternoon storm to look for new shoes. We also went to the Old Country Store, a restaurant and store combination. There we talked with two clerks, Paige and Pam, who introduced us to the owner, Clark Shaw. Clark said he had read our story in the newspaper that morning. He gave us a gift certificate for three people to eat in the restaurant. Pam invited us to come to her church, and we made plans to meet her there the next day.

Sunday, our day of rest, March 21. We arrived at Pam's church early, and entered through a door that had the name of the church on it. This took us down a hall, into the auditorium, and across the stage. Thankfully we weren't coming in late. Somehow we had missed the main entrance—oh, well. Nothing like making a grand entrance.

Several people immediately welcomed us, and Pam invited us to sit with her. The church, named KingDom SeeKers, is an African-American church. Prophetess Teresa Robinson gave the message. It was really a good message taken from Isaiah 1 and 11, and 1 Samuel 9:3.

Her pastor husband, Apostle Larry had seen us on TV the night before, so was quite familiar with our story. He asked us to share with the congregation. Then he handed us a check—a "financial seed gift." This was to plant a seed in our lives to reach out to others as we walked. It really overwhelmed us. God is so good! We thoroughly enjoyed this two-hour service, as well as the warm and friendly congregation. Following the church service we went to meet Russ at the Old Country Store for lunch, where we used our gift certificate. Pam and her friend, Valerie also came. The meal was buffet style, and we ate plenty. Our stomachs hurt all afternoon from stuffing ourselves.

Monday dawned bright and beautiful. There were a lot of people waving and honking and stopping to talk with us. One man had served in Viet Nam and stopped especially to admire Cassie. He told us that the army dogs had always been either German Shepherds or Dobermans. As he left we thanked him for his service to our country. We've tried to make it a point when we meet men and women who have or are now serving in the military, to say "thank you" to them. Too often we find that they feel ostracized by society—especially those who served in Viet Nam—and we want them to know we appreciate them and are praying for them.

This was Russ' first day of driving for us, and we were so happy to be walking together full time. Russ met us every four miles, which seemed to be very comfortable timing for us.

People often asked us gals what we found to talk about when we were together so much. We never seemed to run out of things to talk about, but when we did we were quite comfortable walking in silence. Of course, we stopped to pray whenever we came to a town. Often we talked about our families—how much we missed them, what they might be doing these days, and we prayed for them. Then there were times when we talked about writing a book, and sharing with groups about our Journey.

Late each afternoon when we got tired, we often got silly and saw humor in everything. They say, "Laughter is good medicine," and we figured we should be truly healthy with all of our laughter. While some people had their "Happy Hour" in a bar, we had our "Happy Hour" as we walked, and the strongest thing we had to drink was water or a V-8!

Throughout the walk we had learned to voice our opinions and discuss our differences until we could either agree, compromise, or just agree to disagree. Paul wrote to the Philippians encouraging them to be "united in spirit, intent on one purpose." Throughout the difficult times recently since Sam had gone home, and the vehicle problems, we two had been united in spirit. Sam was still on our hearts, and we missed her incredibly. There was no understanding of why all the vehicle problems were hitting us, but we knew that God was in control, and we would finish this Journey if that was what He had called us to do. Our hearts were at peace, trusting in His timing and leading.

That evening Russ, Joni and I went to see "The Passion" at a movie theater in Jackson. The film was very moving and realistic. The three of us came away from the theater in deep thought, and had a good discussion as we drove back to the Castle. It made us think about how Jesus had persevered in the face of adversity all the way to the cross, where He paid the ultimate price. We knew that because He persevered for us, we must persevere for Him.

## Joni

After we started walking we came to Uncle Bubba's Antiques Store. I just had to look in the windows. It was full of "lovely junk." Ken invited us to come inside, and asked if we were the gals that were walking across America. He offered us cold colas to drink. I told him about my license plate collection and how I had found quite a number on the highways and byways as I walked along. He then took down a 1962 Tennessee plate from a shelf and gave it to me to add to my stash.

Throughout the day many people stopped to talk with us. Late in the afternoon a car pulled off the road and a young couple jumped out and asked if we were the ones walking across America. Laughingly I said we were, and they asked excitedly if they could get our autographs. Lyn and I enjoyed meeting Deacon and Mary from Texas, and

did give them our autographs. As they were leaving, another car stopped and Chase Ames of Jackson wanted to talk.

## Lyn

As we walked up to where Russ was parked waiting for us, a car drove up and a young woman got out with a red, white and blue lei, which she promptly put over my head. Jennifer told us that her husband was in the military, based in Hawaii. She gave us information about him to add to our prayer book for the military.

She was just returning to work at Lofton Chevrolet in Henderson after her lunch break. Her office was just across the street, and she told us the staff there would love to meet us. We enjoyed meeting Rita and Susan. Ronnie Geary, the general manager, is also the pastor of a local church, and he invited us into his office where he said a prayer for us. What a blessing. How thankful we were that we had taken the time to visit Jennifer's workplace.

Someone at Lofton's had called the local newspaper, and Mary Mount came to interview us for the County Independent News. After we finished the interview and continued walking, we came to the Henderson sign on our way out of town. Mary drove up and took pictures as we wrote on the stone and prayed.

At the end of our walking day we got in the van with Russ. He had a gift card for Chili's, so we decided to eat our dinner there. That was a nice change. Our waitress, Katie, was very pleasant and a lot of fun.

On Wednesday, March 24, we seemed to be inundated with people stopping to talk with us. That was OK. It was never a hardship for us to talk with people! Often they asked for our autograph, which never ceased to amaze us. A gal named Suzi told us about a Mennonite bakery further up the road, and we were delighted to pay a visit to this wonderful shop.

Tracy stopped with her twelve year-old son, Ethan, and her baby, Elijah. Ethan blessed our hearts as he told us, "I think what you are doing is a great thing and I wish God's blessing on you for the rest of the trip." Wow! From the mouth of a twelve year-old!

As we were leaving our Memorial Stone number 177 for Bethel Springs, a young man stopped from the Independent Appeal in Selmer to see if he could interview us. He told us that he and his wife were expecting their first baby in October, and we assured Micah that we would be adding him and Amy to our book of people to pray for.

Russ came while we were talking with Micah, and listened in. Then seeing a woman pull to the shoulder across the highway with a flat tire, he rushed over to see if he could help her. She had a small child with her, and was so grateful to Russ for his help. I was grateful, too, as I watched my son give of himself to help a stranded mother.

We continued to the town of Selmer. A family group sitting on a porch began asking us questions. Stopping to chat and take pictures, we learned their names were Becky, Peggy, Wallis, Judy, Katrina, and Richard. A friendly bunch! Richard even gave us a pen and ink drawing he had done. We felt quite honored.

In a gift shop called the "Garden of Eden" we talked with Janice, the owner, and Donald. Janice gave each of us a beautiful red, white and blue flag scarf.

A van passed by, with people inside waving excitedly. A few seconds later they pulled up beside us. They had seen us on TV and just had to stop and talk. Kayla, Karissa, and Tricia were delightful. Little Karissa wanted to try on my hat (this was the flag cowboy hat I always wore that was now filled with state pins and quite faded), so I happily placed it on Karissa's head. Of course, we had to get a picture of her wearing the hat. She looked so cute. Now they had stopped in a driveway, and we noticed that another car was sitting patiently behind them. We assumed they wanted to get out so we said good-bye to our friends. As they drove off we were surprised to find that the second car of people was just waiting in line to talk with us! Robert and Rebecca had also seen us on TV.

Soon after we left them we saw Russ and his dog, Loki walking toward us. We continued to Lady Van Go together. After a meal at Pizza Hut we drove back to the Castle. It had been a fun, but exhausting day.

We had only a few miles left to walk in Tennessee. On the 25th of March we moved the Castle to the Barnes Crossing Campground in Tupelo, Mississippi. Jeannine, the camp manager, was very nice and quite helpful. It didn't take long to get settled in.

Our final day walking in Tennessee was Friday, March 26. It was a lengthy drive back to where we would begin our day. Walking along the scenic route to Guys we saw a sign, "Word Outreach Ministries and Christian Center." We decided to investigate. Jessie and her two teenage grandchildren, Brandon and Valerie invited us in where they explained that they housed and fed those less fortunate. They also helped those that want to "kick the habit" of drugs. We were quite impressed and honored to meet these wonderful people.

At 3:30 P.M. we reached the Tennessee-Mississippi border. Here we prayed for the two states and left Memorial Stones number 181 and 182. Our time in Tennessee had been quite eventful. We had met so many wonderful people, but now it was time to move on into another state, and another part of our adventure.

(See Appendix 5 for some interesting thoughts about Tennessee, as written by Sam.)

# MISSISSIPPI

## *Spring At Last!*

Entered Mississippi.................................................................March 26, 2004

Finished Mississippi ...............................................................April 3, 2004

Actual Days in State..........................................................................9

Walking Days in State........................................................................8

Total Mileage for Mississippi.........................................................101.4

Total Journey Mileage to Date.....................................................2,948.6

Capital ................................................................................Jackson

Admitted to Statehood.............................December 10, 1817 ~ the 20th state

Population.......................................................................2,844,658

Highest Point.......................................... Woodall Mountain ~ 806 feet

Lowest Point........................................Gulf of Mexico ~ Sea Level

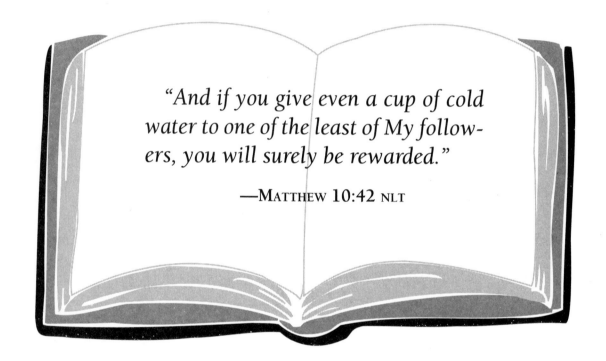

"And if you give even a cup of cold water to one of the least of My followers, you will surely be rewarded."

—MATTHEW 10:42 NLT

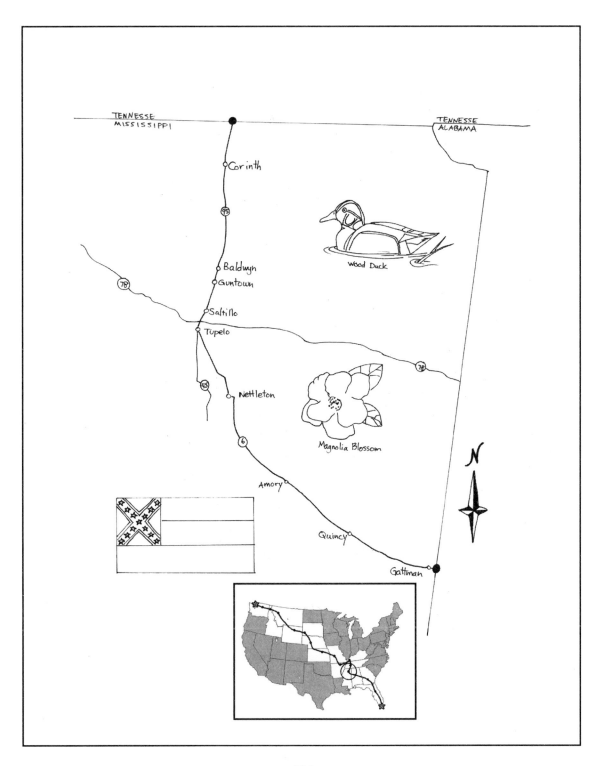

TENNESSE
MISSISSIPPI

TENNESSE
ALABAMA

Corinth

45

Baldwyn

Guntown

78

Saltillo

Tupelo

Wood Duck

45

Nettleton

6

Magnolia Blossom

78

Amory

Quincy

N

Gattman

# Chapter Twenty-Seven

# A CUP OF SUNSHINE

*Lyn*

We were so blessed by people throughout this Journey who gave of themselves for us, thanked us for our prayers, and regularly gave us requests and names to pray for. It never occurred to us when we planned this walk that people would do these things. We wanted to pray for our nation because we believe in America—and most important, we believe in God. We believed that God had called us to walk across this nation to pray specifically for individuals and communities, as well as for the many men and women serving our country in the military.

As more and more people poured out their love to us, and showered us with encouragement, we were amazed. Often we thought of the verse at the beginning of this chapter: "If you give even a cup of cold water to one of the least of my followers, you will surely be rewarded." That "cup of cold water" often took the form of food, or cold drinks (including cold water), cash gifts, or prayers and words of encouragement. We felt very humbled to receive such kindness from so many.

In this chapter we've tried to bring out numerous times when people gave to us from their hearts. Watch for that "cup of cold water" as you read this chapter. See how often acts of kindness were directed our way. It is our prayer that you will reach out to someone today with an act of God's love—a "cup of cold water," and perhaps someone will reach out to you with a "cup of cold water."

The day we finished Tennessee we also walked our first few miles into Mississippi. We went as far as the town of Corinth. The next morning we walked from Corinth to the Mississippi Welcome Center, where we visited the "little girls' room." I was in a stall in the restroom when a lady came in and called out to ask if I was the one carrying a flag down the road. Then the voice asked me to please come inside the Center when I was through. Joni and I went in together and explained what the Journey was all about and why I carried a flag. They told us they like to take pictures of special people, then send them to the local newspaper, and also to their state senator. (*Would they also send a copy to the post office with the word "WANTED" on it?*)

Since we couldn't bring Cassie inside, we went outside to take the pictures in order to include her. Then, leaving Cassie leashed to a tree, we went in for more pictures and some water. We learned that Sherry and Nancy, the two gals working there, were travel counselors for the state of Mississippi. Other than this one encounter, our day was pretty uneventful. Lots of people waved, and a sheriff gave us a quick siren greeting on his way by.

Then it was Sunday, March 28, our first in Mississippi. Our camp manager had told us about her church, so we planned to visit there. The First Baptist Church of Saltillo had an interim pastor, Gary Watkins. He introduced us during the service, and several came to greet us during their "welcome" time. We really enjoyed this church, and felt blessed to be a part of their service.

With rain coming down we took extra time getting our rain gear on. Cassie walked a couple of miles with us, but was happy to spend the rest of the day in the van with Russ and Loki. Cassie loves to walk, but this bit of walking 15 or more miles, and in all kinds of weather, just wasn't what she was thinking of when Joni asked her if she would like to walk across America with us!

Our route took us along Federal Highway 45 into Booneville. Two black dogs joined us through the town. One was a pup and was very friendly. The other kept his distance and had very strange eyes. They stayed with us until we crossed the street, then headed back. They seemed to know their limitations, which was good. We love dogs, but sometimes we felt like pied pipers with our collection of canines lining up behind us.

We met Russ for lunch by a Fossil Park. The rain had stopped, so we were able to take off the rain gear and dry out. Before the break Russ had done some scouting for us and found a quieter road that parallels Highway 45.

Soon we were in the town of Baldwyn, where we met several folks. There was James, who had seen us with our flag a couple of times, and "just had to know what you're up to." Then there was the convenience store, where we met Bobby and his friend, Jason, who liked our hats. Ann managed the store, and Dwana and Keysha were there with her. Along with a prayer request, they also gave us cold drinks.

The Veteran's Memorial in town had three eagles over the plaques with the names of men killed in action. We found that most communities were very proud of those who had served our country. Near the memorial we noticed some funny little dirt mounds, and wondered what these little round towers were. Later Joe told us they were crawfish towers. He said the crawfish use them for a time, then just disappear.

Joni went into another convenience store where James, the owner, questioned her. When she came out she was carrying two bottles of Gatorade and two Granola bars he had given her. Further on we saw an interesting mailbox in the shape of a very large gun. We were getting close to Gun Town.

Russ was waiting for us at the First Christian Church of Baldwyn, where he had parked in their empty parking lot. As he waited cars began to arrive. He asked one of the men if it was OK for him to wait there, explaining what we were doing, and giving him our card. When Joni and I arrived, Joe invited us all to join them for their seniors' luncheon.

Gratefully we accepted the invitation, and enjoyed the meal and fellowship with this group. We met Jim and Ruth, married 48 years; Earlene and Anna; Sydney, who had polio at four-and-a-half months and is now an incredible inspiration to the church and the town; Joe, the retired pastor, and his wife Joan; Morris, the present pastor and his four year-old daughter, Bekka. The food was delectable, even the fried okra!

Russ was sitting next to Morris and Bekka at the luncheon, and later told us that Bekka had wanted to see a rainbow that day. Remembering that we had taken a picture of one that morning, he went back to the camp and printed it out, along with pictures of all the people who attended the lunch. Russ planned to take these back to the church the next day.

Continuing our walk through Guntown and Saltillo to the Natchez Trace crossing, we called Jeannine, our campground manager. She wanted to walk with us for a short distance. This was a sample of what more and more of our days were like. People were definitely curious, and we enjoyed meeting and talking with them. Not once did we think they were hampering our progress. After all, this Journey was about meeting people, and praying for people.

Jeannine walked out to the road with us the next morning as we stepped out of the campground. Our first stop was at the "Tupelo—All America City" sign. There we prayed and left Memorial Stone number 190. We met Russ next to a construction site, where Wayne was shoveling dirt with a piece of heavy equipment. Climbing down, he came over to find out what we were doing, expressing enthusiasm about our trip. When he went back to work, we got some pictures of him on his large tractor.

Errol, a reporter with the Northeast Mississippi Journal in Tupelo, asked if he could interview us over lunch. We gave him Russ' cell phone number so they could arrange a time and place to meet.

Joni bought some rain pants at the Ascent Outdoors sports store. Mandy was very pleasant as she waited on her and helped Joni get the right size. I was looking for a CamelBack waist pack, but Mandy checked and found they had none in stock.

As we left the store, Russ called to tell us that he and Errol, the reporter, were waiting at the restaurant. It took us only a few minutes to get there. The interview with Errol went well, and we enjoyed the time with him. I happened to mention I had been looking for a water pack. Later that day he returned, having found one, and gave it to me as a way of saying, "Thank you for your prayers for our country." I was really touched by his generosity.

We were delighted with the beautiful courthouse in downtown Tupelo. Later we saw what we thought was a monument, but was actually an 1,100 pound meteorite found near Nettleton in 1870.

At the Tupelo Convention and Visitors Bureau we took pictures of the Mississippi flag flying in the breeze. Inside we talked with Sharon and Helen who gave us guitar shaped pins for our hats, and Elvis fans (you know, the kind you wave back and forth in front of your face to cool off). Then Helen saw Cassie through the glass doors and thought she should also have a Tupelo guitar pin for her scarf. We thought that was pretty cool.

Our next destination was the Elvis Presley birthplace, and the home he lived in until he turned thirteen, when he moved with his family to Memphis. I went into the chapel and gift shop and signed the guest book for both of us, When I came out I saw Joni perched on the wall beside the sign, (Elvis Presley's Birthplace, Museum and Chapel). Joni's hat was pulled over her face to shade her from the sun while she slept—what a picture!

Often when Russ was waiting for us, he spent time studying maps and checking out alternate routes. Looking at the maps for the states of Mississippi, Alabama and Georgia, he highlighted a new route that would save us mileage and get us onto roads less traveled. Russ was a great asset to us, and we would have loved to have had him with us for the full Journey.

### Joni

Walking along State Route 6, the exotic fragrance of wild wisteria climbing over trees, telephone poles, and lampposts wafted over us. Trees were budding out with green leaves, and redbuds, dogwoods and azaleas were a profusion of color. Fields of buttercups also brightened our day.

Passing through a construction zone we stopped to talk with Truman, the flagman. He had seen us a few days earlier in Saltillo and was glad to get the chance to find out what we were doing. Candace and her mother greeted us from their front porch and told us they would be praying for us.

We walked through Nettleton with its population of 2,462, a reasonably large town for this part of Mississippi. Charlie showed us the house he was remodeling for himself and his wife, then gave us some juice and bottled water. Huge paw prints were painted on some of the streets of Nettleton, which Charlie explained were tiger paws leading to the school where the Nettleton Tigers team plays.

*Lyn*

At the end of the day when Russ picked us up, we drove back to Tupelo to eat at Logan's Roadhouse. Our waiter was Mitch. Now this is one of those places where they like to introduce special guests, and sing "Happy Birthday." At some point Russ had slipped out and told Mitch about the Journey we were making across America. Part way through our dinner, all the waiters marched to our table and called for everyone's attention. They introduced us and told what we were doing. The people around us wanted to know more.

That night back at camp Dave called. His special news was that a letter had come from President Bush, in response to the letter we had written to him when we were in Branson, Missouri. How special that he had answered our letter. We appreciated the response.

As we walked through Bigbee the next day we stopped at the Tenn-Tom Sports Shop and talked with Gene and Gail. Later that afternoon Gail came by as we walked and gave us ice cold cans of tea. Delicious!

We walked across the bridge that stretches over the Tennessee Tombigbee Waterway and Locks, known by locals as the Tenn-Tom. A large boat was coming through the locks, so we watched awhile and took pictures.

Coming to the "Welcome to Amory" sign, we looked to see if we could find a stone to use for a Memorial. We noticed a store called "The Sunshine Outlet" and went inside. As we talked with owners Charlie and Billie, Charlie grabbed the newspaper and showed Billie our picture in the Tupelo Daily Journal. They called a reporter from the "Amory Advertiser."

We explained that we were getting ready to leave a Memorial Stone for their town, and Charlie and Billie asked us to write on the large stone in front of their store. By this time Chris Wilson, the reporter, had arrived, and Russ had come looking for us as well, so we all gathered around this large, partially buried stone. Joni and I knelt to do the writing, but wanted to pray first, so everyone else knelt down with us and we prayed for the town of Amory. Then Billie prayed for us. We felt as though we had been handed a cup of sunshine. What a beautiful time.

Continuing through the residential area of Amory, we passed beautiful homes with lovely gardens, their trees and flowers in full bloom. A sign in front of one proclaimed it to be the "Yard of the Month."

We continued to the community of Quincy, where Stan stopped and told us he had seen us earlier near Nettleton. Then Mario and Alice drove up and handed us each a bottle of water. Later, Ann asked us to autograph our picture from the newspaper. Karol saw us as she drove past and sensed that God was telling her to stop and talk with us. She asked us to pray for her husband, who was in the military, and also for a friend who had leukemia. We felt blessed by God to have met so many loving, caring people that day.

April 3, our final day of walking in Mississippi! We stopped at the Cason Baptist Church in Amory where we met Greg and Gail. They were getting ready for an Easter Egg hunt that day, and were expecting over 200 children. They have an awesome puppet ministry for kids, and they showed us their large variety of figures. We were astounded at the craftsmanship and changes of clothes for these puppets. What an incredible outreach this church has.

Just past Quincy a car pulled up in front of us, and four well-dressed adults got out with cameras at the ready. The Cunninghams, Mother Tess, daughters Janice and Paula, and son Gregg were in Mississippi for a family reunion (the first in seven years). We really enjoyed talking with them and took pictures of each other.

At Greenwood Springs, Rodney told us he had been touched by our story in the newspaper and wanted to meet us.

Soon after Priestville, Keith drove up with a paper in hand. It was a copy of one of our cards that someone had given him. He was with the Lamar Leader in Sulligent, Alabama, just across the border. He took pictures and asked us some questions, then left.

Our final town in Mississippi was Gattman, where we wrote Memorial Stone number 199. At the border we left Stones number 200 and 201 for Mississippi and Alabama. It was 3:00 P.M. when we crossed the border into Alabama. We were delighted and amused to see Russ sitting in a folding chair down in a shallow ravine, checking our computer map program. We rested for a while, then continued walking.

# ALABAMA

## *Fragrance In the Woods*

Entered Alabama..................................................................April 3, 2004

Finished Alabama ...............................................................May 3, 2004

Actual Days in State.....................................................................31

Walking Days in State..................................................................21

Total Mileage for Alabama........................................................285.6

Total Journey Mileage to Date................................................3,234.2

Capital ....................................................................Montgomery

Admitted to Statehood.............................December 14, 1819 ~ the 22nd state

Population.............................................................4,447,100

Highest Point................................................Cheaha Mountain ~ 2,407 feet

Lowest Point........................................................Gulf of Mexico ~ Sea Level

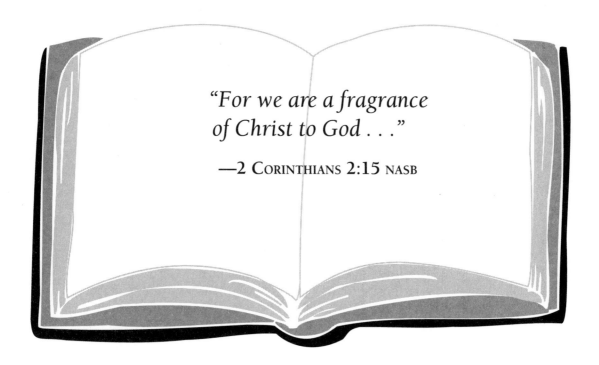

*"For we are a fragrance of Christ to God . . ."*

—2 CORINTHIANS 2:15 NASB

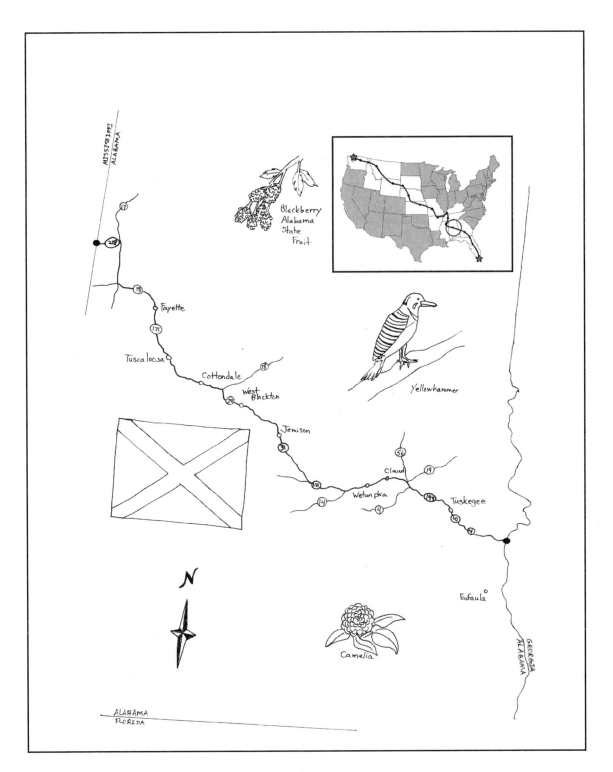

MISSISSIPPI
ALABAMA

17

278

18

Fayette

171

Tuscaloosa

Cottondale

18

West
Blockton

20

Jemison

31

56

Claud

14

11

Wetumpka

14

82

Tuskegee

9

10

7

Blackberry
Alabama
State
Fruit

Yellowhammer

Camelia

Eufaula

GEORGIA
ALABAMA

N

ALABAMA
FLORIDA

*Chapter Twenty-Eight*

# "Y'ALL COME BACK NOW, YA HEAR?"

**Lyn**

After leaving Mississippi we continued enjoying the scenic farmlands in Alabama. We were especially interested in the light tan colored cows with long floppy ears and humps on their backs. They had very sweet faces, but what was their breed?

Nearing the first Alabama town of Sulligent we noticed signs welcoming home the guardsmen of Troop 877. It would be another few days before we would find out more about this Troop. For now it was time to return to our campground for the night. The sun was just setting as we drove back to Tupelo.

Palm Sunday, April 4. Russ had suggested we attend the First Christian Church of Baldwyn, Mississippi where we had enjoyed lunch with the senior group. Since we were still camped nearby we agreed. Many of them had seen us during the week, and one man was surprised we were still in the area, thinking we would be further down the road by now. Pastor Joe Carraway greeted us, and others recognized us as well. It was a great service.

The next day was moving day—from Mississippi to Alabama, known as the "twin states." Looking at them side by side on a map one can see why they are called by this name. They're basically the same shape in reverse, so that if you flip one over onto the other, they nearly match.

As we left the camp in Tupelo, Jeannine, the manager, gave us some prayer requests. We hugged each other and said good-bye. Jeannine was one of many very special camp managers we had been fortunate to meet.

After we got gas, the motor home had a hard time starting. With prayer and perseverance it finally caught, and we were on our way again.

Russ had gone ahead to find a campsite at Lurleen Lake State Park near Tuscaloosa. The camp host was next door, and we came to greatly appreciate Billy as we got to know him. It was a few days before we met his wife, Debbie, and daughter, Lori.

On Tuesday we were glad to get back to our walking, starting out the day in Sulligent. This town was full of yellow ribbons welcoming home Troop 877, the local engineering corp of National Guardsmen. Several signs were in front of homes welcoming loved ones back from their deployment. It was really great to see the affirmation this town gave its returning servicemen and women.

Turning south we noticed a lot of Kudzu growing over trees and other plants. Giant "spider webs" partially wrapped around the trees became a regular part of the scenery.

Eventually we arrived at the "Welcome to Vernon" sign, where we prayed for the community. After lunch Russ walked with us, guiding us into a building saying he wanted us to meet some friends. Earlier he had gone to this radio station and arranged for us to be interviewed by Eric and Curt, "his friends," at WJEC.

As we left the radio station we were suddenly enveloped in a wonderful fragrance. Breathing deeply to take in as much of this pleasant scent as possible we continued on. Then we saw it—wild wisteria climbing up and around some tall trees along the road. Not only was the fragrance wonderful, but also the sight before our eyes was magnificent. What a pleasant walk as we continued to behold, and inhale, the beauty of the earth.

The wisteria made me think of the verse from 2 Corinthians that says we are the fragrance of Christ to God. It was my prayer that as we walked, people around us would sense a fragrance of Christ—a sweet smelling fragrance that would attract them to the One from whom comes this exquisite perfume. Our actions as we walked could either attract people to Christ, or cause them to turn away in disgust.

I knew there were times in this Journey when my actions around my teammates had not been the best. How sad I felt thinking about how those actions might have turned the beautiful fragrance of Christ into a spoiled or rotten smell. I could only pray for God's forgiveness, and for more opportunities to pass His fragrance on in a clear and sweet way, both to my friends and to those we met as we walked.

In Vernon we headed to a McDonald's to get hot fudge and caramel sundaes. When we walked in, the whole crew greeted us warmly as though they were expecting us. Well, they were! Russ had been there ahead of us. Roberta (the manager), Crystal, Olivia, Maxine, Kimberley, Heather and Lynn spent a long time asking questions. They had beautiful deep southern accents, and enjoyed teaching us how to say phrases with the right inflection. As we left they all called out to us, "Y'all come back now, ya hear?"

As we were leaving, a lady stopped to ask how long we had been walking. Her husband was the pastor of a church nearby, and Barbara expressed a strong enthusiasm for what we were doing. When we finally left the McDonald's parking lot we realized we had spent three hours with the crew and guests. In another mile and a half it was time to quit, and the mileage wasn't as much as we would have liked. But we prayed that

God would turn those miles into an abundance of sweet fragrance in the lives of those we saw and talked with that day.

The next morning saw us back at McDonald's to eat breakfast and meet the morning crew: Sadie, Sherrie, Erin, Al, Shannon and Roberta. Barbara (our parking lot lady from the day before) was there with her husband, Norman. We also met Ernie, a game warden, and Howard, Editor of the Lamar Democrat in Vernon, who came to interview us.

We soon turned onto State Route 18 heading for Fayette. "Welcome Home Jeff and the 877th." This sign stood in front of a home on our route. Two women, Martha and Patricia, the mother and wife of Jeff, shared their excitement that he was returning home from his tour of duty. We wished them well and promised to pray for them.

At the Crossville Fire Department we met Hoyt, a brother to the fire chief. He told us we must stop and look at a house down the street—a local point of interest. We saw the house completely covered with old license plates. Joni's eyes lit up, and I joked, "If you could collect enough license plates along the highways and byways, you could cover your house with them too."

We turned onto a peaceful and quiet side road where we could let Cassie run free for a while. Clouds were gathering and we could see lightning in the distance and hear rolling thunder. After a rain shower the sun appeared, giving us a beautiful rainbow. We prayed for the town of Coven as we passed through. That evening we decided to have pizza. Our waitress was Stacy, who very efficiently brought Joni the kids' puzzle to work on while we waited—hmmm, second childhood?

We walked through Fayette, past the County Courthouse with its shiny gold rotunda. As we started to walk away a lady rushed over to ask if we were walking across America. Wow! That surprised us. She and her co-workers had seen us from an upstairs office window. They discussed among themselves what we must be doing, and Beth told them we must be walking across America. They suggested she should go ask us. So here she was! We told her about our Journey and its purpose. Beth had lived in Fayette all her life.

## Joni

Our route was going southeast now. The days were nice, and Lyn and I were finding ourselves laughing easily, and really enjoying walking together. Russ often found interesting side roads for us to walk on. One of these was Moore's Crossing. On this road we met Stanley Moore, whose family had lived in the same house for four generations. These are the Moores for whom the road was named. Stanley had his dog, "Miss Alabama," with him. We loved hearing the different names people gave their dogs.

On Friday, April 9 we celebrated a day of "three's." We had fun coming up with some of these "three's" and thought you might enjoy reading about them. First, it was April 9 (3x3), then it was Day 333 of the Great American Journey, and we reached mile 3,000 that day. Russ later calculated that we had about a thousand miles left to walk, which would take 333 1/3 hours walking at 3 miles per hour.

Our 3,000 mile mark came at the junction of Highway 171 and Moore's Crossing Road. There we placed a special Memorial Stone commemorating this event. We prayed for the whole area. Then we took pictures and hugged each other and had some special candy bars to help us celebrate. Lyn is the only one of the team who has actually walked every step of the 3,000 miles. Congratulations, Lyn.

## Lyn

Later, crossing to the other side of Highway 171, the name of our road changed to Moore's Bridge Road. Here we met Alton and Judy and their grandson Grayson traveling in a small pickup truck and towing a trailer with a huge bundle of hay.

At our camp at Lurleen State Park we met Ranger Mike Storm, who told us he had just returned in February from Kuwait with his Division 266. We were grateful for the opportunity to talk with him

The beautiful side roads that Russ found for us allowed Cassie to play in streams and lie in the water to get cool. Having lunch in a church parking lot, we talked with Kathy and her granddaughter, Courtney.

Clouds were gathering as we neared the end of the day and the week. Arriving at the van we began to hear thunder. Then the first rain came, just a sprinkle. But before long it was a real downpour, with wind blowing every which way. It turned into a real "gully washer." Thankfully we had finished our day and would soon be back at camp, where we could enjoy the comfort of our Castle.

April 11 was Easter Sunday. Our camp host, Billy, was one of two chaplains for the Truckers Chapel at the Truck Stop in Cottondale, and he had invited us to attend their Easter service. We were thrilled. Telling them about our Journey and the purpose for it, we shared with them that, as we walked, we found the truck drivers to be friendly and courteous.

Billy preached the sermon that morning, and his wife, Debbie and daughter, Lori, sang a duet during the service. It was a wonderful experience for us, and again we felt certain that God had picked this church. Billy and Debbie are co-Chaplains with James and Diane, and together God has given them a wonderful ministry with truckers.

The chapel itself was a very simple portable building, but the stained glass windows had a most interesting design. Each window had a cross with a truck in the center and crossroads going out from the truck in all directions.

A reporter, Markesha, from the Tuscaloosa News, along with a photographer, Michael, came out to our camp that afternoon to interview us. Michael had also been asked to get several photos of our feet in our walking shoes. So we got our feet ready for walking and he snapped away. We had a good time with Michael as he kept taking pictures.

Having seen our story in the newspaper, Jim and Dottie, with their five-year old grandson, Jake, stopped to visit while we walked through Tuscaloosa. Russ took a picture of the five of us, and we promised to send them one. Hopefully we sent the picture, but if not, please let us know and we'll get one to you.

A man named Jim Randell pulled over in a car to give us some water and talk. He had actually gone out to our Castle and left us a note and some state pins, as well as a copy of the newspaper that had the article about us. We would see Jim again soon.

Russ told us to be sure to stop at the Hampton Inn and say "Hi" to Tonya. She introduced us to the rest of the staff and we took pictures of Joey, Jana, Tonya, and Toby. They told us to help ourselves to donuts. So we enjoyed the custard-filled chocolate-covered pastries. Ummmmm, good.

Soon we were walking on Helen Keller Road, named for Helen Keller, of course, who was born here. We would have loved to have spent a little more time exploring this area, but we needed to keep walking.

A lady in a van pulled over to talk with us. Katey had her daughter, Alex with her, and asked us to please pray for her. She had seen our story in the paper and had been watching for us. Alex was born with Spina-Bifida. Katey asked us to please pray that Alex would always know that God had a purpose for her in life and that she would be content to let God use her just as she was.

Katey also wanted us to pray for wisdom for her as a mother to raise Alex in the way she should, to be patient and trust God for His best in all of this. We stopped and prayed with them right then, and later added them to our book of prayer requests.

A picture of Katey and Alex hangs in the hallway of my home as a reminder of the courage and faith of the many people in this country we were privileged to meet. We show their picture and tell their story in our presentations as well. They touched our hearts in a special way in our Journey across America.

When we saw a sign for Struggle Hill a bit later, we began to talk about our own struggles and how God has been with us through every one of them. Our prayer books are full of names of people going through one sort of conflict or another. Our prayer is that these struggles will draw people closer to God as they allow Him to work in their lives.

*Consider it pure joy, my brothers, whenever you face trials of many kinds, because you know that the testing of your faith develops perseverance . . . Blessed is the man who perseveres under trial, because when he has stood the test, he will receive the crown of life that God has promised to those who love Him. (James 1:2, 3, 12)*

*Chapter Twenty-Nine*

# ORDERED INTO A POLICE CAR

*Lyn*

That evening as we drove back to the Castle, we stopped in a parking lot, where I had good cell reception to make a phone call. Cassie and Loki got out for a stretch and a break, but were suddenly at each other's throats. Joni and Russ quickly got them separated, but not before Loki had torn Cassie's eyelid.

Now, lest you think that Loki is some kind of mad dog, we had best explain the relationship these two have had. Both Cassie and Loki were dominant dogs and strongly disliked each other. In the Castle we kept them at opposite ends, but every so often we'd catch them looking at each other with what we called the evil eye. Usually we could tell them "NO!" and they would quit looking at each other. But one other time, they had given each other "the look" and Cassie managed to tear Loki's ear. So you see, neither one is innocent.

Back to Cassie's torn eyelid. We didn't know if the eye itself was damaged or not, but we were unable to find a veterinary office still open. We decided to go back to the Castle and put cold compresses on her eye, watch her carefully, and pray. Cassie always slept on Joni's bed, but this night she was restless and wanted to scratch the injured eye. Joni woke up in the night and saw that Cassie had gone to the front of the Castle, and that Russ was sitting up with her, petting her to keep her from rubbing her eye. This really touched Joni's heart to see how lovingly Russ was treating Cassie.

The next day we were all quite concerned about Cassie. Her eye looked pretty bad. It didn't take long to find a veterinarian and we deposited Joni with her "furry partner" in the waiting room. Doctor Harold Threadgil cleaned her eye, gave her an injection, stitched the eyelid and assured Joni that the eye was not damaged.

None of us blamed either dog, or their masters, for this incident. It was just one of those things that happen with dogs. We were all so grateful that the injuries they inflicted on each other weren't any worse, and we watched them even more carefully than we had before.

I had a call from Jim Randell, whom we met yesterday. He wanted to know if we would be able to meet him at the McFarlin Mall in Tuscaloosa at noon to be on a television talk show, "Good Day Tuscaloosa." We were happy to accept this invitation, and made the arrangements to meet.

While Joni was at the veterinarian, Russ and I went to get my cell phone repaired. At the Customer Service counter Kira waited on us. She checked the cell phone and concluded it couldn't be repaired. Since it was still under warranty, she was able to exchange the phone for me and transfer all the data from the old to the new. What a relief. Kira was an excellent Customer Service Representative and we appreciated her help in getting everything taken care of quickly and efficiently.

When we met Jim at the mall he introduced us to Michelle, the program hostess. She briefed Joni and me on the types of questions we would be responding to. We would only have five minutes, since we were added to the program at the last minute. However, she told us that our walk was something people should hear about. Our appreciation to her was genuine, since we believed that every chance we had to speak publicly gave us an opportunity to share the love of God with people. When our turn came we were able to pack an awful lot into that five minutes.

Jim very kindly took us to lunch at a Chinese buffet after the program. It was a good opportunity for us to share together and ask him if we could add him to our prayer list.

He also told us about the University of Alabama Arboretum and asked if we would have time for him to show the gardens to us. We decided this would be a good idea. There wasn't much of a day left for walking, and Cassie was better off taking it easy.

There were trails wandering through the Arboretum, so we could get a close look at the variety of plants, trees and flowers. It really was a beautiful place, and we were not sorry we had taken the time to see it. We thanked Jim for all he had done for us that day.

The next morning we got ready to move the Castle to our next location. I turned the key and nothing happened. Thankfully Russ was with us. He set right to work. He very patiently persevered until he got it running again. It was four in the afternoon, and we headed for the Peach Queen RV Park just outside of Jemison, Alabama.

When we found our campsite and began to set up, we discovered that we had brought along a cupboard full of ants. We had been plagued with them at the last camp, but thought we had gotten rid of them. A number of things had to be tossed out, and cupboards cleaned, before we could even think about fixing dinner. Finally, after taking care of our many evening details we were ready to fall into bed and sleep. It was a very long day.

The next day we got a very late start—noon—but still managed to walk 15 miles. Our route took us along Highway 11 to Lower Coaling Road, where we discovered some horses with a bad hair day—at least it looked that way to us, with the wind blowing through their manes.

A gentleman stopped to tell us he had read about us in the Tuscaloosa paper, and he wanted us to know he and his congregation were praying for us. His name, believe it or not, was Rock Stone, and he was pastor of the Coaling and Duncanville United Methodist Church. Our hearts were truly touched and encouraged by the many people who told us of their prayers for us. We soon passed the church that Rock Stone pastors, and chose to leave our Memorial Stone number 211 for the town of Coaling beside their church sign.

A trucker named Jeff stopped to tell us that he would be leaving soon for Iraq with the 122nd Corp Support Group. We assured him that he and his whole troop would be added to our prayer list.

Eighty-two year-old Mary, a very spry and delightful little lady, was working in her garden. Another lady called to us from her porch and handed us a donation to help us along on our Journey. We were able to add several more people to our prayer list.

April 15 is a very special day at "Hanush Haven," the name of our home in Paso Robles. My husband is a CPA, so this day marking the end of the official tax season is a day to celebrate. In honor of this day, Joni helped me write a song to be sung to the tune of The Twelve Days Of Christmas. The title for the song is "The Fifteen Days of Taxes." Perhaps you'd enjoy singing it to your tax person next April 15th. Smile!

*On the first day of April my tax man gave to me a long form prepared for me.*
*On the second day of April my tax man gave to me two calculators.*
*On the third day of April my tax man gave to me three sheaves of papers.*
*On the fourth day of April my tax man gave to me four staplers stapling.*
*On the fifth day of April my tax man gave to me five golden pens.*
*On the sixth day of April my tax man gave to me six clips a clippin'.*
*On the seventh day of April my tax man gave to me seven secretaries typin'.*
*On the eighth day of April my tax man gave to me eight tax men leaping.*
*On the ninth day of April my tax man gave to me nine computers 'puting.*
*On the tenth day of April my tax man gave to me ten mouses scrolling.*
*On the eleventh day of April my tax man gave to me eleven phones a ringin'.*
*On the twelfth day of April my tax man gave to me twelve audits pending.*
*On the thirteenth day of April my tax man gave to me thirteen post clerks stamping.*
*On the fourteenth day of April my tax man gave to me fourteen clocks a tickin'.*
*On the fifteenth day of April my tax man gave to me fifteen extensions filed.*

At the end of our walking day I called Dave to wish him a happy end to the official tax season, and sang this to him. Yes, he listened patiently to the whole song.

April 16 was one of our more memorable days, and a big highlight for this state. As we entered the town of West Blocton, we stopped at the sign and prayed, then began to write our Memorial Stone. Suddenly a police car pulled in behind us, and out jumped two policemen. Asking if one of us was Lyn, they told us to get into the back of their car! Explaining that they had met Russ, and hearing about the journey, they wanted to meet us.

Officers Ralph and Cliff were brothers working together. They waited while we finished writing our Memorial Stone. Then the three of us, Joni, Cassie and I, got into their car and we went to find Russ. With Russ following, they took us first to the mayor's office, then to the Whitfield Café. Ralph and Cliff also called their pastor to join us for lunch.

Pastor Danny Glover asked a lot of questions, and agreed with Cliff and Ralph that they would like us to come to their church on Sunday and share with their congregation. We knew that God had just picked our next church for us. Kristi our waitress, and Lisa, the owner of the café, talked with us and took pictures of us to hang up in the restaurant.

Back to walking that afternoon, we took a small side road and saw a sign that said, Alligator Creek Hunting Club. We just had to take pictures of ourselves beside the sign, figuring we must be in alligator territory now.

We were enjoying the late evening walk and noticed distant lights through the trees. Yet these lights didn't seem to stay on too long. Suddenly it dawned on us: these weren't distant lights. They were fireflies flitting around in the woods alongside the road. We were fascinated. Coming to where Russ was waiting, we found he, too, was watching the fireflies in fascination. What a perfect ending to a wonderful and exciting day. God had truly blessed us this day.

## Joni

The next day we walked along a narrow road through villages with no names, small clusters of homes, lots of trees, wildflowers and ponds, and Cassie enjoyed chasing small critters and bounding through the tall grasses. Two men sitting on a porch called to us pleasantly, wondering if we were taking a little walk. We loved it when people made comments like that. Of course, we had to explain to them what we really were doing. Well, Joe and his brother Terry just couldn't believe it and exclaimed over and over, "You're really walkin' all that way?!" Of course, we had to take their photos.

A sign soon told us that the road ahead was closed in 1,000 feet, then 500 feet, but we kept walking and never did see where it was closed. The bridge that was supposedly "out" looked brand new. We figured they must have just forgotten to take down the signs.

## Lyn

Sunday, April 18, we drove back to West Blocton to attend Mount Carmel Baptist Church. We enjoyed a morning of good music, good preaching, and good people. The choir sang their opening song, and the leader gave some announcements and welcomed guests. Then Pastor Danny Glover had us come up and share about our Journey. He announced that they would take a love offering for our team. We were overwhelmed with the gift they gave us. Even the little children put their coins in. What a blessing, and we knew that this church was also experiencing God's blessing.

After the service many came to us with prayer requests, and we put them in our book. Others came to ask questions and share their appreciation for what we were doing.

That afternoon on the way back to the Castle we stopped on Plant Road. Along both sides of this road were beautiful rocks of varying sizes, many of which would be perfect for our Memorial Stones. We collected quite a number of them and included some for our home collections as well. We ate our Sunday lunch at the Sleepy Hollow Restaurant in Jemison, where we found the candied yams to be superb.

On the walk into Jemison we met 72 year-old Nathaniel. He had lived in Jemison all his life. His wife and three of their children had been killed in a house fire many years ago. Now the town has adopted him as the "town handyman."

We then went into an Antique store where we met Betty, the owner, and her friend Roxanne. Roxanne, a mannequin, sits and greets people and is dressed in different clothes for each season. As we left, Betty gave us beautiful flag pins to wear on our team shirts.

*Chapter Thirty*

# CHANGING OF THE GUARD—OR DRIVER

**Lyn**

One of the towns on our route was Thorsby, where we placed Memorial Stone number 217. This stone also served as a memorial for Russ' dog, Thor, who died on July 7, 2001. Thor was a very special dog to Russ, and we thought it fitting to have a memorial for him at this town that bore his name.

On our way through Thorsby we went into an old fashioned drug store and met Terri, Debbie and Jerame (pronounced Jeremy). They gave us iced water and asked lots of questions.

Along a stretch of road construction, we started to take a picture of the crew. As we held up our cameras, the men quickly grabbed their hard hats and slapped them on their heads, then smiled for the camera. The Engineering firm inspector came over and talked with us.

There was a reporter, Scott, with the Clanton Advertiser, who told us someone had alerted him that we were coming his way. We happily agreed to an interview for the paper.

Russ was waiting for us at the Assembly of God Church, and had been there long enough to meet several people. He introduced us to Donna, the pastor's wife, and to three young people, Aaron, Tonya, and Matt. They were getting ready to do some filming, and decided to do a film clip of us to show their youth group.

We were invited inside and given a tour of the building. A beautiful, eye-catching picture graced the foyer. It was a painting of a harvest, with people working in the fields and the hand of Christ in the corner. They told us that the theme of their church was "Harvest Time."

They also displayed pictures of many missionaries that they help support. The three young people we talked with were planning to go out in the summer to the Canary Islands to do short term missions work. What a blessing to talk with them.

We continued on and met a few more people, including Angie and then Hazel. Hazel had passed us a couple of times and just sensed that she needed to come back and talk with us. She drove a van that was as full as she could get it, and told us she had just been evicted from her home and had no place to go. We listened to her story and prayed with her, but knew we had to do more. God had blessed us so much. Now we must share some of our blessings with this dear lady. It was obvious that she wasn't just telling us a story to get money. In fact, she refused to take anything from us at first, but we gave her enough to cover a motel for a night or two, and suggested she visit the Assembly of God Church the next day, where we had stopped earlier. We told her the money was from God, not from us, and only then did she agree to take it. We felt privileged to be used by God in this way.

Tuesday, April 20, was to be Russ' last day of driving for us. It was with mixed emotions that we headed out that day. Russ had been such a help, so dedicated to serving our needs so that we could concentrate on walking and meeting people. We knew we would miss him sorely.

As we were preparing to start walking, a man saw us carrying our flag and had to know what we were doing. This was in the town of Clanton, "The heart of the heart of Dixie," and this delightful gentleman was a former mayor of the town. His name was Basil Clark, and we stood and talked for quite a while. He told us story after story—some serious and some very funny.

Basil told us about giving a possum to Jimmy Carter to eat (before he was President), and Jimmy told him he liked possum. We had a hard time knowing when Basil was telling us about a real incident, or when he was joking. It was all very interesting, and gave us a good laugh with which to begin our walking.

One of the more serious, but true stories he told us was about an incident during the Civil War. Most towns around this area are known for the battles fought in or around them. But Clanton boasts about the battles that weren't fought there. Some soldiers from each side met in this area, and realizing they were all so tired of the war, they just quit fighting. They all became friends and ended up living in the Goose Pond Park area until the war was over.

After walking through much of Clanton, we turned onto Greasy Ridge Road, a rather interesting name. Here we took a back route through a more residential area. Eventually this brought us back to the main highway and on through the rest of Clanton. This town is about eight miles long, and it seems to be longer than it is wide.

We had a short day, since we had to drive to the airport in Birmingham to pick up our next driver. The Heart of Dixie Cheerleading Academy was a convenient place to end our day, and would be easy to find when we picked up our walking again in a couple of days.

### Joni

The drive to Birmingham was pleasant and we were there in just over an hour. Lyn and I met Ronni Schoch in the baggage area. I had met Ronni when we were young women in Sydney, Australia, sharing a flat together until I married Karl in 1962, but we had stayed friends over the years.

She had a very large suitcase coming onto the conveyer belt, and needed some help lifting it. Russ was coming in just then, so I said to Ronni, "Let's see if we can find a strong young man to lift this suitcase for us." Picking up my lead, Lyn went over and asked Russ to get the suitcase off the belt and take it to our van.

Now Ronni had no idea who this young man was, and wasn't sure she wanted a stranger walking out the door with her suitcase. We couldn't leave her in suspense any longer, so we introduced her to Russ. Ronni had a good laugh, and told us she thought we were "cheeky blighters," asking a stranger to come lift her suitcase and carry it out to the van. We could see it was going to be an interesting time with Ronni's strong Australian accent and unique phrases.

We drove back to the Castle and got Ronni set up and oriented. Then on to Clanton, to the Cattleman Café, where we had a combination farewell/welcome dinner for Russ and Ronni. Steaks were ordered for the occasion—excellent, by the way.

## Lyn

The next day was moving day, so we were all up early, busily preparing the motor home. Russ needed to go to the Piggly Wiggly grocery store to get supplies for his long journey home, and Ronni wanted to pick up some things as well. The two of them left, taking extra time for Russ to teach Ronni the in's and out's of driving Lady Van Go, and helping her adjust to driving on the right side of the road!

When they returned, we took a few pictures and hugged Russ good-bye. The three of us who had been together for the last month had a really hard time holding back the tears. It had been an incredible month together. He had spent many hours working on the RV engine, tuning it up and making repairs, and we appreciated his efforts so much. I was also grateful that God had allowed me to spend this whole month with my son.

Soon Russ headed off on his long drive. He planned to do camping and sightseeing along the way. (For Russ' view of his time with us in Tennessee, Mississippi, and Alabama see Appendix 6.)

The Castle was packed up and ready to go soon after Russ left. After all the work Russ had put into the engine, we felt pretty confident starting out. Ronni rode with Joni in Lady Van Go, while I drove the RV. At the edge of Wetumpka I went into a convenience store to ask about a campground, but once I returned to the RV, it wouldn't start.

Talking it over, we decided we needed to go into town to find someone that could work on the motor home. It was not parked in front of gas pumps this time, so we got permission to leave it—not that we had much choice. On the outskirts of Montgomery we found "All Roads Transmission," owned by Brian and Cindy. We told them about our problem, and about our Journey, then made arrangements to bring the RV in.

We went back to see if the engine would turn over, and it did! Then we drove it to All Roads and parked it where Brian had prepared a space. We appreciated that they stayed late to work on it, so we could have our Castle for the night.

While they worked we made phone calls to campgrounds. When the Castle was ready we drove to one on the east side of town. This turned out to be a not-so-well maintained, highly priced campground—crowded, noisy, and with a bathroom that we didn't even want to walk into. For the next week we used our extra large size wet-ones in place of a shower. Fortunately we didn't have to spend a lot of time in the campground itself. Poor Ronni was quickly initiated into life on the road (and in campgrounds) with Joni and me.

Our first day with Ronni as our driver turned out to be a very busy and active day. Our story was in the Clanton newspaper and several people stopped to talk with us, take pictures, or ask for our autographs. It always amused and humbled us when someone wanted our autograph. We really didn't quite know what to think of it, and even felt a little embarrassed by the attention. We did like the opportunity it gave us to share about praying for our nation. It was our desire to talk with people, and share with them about the love that God had put in our hearts.

In the little town of Verbena we met three men inside an Antique store. They looked up when we came in and said, "We just read about you ladies in the newspaper." We talked with John, Louis, and Johnny about their historic town. Johnny took us on an interesting walking tour of Verbena. Among other sites, we saw a large home built by a Confederate Colonel, and two old churches—one recently restored, and one built in 1871. Johnny said the town was named for the beautiful verbena plants growing wild.

# Chapter Thirty-One

# LOST IN AMERICA

*Lyn*

Spring was definitely in the air, and we had a continuous grand floral display most of the day. Looking through a gate we saw a whole field of bright flowers, and on the other side a feathery pale green tree. We had seen a few of these around, but could find no one who knew what they were. There were awesome fields of red clover and Mexican roses along the highway, and fragrant honeysuckle grew over the trees along the road.

Over the next few days quite a few people stopped to talk with us. Rounding a corner in Elmore we heard a voice ask, "Are you ladies thirsty?" We stopped and talked with John Glasscot, explaining what we were doing. He was in a state of shock for a bit, but we enjoyed the surprised look on his face as we took his picture.

In the downtown area we noticed the beautiful First Presbyterian Church of Wetumpka, founded in 1836. We prayed and placed our Memorial Stone there.

(Weeks later we received word that, following a wedding at the First Presbyterian Church, someone noticed our stone by the sign. Reading our inscription, they were so touched by the fact that someone was praying for the nation and their town that they wanted to know more about the people who left the stone. They gave the information they had to their local newspaper who did some research and found out about our walk of prayer. They did a story about the rock in the newspaper and a copy of the article eventually reached Dave in Paso Robles. After Dave told us this story, we began putting our web site on the Memorial Stones.)

We crossed over the Coosa River on the old Bibb Graves Bridge. The large river flowing beneath reminded us of the bayous near the Mississippi River. Ronni was waiting on the other side of the bridge, and we ate lunch in a park. Then walking into the evening we enjoyed pretty creeks, rocks and shady trees. We also saw a house where old fashioned gaslights lined a long driveway.

Our church for Sunday, April 25, was the Crestview Baptist Church of Prattville, where we received a warm welcome. We enjoyed the music by the choir, and a good message titled "Perfect Peace" by Pastor Larry Teal.

Coming into Tallassee it was raining, but later the town was bathed in bright sunshine. On the Thurlow Dam Bridge over the Tallapoosa River, we met Billy coming out of the library on the other side. He had lived in the area all his life, and told us the history of the dam. It was one of a series of three, and was built by using the huge slabs of rock already there and adding metal segments to complete it. It was an amazing sight.

We met Willy Mosley standing by his car with a camera hanging around his neck. He was a reporter from the Tallassee News. Willy saw us yesterday walking in the rain, so when he saw us a second time, he thought he might have a story.

Joni and I made the turn from Highway 14 onto 199 and walked for some time, but we saw no sign of Ronni. We had told her the highway number where we were turning, and it was well marked, so we weren't worried.

Ronni called to say she was waiting at a church cemetery on the right side of the road, and we should look for her under a tree. Soon we came to a church with a cemetery on the right side, but didn't see Ronni anyplace. We tried calling her, but no response. Finally she called us and said it was a Baptist Church she was parked at. The one we had seen was a Presbyterian, so we kept going and going, and still no Ronni. She called again, thinking by now we must have passed her. A few minutes later we began to wonder if she had missed the turn and was waiting by a church on a completely different road.

When Ronni called again, we asked if she was on Highway 199. After a short hesitation she figured she may have missed the turn. She had indeed missed the turn, but was soon on the right road again and found us still walking along. By now we had walked about 15 miles. At last we found a quiet place to sit, enjoy our lunch and rest awhile. Poor Ronni—she had quite a time getting used to the different styles of signs for county, state and federal highways. In America only a few days, and lost already.

Moving day! We got up and packed, ready to take the Castle to All Roads Transmission for some engine work. In our prayers we prayed that the motor home would start, and it did! While Brian and his crew worked on the RV they discovered that the engine size was a 440 and not a 360. After finishing the work, Brian and Cindy gave us the bill, an incredibly low amount, saying that we had been through enough and didn't need to have a big bill to add to our recent troubles with this vehicle. We hugged them and thanked them for their generosity, and were on our way.

It was after dark when we arrived at our next campground at Eufaula. The RV had run smoothly all the way, and we were so grateful to God for providing us with a great mechanic to get it in shape.

Our route took us through Tuskegee, where we saw our first magnolia Tree in full bloom. This was a quaint town with beautiful buildings. We especially enjoyed the county court house with its clock tower. In the square was a memorial to the Confederate soldiers of Macon County.

## Joni

Friday, April 30! Today I am 67 years old. I don't feel old—plenty of energy, but oh, how I hate looking into the mirror and seeing all those wrinkles!

As we drove through town we looked for a restaurant because "the girls" wanted to take me out to eat after we walked. I decided on the Golden Corral. Then, at the post office, the clerk handed me a whole pile of birthday cards. Having a birthday is sure fun! As I read the cards it brought my family and friends closer to me. When the postal clerk found out about us praying for people, he asked us to put his wife on our list, as she was suffering from severe neck and back pain.

Walking into Hurtsboro, we met a man who commented that we must be part of the team of walkers. His name was Rick and he ran the local hardware store. He had opened the library so that Ronni could get her e-mail. Ronni then bought a step-stool from him to use for climbing into her bed above the cab in the Castle.

Lyn and I continued walking through town and out into the country. We came to Creek Stand Methodist Church and I wandered around the old cemetery reading the names and dates on the tombstones. (Lyn's note: Joni loved looking at old tombstones, so I let her look at them to her heart's content for her birthday gift!)

It was raining slightly, but we continued on. Soon it was raining harder and harder and we were soaked, but still having fun. Ronni had been using the computers inside the library and had not realized it was raining until Rick came back and told her. She then rushed to the van to come and get us.

Driving back to camp, we were so wet that I said I would prefer to eat out some other time for my birthday meal. So we went straight back to camp and got dried off. Lyn cooked me one of our famous Castle concoctions for dinner.

## Lyn

In our campground by the lake we met Bill Nuckles, who grew up in California and went to junior college in Bakersfield. When I asked where he grew up, he said, "Paso Robles." In fact, his family used to own the acorn building that came down in the December 22, 2003 earthquake. He had also lived in Shandon for a time. These were all very familiar places to me. For now he was living in the Park where we were camped, doing construction work in the area.

With only two more walking days in Alabama, we found ourselves walking on country roads with occasional clusters of homes. This area was called the "Black Belt." We found the people to be very friendly and inquisitive about our Journey.

One night I had been unable to sleep, so at 2:00 A.M. I decided to read my Bible and journal. Here is what I wrote that morning.

*I was starting 1 Samuel today. 1 and 2 Samuel and 1 and 2 Kings are some of my favorite books of the Bible, with so many lessons to learn. How slow we humans are to learn, and I think I'm one of the slowest. So many times I've blown it, but, oh, how patient God is. The examples from these books of the Bible encourage me so much, for certainly the people here often reacted terribly to circumstances, yet God's grace is sure and steady. I keep thinking I've learned the lessons God has for me, and about that time He comes up with a new lesson for me to learn, or a repeat lesson that I thought I had learned, but hadn't. (Sigh.)*

May 2nd was our last Sunday in Alabama. As we prepared to go to church we heard a knock on our door. It was Steve, a man we had met the night before. He wanted to know if he could go to church with us that morning. We picked him up at his camper a few minutes later and drove through town looking for a church.

As we drove by Parkview Baptist Church in Eufaula several people were just going in, so we stopped to ask what time the service started. The timing was perfect, and we parked and went inside. Rick Stanley was the special speaker that morning—he happened to be a stepbrother of Elvis Presley. Rick preached a powerful sermon, and we were happy to see Steve go forward to rededicate his life to God.

We talked with several people after church, including Jerry and Margaret who invited us to go to lunch with them. Jerry told us he went to high school in Paso Robles. That is amazing—two people in this town in Alabama who used to live in my hometown. We enjoyed a great meal at a buffet with good southern cooking.

Later that afternoon Steve took Ronni and me in his boat out on Lake Eufaula to look for alligators. Joni did not want to take Cassie along, so she chose to stay with her at the Castle. At first we saw a lot of turtles, herons, egrets, and ducks, but no alligators. Then we met a couple fishing from the bank, and they told Steve where there were some alligators by the island. Sure enough, we saw a large bull 'gator and a sow 'gator. We also saw a water moccasin swimming in the water.

Shortly after returning to the Castle, Dave showed up at the door. We were expecting him, but thought he would be calling to find out where the camp was first. I was so excited to see him! It had been four months!

Finally, our last day of walking in Alabama. We only had another 5.3 miles left to the border! We crossed on a bridge over a swamp. We saw what looked like a snake swimming in the water, but as we continued watching we saw that it was an alligator.

Even Cassie liked hiking with John - as long as Joni was close by

Pastor Terry and Betty with their son, Jason, at "His Place Ministries"

Manatee mailboxes were not uncommon in Southern Florida

From the white sands of Florida to the white sands of California - Lyn flew to the west coast for her granddaughter's beach wedding near Carmel - Josh and Brenda

Leaving Memorial Stone Number 268 at Vero Beach, Florida - we were told that this stone is now inside the Fire Station under glass

Michael Hatch wanted to be in our book - how could we say "No?"

A very dignified Cassie - she's proud to be American

Lady Van Go got stuck in the sand beside the road

Ranger Bill stands at the restroom at Seabranch Preserve State Park where Ronni got trapped for a time

Lyn is dwarfed by the tall hedges of Palm Beach, Florida

The city of Miami, Florida

Dellie from California "returns" to Florida to walk with our team

Dellie got to visit her Alma Mater

Patrice was an "angel" sent by God to pray for us

Scott and Kathy with their children, Sarah, Kelly and Karen
treated us to our first Cuban meal - delicious!

Eva, Mary, Ilene and Joe of the Islamorada Chamber of Commerce

Only 50 miles to the end of our Journey across America

We never knew what we might find on the bridges going through the Keys of Florida - but an octopus?

JoAn and Dellie join Joni on a trail through some of the Florida Keys

The Seven Mile Bridge from Marathon Key

Laura and Chris with WW US 1 Radio

Juan and Alfredo looking for their rooster

Bill of US 1 Radio interviewed us

Who is that man getting into my picture? - It's Dave!

The night before the walk ended Dave and Lyn celebrated with dinner at Shula's on the Beach in Key West

Diane and Mike had a son in Iraq

The whole team gathered to walk the final mile - JoAn, Joni with Cassie, Dellie, Ronni and Lyn

The final Team photo - Lyn, JoAn, Ronni, Dellie, and Joni with Cassie

Surprise! Clayton met us at the end! He had roses for all of us!

Michael filming the end of our walk

Our final Memorial Stone

Dave and Lyn lead the gathering of well-wishers in "God Bless America"

Lyn pours water over Sam to celebrate crossing the Montana border into Wyoming. Waliluke and Cassie try to stay dry

Road construction on the Crow Reservation near Pryor, Montana included cutting down some trees

Clay Center Christian Church in Kansas included us in their Appreciation Evening

Lyn and Sam walk where the buffalo roam, and the deer and the antelope play: Wind Cave National Park, South Dakota

Janell with Lyn and Sam at dinner in Topeka, Kansas

Eric was just home from Iraq when we met him near the Kentucky/Tennessee border

Joni and Lyn pray and place a Memorial Stone at the foot of a cross in Doerun, Georgia

We had lunch with Danny Glover who was pastor of the Mount Carmel Baptist Church in West Blocton, Alabama

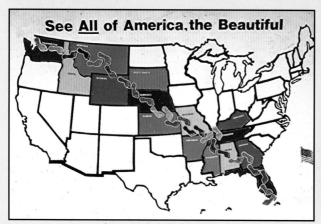

The map on the back of our Castle

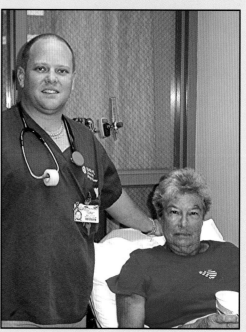

Another trip to the emergency room for Joni - This time in Ormond Beach, Florida

At 11:30 A.M. we crossed the Chatahoochee River and the border between Alabama and Georgia. Dave dropped Ronni off to walk across the bridge and into Georgia with us.

Alabama had been a great state for us—wonderful people, scenery, and lots of fragrant flowers in bloom. But we were happy to at last be in our fourteenth and next to the last state of this Great American Journey.

# GEORGIA

## *Southern Hospitality*

Entered Georgia.................................................................May 3, 2004

Finished Georgia .............................................................May 24, 2004

Actual Days in State...................................................................22

Walking Days in State.................................................................13

Total Mileage for Georgia.......................................................193.2

Total Journey Mileage to Date..............................................3,427.4

Capital ................................................................................Atlanta

Admitted to Statehood.....................January 2, 1788 ~ the 4th State

Population..........................................................................8,186,453

Highest Point....................................... Brasstown Bald ~ 4,784 feet

Lowest Point........................................ Atlantic Ocean ~ Sea Level

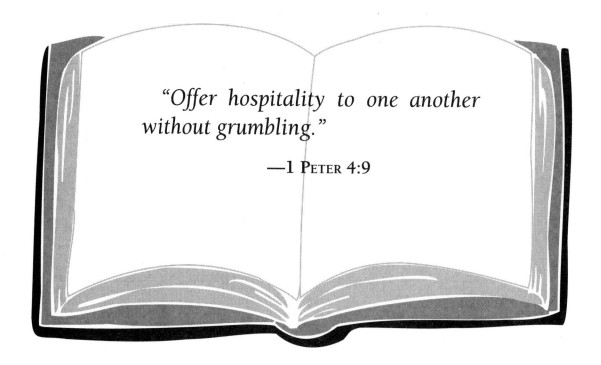

"*Offer hospitality to one another without grumbling.*"

—1 PETER 4:9

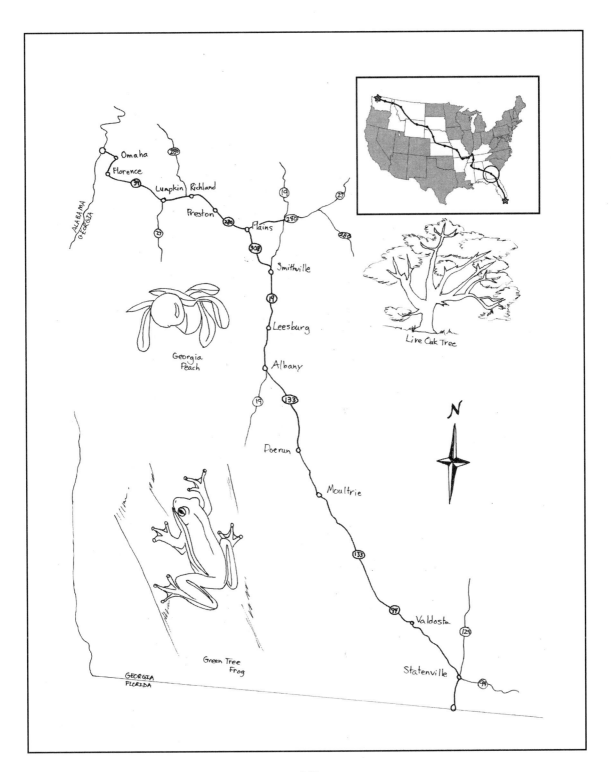

Omaha

Florence

Lumpkin Richland

Preston

Flains

Smithville

Leesburg

Albany

Doerun

Moultrie

Valdosta

Statenville

ALABAMA
GEORGIA

GEORGIA
FLORIDA

Georgia
Peach

Live Oak Tree

Green Tree
Frog

N

*Chapter Thirty-Two*

# STOPPED BY THE POLICE

### Lyn

The Secret Service men searched through our things, looking for whatever might be suspicious. We had been careful to remove the scissors we usually carried. They sent us on into the main room where we were all told to take our seats. Tension was high as we waited with the crowd.

Soon after we took our first steps into Georgia we saw snakes, snapping turtles, and an alligator. Our minds told us this state was destined to be exciting. Even the rivers and lakes had strange sounding names like "Chatahoochee" and "Chehaw." The date was May 3, and we were just beginning to walk through the Peach State.

Benny, Norma and a few others made up the small group of people waiting to greet us as we made our way into the tiny town of Omaha, our first in this state. No doubt we were an oddity in this little community that seldom sees anyone from further away than Cottonton, Alabama.

### Joni

Laughter filled the air as we walked from Florence to Lumpkin, enjoying the swamps and bayous and a canyon named Providence. Our spirits were high as we looked over an area covered with tangled Kudzu. This vine that was brought in so innocently from Asia to be used for erosion control had gotten totally out of control. Ranger Patterson told us it grows twelve inches a day in its growing season. Lyn and I often joked about sending in a rescue team if one of us didn't return from the woods after using the "facilities." We even entwined ourselves in the wacky vine for a few pictures to emphasize its wrapping qualities.

Ronni called us excitedly from the Lumpkin library and urged us to come as soon as possible. The librarian wanted to interview us for their local paper. When we arrived Winnie Patterson, the librarian, took our picture and asked us questions about our Journey. As we were leaving, Pat Patterson, the ranger we met earlier, walked in. He was as surprised to see us again as we were to see him, and he told us that Winnie was his mother. Then we headed out of this small country town with its quiet streets and lovely gardens.

We continued going east, walking into the late afternoon. Coming to an isolated church we saw a man working outside. Lyn and I talked to Eddie, whose great-grandfather had built the church. His wife Dianne was the pastor, and the two of them showed us inside the old building. Eddie had seen us that morning at Providence Canyon Park, and Dianne saw us earlier when she drove into town. Both said we had waved to them, so we told them that meant they had been prayed for.

## Lyn

Moving the Castle had become a time to dread. We never knew if the engine was going to start up or not—or if it did, would it keep going? Our move from Eufaula, Alabama to Albany, Georgia was no different. This time the engine turned over nicely, but refused to catch. Help came by mid-afternoon, and soon the repairs were complete. Our joy was short-lived, however, for the engine stopped as soon as we turned on the headlights. It refused to start again. Bernie came back out and took care of some more problems, but by the time it was ready to go, it was late evening. We decided to wait until the next morning to head out.

As we got ready to go the next morning, we stopped for our usual morning prayers, with special emphasis on praying for the engine to start up and keep running. The suspense was killing us all as I turned the key. It started! And, yes, it kept running. We let it idle for a while, then shifted into gear. A big smile crossed my face as I drove out of the campground and headed down the road, followed by Joni, Cassie, and Ronni in Lady Van Go, and Dave in the rental car.

About thirty miles down the road, I suddenly felt the engine quit. I desperately looked around, realizing we were on a small road with one lane going each way. There were no shoulders, only small gullies on each side. It would be dangerous to stop in the middle of the road, but what choice did I have? I quickly prayed that God would open up a spot for me. Just then I noticed a big flat dirt area across the road and just ahead. Quickly glancing ahead, I saw that the road was clear of traffic, and I shot across onto the big flat area as the other two vehicles in our caravan followed. Traffic had been heavy all morning, but God had opened a space to get me across to a safe spot to stop. The big dirt area was a miracle in itself, since the ditch along the road had no breaks anywhere around, except right where I needed it.

After the engine cooled down I tried it again, and it started right up. The engine conked out on me two more times that day, but each of those times there was a good place to pull over and let it cool.

But what happened next was totally unexpected. Shortly before I reached Albany I noticed a patrol car staying right at my side. I glanced at the speedometer—a bit under the speed limit, yet he was definitely staying right with me. Then I saw him pull in behind me and hit the red lights. I ran through a checklist in my mind, trying to figure out what I was doing wrong. With all the problems we were having with the engine, I sure didn't need this now. I pulled to the side of the road, put the brake on and got up to let Officer Reggie in. He was very kind and assured me I had done nothing wrong, but told me that the date on my license plate was unreadable. After looking over my driver's license and other papers, he gave me a "courtesy warning."

I gave him one of our cards with information about our Journey across America. He was enthusiastic about this, and about the fact that he was the first policeman to stop me in the 46 years that I'd had a driver's license. Of course, I had to get a picture of him, and he happily obliged after I promised not to put it on the internet—it seems he is an undercover officer. He did give permission to write the story for our book, though. We later found out that "Meth labs" are often kept mobile and away from the police by using old vans or motor homes. Most likely this very nice officer had stopped me for a superficial reason, in order to get inside the motor home to look around. This was certainly not the first time on this Journey that we were looked at with suspicion.

Finally we got settled into Devoncrest RV Park, where a resident repairman gave us an estimate of about $1,500 to repair our motor home. Perhaps it was finally time to say good-bye to our beloved Castle. We made phone calls to some of our prayer partners, and within a few days we had come to the decision to leave the Castle behind. Continuing to use the Castle until we were ready to move from this area, we began to check out storage possibilities.

During the time we were camped in the Albany area, we had some exciting walking times. Plains, Georgia, a National Historic Site, is well known as the home of President Jimmy Carter. Our route went right past the Carter's home. When Russ was with us back in Alabama, he had rearranged our route specifically to take us through Plains so we could visit President Carter's church.

On our way to Plains we walked through Richland, where Gary and Jason stopped to talk with us. At the Courthouse in the center of Preston were three sisters, Chelsea, Ashley and Sachiaka, who posed enthusiastically while we took their pictures. On the steps of the Courthouse, we chatted with Stephanie and Alexandria, on a day trip from Webster County School in Preston. They watched as we wrote our Memorial Stone for Preston, and Joni asked them if they would like to place it by the Courthouse for us. They were delighted to do so.

Across the street we saw some beautiful murals at Mom's Café. One was of the "Lord's Supper." Back at the Courthouse we also met Maurie and her sister, Lorene, the probate judge of Webster County. She was running for re-election.

The Presidential Highway of the Georgia Presidential Pathways Travel Region began about nine miles from Plains. As we walked along here the shoulders of the road were a mass of wildflowers including delphiniums, cosmos, and poppies.

Plains is not a large town. President Carter's residence was on our left as we entered and it was the only home he and Rosalynn had ever owned. It was quite unpretentious and nestled among the trees. The train station where Jimmy Carter had his campaign headquarters was on our right, and we walked past it to the main street of the town.

Stopping in at the local pharmacy we met Mayor L. E. "Boze" Godwin and his wife, Betty. Mayor Godwin held this office for the last 26 years. I presented the mayor with a packet of information about Paso Robles and gave him greetings from Mayor Frank Mecham. We learned that a number of the people who lived here were related to the former president. Stopping at several stores in town, we discovered that Ronni and Dave

had gone before us, and many people were even expecting us. There were a few tourists who asked if they could have a photo taken with us. A group of motorcyclists passing through wanted us to pose with them so that, "When we appear on the cover of Time Magazine, they could say they met us in Plains, Georgia." That seemed pretty funny to us, but we were still happy to pose with them.

After we finished walking, Dave drove us to Jimmy Carter's boyhood home, a plain white farmhouse where all the children had to do their share of chores. Even the bathroom had a rigged up shower using a metal bucket with holes in the bottom. One of young Carter's assigned chores was to sweep the hard packed dirt ground in front of the house regularly.

That Sunday, Mothers Day, May 9, we attended President Carter's church. We had to arrive early, and it was here that our purses were searched by the Secret Service. About fifty regular church members were present. The other three hundred were visitors. Every Sunday this church hosts from three to six hundred guests. President Carter teaches the adult Sunday School Class about three Sundays a month, when he is in town. We enjoyed listening to his study and thought he did a fine job of teaching.

After Sunday School we stayed for the church service. Dave, who had been with us for a week now, was invited to sing with the choir. He was delighted. Guest Pastor H. C. Harvey spoke on "The White Carnation" with Proverbs 31 as his text.

Following the service we all lined up for pictures with President and Rosalynn Carter. This was all very organized, with church members on hand to take the visitor's camera as they posed with the president and to snap their picture. We were grateful that four members each took one of our cameras and took our pictures from different angles. Normally they used only one camera per group. Also we were not to speak to the President unless he first spoke to us, and then only to respond to his question. He did ask about our team shirts, so we were able to quickly tell him what we were doing. Then President and Mrs. Carter were gone, and we went back to being "normal people" again.

Dave left for home the day after we saw President Carter. His next trip out would be more than just a visit. He would come to see us finish the walk, and then take me home, in just over two months. (To read Dave's account of his time with us in Alabama and Georgia, see Appendix 7.)

# Chapter Thirty-Three

# FAREWELL TO THE CASTLE

*Lyn*

Coming out of the post office in Albany we saw a large bug on the ground and paused to look at it. A man behind us said, "It won't hurt you, it's sleeping." Of course we knew it was dead. Then he asked if we were twins, and when we explained our story, he introduced himself and asked if we would be open to a little publicity. Lee County Commissioner Jacky McCorkle with the Albany Fire Department called the local newspaper and TV station and arranged for them to meet us.

First there was WALB-TV with Kathryn Simmons and a crew who came out to spend most of one morning with us. One crewman walked forward watching for obstacles while Kathryn and the cameraman walked backwards interviewing and taping our progress. Suddenly he stopped everyone. Right there in our path was a large black snake with a rather flat head. I used my walking stick to get it to move as the cameraman shot some footage of it. The snake seemed a bit angry that we were disturbing it. The TV crew spent most of the morning with us.

We had just placed our Memorial Stone by a flag at the Leesburg County Courthouse when Jim Quinn of the Leesburg newspaper came to take our picture. He had already checked our web site and gotten much of the information he needed, so he did not spend much time with us.

That evening we went to Mama Gina's Ristorante Pizza Restaurant to watch our interview on the news. After hearing our story Jack, the young owner, came out and told us our meal was on the house that night. We were happy with the news clip when it finally came on. Our waitress had called Sissy of the Albany Journal who came to the restaurant to interview us.

The next morning we picked up a local paper to find our picture on the front page with the large heading above it reading something like, "Three Prostitutes Arrested." Our story was actually underneath the picture, but it gave us a good laugh to start our day.

The day after our Albany TV interview was May 12—one full year since we had begun the Great American Journey. As we began walking we found ourselves inundated with people calling out to us such thoughts as "God bless you," or "We're praying for you." Many stopped to talk with us, ask for our autographs, give us prayer requests, or even to take our picture. At one store, Kathy, the manager, gave us a bag of boiled peanuts (a very popular snack in the south). Her daughter, English, and grandchildren, Savannah and Jacob were there as well. English gave us her husband's name, Joseph, for our military prayer list.

Graham of the Albany Police Department greeted us with an invitation to come to the Albany Area Emergency Services Cook-off at lunch time. Before going to the cook-off we met many others, too numerous to mention.

It took us three-and-a-half hours to walk five miles that morning. Perhaps we weren't making very good progress in mileage, but certainly we were fulfilling one purpose of our Journey as we met many people who are a part of this great country.

At the cook-off we were delighted to meet many fine police officers, firemen, paramedics and other emergency personnel. Among them was "my old friend," Reggie, the officer who stopped me in the motor home for having a "dirty" license tag. He said he had seen us on TV the night before, and was surprised but pleased to see us here. His friends there that day told us they planned to rib him plenty for stopping us "sweet ladies." "Sorry, Reggie." We also met the chief of police and a juvenile court judge.

We considered the team with Officer Graham as "our team" in the cook-off. They won first place in chicken and second place in hot wings and ribs. We were very proud of them and offered them our hearty congratulations.

Back on the road, three men in a truck stopped to talk with us. They told us they worked with the city and even allowed us to take their picture. As they drove off it struck us that the two passengers were in orange jump suits. Several times in Georgia we had stopped to talk with guards and a few prisoners working on roads. The guards generally initiated these conversations, but we were happy to talk with them and found them quite congenial. We knew that Jesus would not have hesitated to talk with these men, so why should we. After all Peter tells us to offer hospitality to one another without grumbling. Perhaps being kind and willing to visit was one way of offering hospitality to prisoners.

We continued walking through Albany and greeting people. Some handed us bottles of ice water or cans of soda pop. One of these was Luther, who stopped in the center turn lane, jumped out, opened his trunk, pulled out four bottles of ice water and ran in front of traffic to give them to us along with a big hug.

The "icing on the cake" came late in the day shortly before we headed back to camp. Ernie and Joyce pulled up in front of us with camera in hand. Joni and I enjoyed their company, and after taking pictures, they asked if they could pray with us. Right there beside the road we four held hands and prayed together. Wow! That was beautiful. We really are overwhelmed at the outpouring of love from people in Albany. We love you Albany, Georgia!

Having decided to leave the motor home behind, we took a few days off from walking to pack up our stuff. As we were packing, some people from down the lane in the RV Park knocked on our door. It seems that a young couple had been living in a borrowed trailer, but the owners wanted it back. This couple would soon be homeless. After making some phone calls and giving it some thought and prayer we decided to give the Castle to them. God had provided this Castle for us, and now He gave us the opportunity to bless someone else with it. On May 14 we signed the papers with Scott and Pam. This happened to be exactly one year after Dave and Russ brought the motor home to us when we began the walk in Washington State.

There was still more packing to do, so we kept at it. We rented a small storage unit and boxed up everything that we wouldn't be taking with us. For Joni and me this was a very traumatic time. This was our Castle, the home that moved with us from place to place. Our beds were familiar and quite comfortable. As we continued packing we frequently broke down and cried. There were lots of memories in this place.

We took the last of the stuff to storage, packed Lady Van Go with the things we'd be taking with us, then let Scott and Pam know we were ready to turn the keys over to them. We held hands with them and said a prayer of dedication for them in their new home, then gave them the keys. As we drove away Joni and I made the mistake of turning back for one last look. The tears came and wouldn't stop. Though we had lots of tears, we also had total peace about this. A lot of prayer and discussion had taken place and we were sure this was God's leading for us at this time.

May 16, our last Sunday in Albany we went to the First Baptist Church in the downtown area. It was a big beautiful church with stained glass windows. Keith Gaines preached from John 20:19–31. It was a good service and we were glad we had chosen this particular church. Several came to talk to us and said they had seen us on TV.

For the next several walking days in Georgia, people continued to recognize us from the WALB-TV News. Hansel and Imogene were working in their yard as we came by, and they headed to the road to intercept us as we walked. They had been watching for us for several days and had pretty much given up, thinking they must have missed us somehow. We sat outside their home and visited for a while with glasses of ice water. Before we left, they asked if they could pray for us, so for the second time on the same road a couple held our hands and prayed with us. What a blessing.

When we saw a bicyclist riding toward us with an American flag flying we had to ask where he was headed. Kevin told us that he and his buddy, Dave, were heading to

Alaska and had started in Florida. They were cycling the opposite direction of what we were walking, but it would take them a lot less time.

In the town of Doerun, after walking past large pots of coleus with beautiful deep colors, we met Lieutenant Burnett of the local police force. Then there was Roy, a paraplegic for 18 years, and his brother Leon. I thought Roy's long beard was priceless. Cathy gave us money to buy dinner; and Katey brought some water for Cassie. Many others honked and waved as they passed by.

In a very nice town in Georgia, Ronni's big black bag was stolen from our van. We stopped at the police station to report it, and they had her fill out papers. After that, whenever we passed through this town in the van we stopped in at the police station to see if her bag had shown up. Twice they thought they had it, but it turned out to be another bag. Ronni said that the main thing in it were her expensive glasses. She was able to get those replaced. We were all saddened that such a thing had happened.

Walking down a street in Moultrie we met newsman John Mercer from the Moultrie Observer. He took photos and talked with us. Then heading out of town we saw Katie, an 82 year-old lady from Hartsville, who had seen us on TV and was standing beside the road waiting for us. She was a delight.

Our last two nights in Albany were spent in a motel, but now it was time to move on to Valdosta, Georgia and look for a motel to stay in for a full week. After explaining our Journey to clerks at several motels, one manager told us they would be happy to put us up for the full week free of charge. This was totally unexpected. We gratefully accepted and got busy moving into our new home for the week. Our room allowed us to have Cassie with us. There was a refrigerator and microwave so we could prepare our dinners in the room, and the motel served full breakfasts for their guests. God had supplied above and beyond anything we could have asked for. Thank you, Evelyn, Norma and the staff of the Ramada Limited. There were no more free motels, but we were always given special rates, which we appreciated.

Many people stopped to share a moment with us, as we wound up our walking time in Georgia. Sheryl invited us inside to share at the Green Oaks Center for Developmentally Disabled Adults. Another staff member, Jackie, told us, "I am a child of the King." What a joy to meet so many who believed in Jesus, our Lord and King.

One young man asked us to sign our autographs on a shirt he had with him. That was certainly unique! A seventy-two year old cabbage truck driver had honked tunes to us each time he passed by in his truck. Finally, Kenny stopped to talk with us as he headed home.

Two home-care physical therapists, Geri and Marianne, came looking for us as soon as they finished working with a patient. Then Carol Ann and Angie stopped with their baby to see if they could snap a picture of us with Cody, to put into his baby book. A police officer offered a ride through town in his police car (we declined).

As Joni and Cassie walked in the grasses by a pond one day, we met Ray who works at the nearby Maule Airplane Factory. His beautiful black German shepherd, Willy, walked proudly beside him. He told us about the Maule airplanes that have been used in several movies and written up in many magazines.

Then, continuing by the large pond, we saw two nests of duck eggs—nine eggs in one and eight in the other. Cassie, meanwhile, was having a great time frolicking in the pond among the reeds.

As we neared Valdosta late one evening, a young man and his wife, with their two children, stopped and gave us each a beautiful feathered rose. The husband proudly told us that his wife made them.

The weather was becoming hotter, and we found ourselves dripping by 8:30 in the morning. We were walking early mornings and late afternoons and evenings these days to avoid the midday heat and humidity.

Late one day Stephanie and James, with their two boys Ethan and Christopher, stopped to say "hello" to us. Sarah had seen us on the WALB-TV news, but nobody believed her. Now, she was ecstatic to meet us and have us autograph one of our cards for her to show her friends and family. A runner crossed the street to tell us that he had seen us on TV, and to wish us well. Chuck called out a little later, saying that he believed in what we were doing. Another truck driver wanted to take our picture. All these friendly visitors continually encouraging us were a confirmation of the kindness of the people of America.

May 23rd was our last Sunday in Georgia, and we had decided to visit our motel manager's church, where we were warmly welcomed. At Rosedale Church of God, it was pastor appreciation day. The small congregation really loved Pastor Butler. We were moved by their display of gratitude for this gentleman. Without exception the churches across America made us feel right at home. What a testament to the heart and soul of our country's church people.

Food in the South was exceptional. Our Sunday lunches were usually at local restaurants. Menus often included such things as okra, roast beef, southern stuffing made with cornmeal, and sweet potatoes prepared in a variety of ways. Then there is almost always banana pudding, plus a variety of other desserts.

Our last day of walking in Georgia featured forests, bayous and swamps. Birds were singing, frogs were croaking, and we saw a large turtle jump into a pond as we headed toward Statenville on Highway 133.

During our first couple of miles, a man in an official looking truck stopped to ask us about our walk, and also about Cassie. He was from Animal Control and wanted to be sure we weren't overworking her in this hot weather. We assured him that she only walked the first mile or two with us on these hot days, then retired to the air conditioned van for the rest of the time. Pleased with our answer, he held out a dog cookie to Cassie. He then gave the rest of the box to us to give her whenever we wished.

The day had begun with 19.7 miles to the border, and we were closing in on it. Joni had some pretty miserable blisters, but said that she was going to make it to the state line today even if she had to crawl! I was more than ready to take pictures of Joni crawling over the state line.

Four-and-a-half miles before the border, we saw a street sign for Hester Road. I took a picture of the sign, and we dedicated the last miles of Georgia to the memory of my deceased mother, Hester Black.

The last two miles to Florida we both picked up our speed. We were so excited to be entering our final state of this Journey. Ronni was waiting with the van at the border. As we stepped over the line into Florida, Joni and I hollered and screamed and hugged.

Ronni honked Lady Van Go's funny sounding horn over and over. We could hardly believe that we were now in our final state.

Florida: a land of armadillos, alligators, palmetto bugs, manatees and other creatures (both two and four-legged). We knew that Florida was a long state, but at least we were now in it, and ready to walk those final miles!

# FLORIDA

## *Land Of Palms—And Armadillos*

Began Florida..............................................................May 25, 2004

Finished Florida........................................................ July 23, 2004

Actual Days in State..............................................................60

Walking Days in State............................................................40

Total Mileage for Florida ....................................................599.1

Total Journey Mileage ......................................................4,026.5

Capital .................................................................... Tallahassee

Admitted to Statehood ....................................March 3, 1845 ~ the 27th State

Population.................................................................15,982,378

Highest Point.............................................. Britton Hill ~ 345 feet

Lowest Point........................... Atlantic Ocean and Gulf of Mexico ~ Sea Level

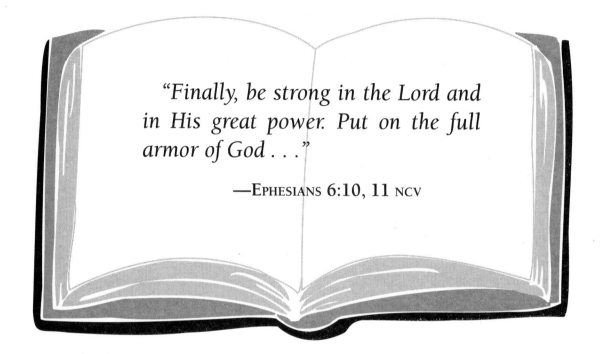

*"Finally, be strong in the Lord and in His great power. Put on the full armor of God . . ."*

—EPHESIANS 6:10, 11 NCV

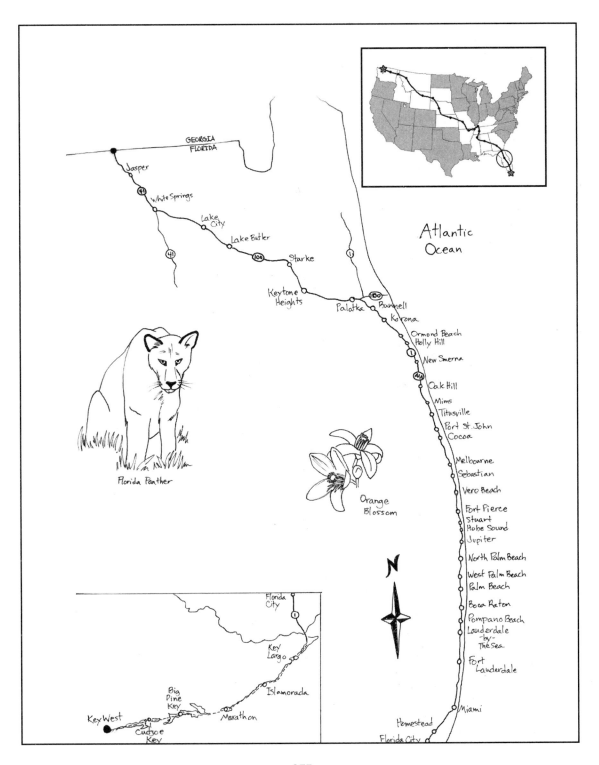

GEORGIA
FLORIDA

Jasper

White Springs

Lake City

Lake Butler

Starke

Keytone Heights

Palatka

Bunnell

Korona

Ormond Beach
Holly Hill

New Smerna

Oak Hill

Mims

Titusville

Port St. John
Cocoa

Melbourne

Sebastian

Vero Beach

Fort Pierce
Stuart
Hobe Sound
Jupiter

North Palm Beach

West Palm Beach
Palm Beach

Boca Raton

Pompano Beach
Lauderdale
-by-
The Sea

Fort
Lauderdale

Miami

Homestead

Florida City

Atlantic
Ocean

Florida Panther

Orange
Blossom

N

Florida
City

Key
Largo

Islamorada

Big
Pine
Key

Marathon

Key West

Cudjoe
Key

# Chapter Thirty-Four

# LAND OF THE SWANEE RIVER

### Lyn

*J**oni, Look!*** I spoke softly, but with excitement. We didn't want to scare the small armadillos off. Just then, Cassie sniffed the scent and quickly pulled free from Joni's grasp, running into the bushes. The moment was over.

Our beginning miles in Florida were met with hot, humid weather. We did our best to start walking early in the morning, but still our skin glowed with perspiration from the time we stepped out the door of the motel. At one point in the hotter part of a day, we saw a few dozen buzzards circling over the nearby forest. Jokingly we checked to make sure we were still moving and hadn't become lunch for the buzzards.

Most of the time now we either heated TV dinners in our motel microwave, or stopped at a fast food restaurant to eat. One day after we had ordered our meal it was quite a surprise to have the gentleman behind us step up and pay our bill. It amazed us still, even after thirty-four hundred miles, that the people of America were so generous.

Our route took us through the famed White Springs where the Suwannee River flows. Stephen Foster had immortalized this area in 1851, when he composed his well-known song, "Way Down Upon the Swanee River." We were surprised to learn that

Stephen Foster never actually saw the Suwannee River. He picked the name from a map because it fit the music he had written. I'm sure you noticed the two different spellings above—both are correct. In the song Stephen Foster simplified the spelling to Swanee. But it actually reads Suwannee on the signs in the White Springs area.

Memorial Day weekend is the time of the Florida Folk

Festival in White Springs, and it just happened that we were walking through the town as it was getting started. We would have liked to check it out for a while, but the cost of going in for just half an hour or so seemed a bit extravagant. This was Florida, and we were anxious to be moving on, so we bid farewell to White Springs and kept on going.

For a few days we had been walking along the same road, and people who traveled back and forth were beginning to recognize us. Some honked and waved, and others stared in disbelief as they continued to see us farther and farther away from their first sighting. One trucker in particular always greeted us with a singsong beeping of his horn. We had begun to watch for him each morning at around 10:30 or 11:00 o'clock. The last time we saw him he smiled broadly and waved with enthusiasm after his familiar "beep-e-dy-beep-beep-beep-beep." Soon after that we turned onto a different road.

One of the interesting things that mystified us all the way through Florida was the number of streets with such names as "Summit Road," "Hilltop Drive," "Mountain Top Drive," "The Heights," or other similar names. This seemed especially funny, since the highest point in all of Florida is Britton Hill at 345 feet. Maybe we thought this was strange because we come from California with many high peaks, the highest being Mount Whitney at 14,494 feet. Perhaps these names were "wishful thinking" on the part of Florida. We loved these names regardless of the reasoning behind them, and we loved the people and many sights we saw as well.

One day the sight of a very small cemetery intrigued us. A sign proclaimed it as "Mt. Zion Slaves Cemetary." The spelling here is as it was on the sign. It was just alongside the road and wouldn't be noticed unless one was walking here or specifically looking for it. We read that it had been established in 1910, and the sign was "erected in 1996 in memory of Joseph Anthony's relatives and friends who lived and picked cotton for their livelihood in a by-gone era." Our minds wandered to those "by-gone days" as we wondered what the lives of these people might have been like when they lived in these parts.

On May 30, our first Sunday in Florida, we attended the First Christian Church in Lake City. There we were warmly greeted by the pastor and introduced to the congregation. Pastor Hugh Sherrill gave his message on "Where Are the Nine?" from Luke 17:11–21. Quite a few came to talk with us after the service. One gentleman, Ray had a particularly striking necktie—a white background with purple rectangles and glowing crosses in the rectangles. My husband collects neckties, so I noticed this unusual tie right away. The man wearing it was quite delightful, and we later saw him at the restaurant where we ate lunch.

A soloist at this church sang a song that really touched my heart. The song talks of Jesus being on the cross and each of us being on His mind while He hung there bearing our sins. I was grateful for the reminder of these words. He hung there, looking ahead in time, seeing each person with His heart full of love. We were unworthy, but He loved us and poured His life out for us. Tears trickled down my cheeks as I listened to Joyce singing this song. After the service I asked Joyce if I could get a copy of the words. She pulled out the sheet of paper with the words and handed it to me.

At lunch that Sunday afternoon our waitress informed us that our meal was paid for by a gentleman who had asked that his name not be revealed to us. How blessed we were by that experience.

Our stay in Lake City had turned into such a wonderful experience. In fact, our original plan had been to stay in a town farther down the road. However, when we had gone to that next town, we had been met with unfriendliness, high prices, and a lack of available rooms. For that reason we had backtracked to Lake City, where we immediately noticed a difference. Everyone we met was very friendly.

## Joni

During the time we stayed in Lake City we were at the newly renovated Econo Lodge. Three different people staying here asked us to pray for them. One was a motel maid, Shelly, whose dog had been hit by a car (he survived). Another was a lady whose husband and dog had been in a car accident and she was staying there while he recuperated. Still another woman's husband had had a heart attack and she, too, was staying there while he recovered. Somehow we felt that God had placed us in this town and in this specific motel for a reason.

I had been plagued with blisters in Washington state for the first two weeks, but had not had any more until Georgia, and now in Florida. The heat and humidity seemed to bring them on again.

In Keystone Heights, Florida, one of my blisters burst. It soon became too painful to walk and we quit early that day. While my feet rested for the next couple of days we made our move to a motel in Ormond Beach. Lyn wanted to go to a doctor about an ear problem, and I checked with him about ideas for escaping the painful blisters. We both came away from the clinic greatly relieved, and went to find a special powder for my feet.

On our move from Lake City to Ormond Beach we had one of those "What if . . .?" experiences. Nearing Keystone Heights on the drive, we noticed a lot of smoke. We had walked through this town the day before. Now the police detoured us around a forest fire that was threatening the area. The detour took us to the south end of Keystone Heights. We stopped and took photos of smoke and flames rising beyond the north end of the town. Had we been a day later walking through this area we would have had to take a big detour, adding hours to our walk. God graciously got us through there before the fire hit.

Come to think of it, God had us one day ahead of the flood waters of the Mississippi River, and now one day ahead of this fire. His timing certainly seemed to be right on. It made us wonder if there were other times when similar things happened that we just weren't aware of. How good to know that God is in control. Eventually we did get settled into a Day's Inn motel, just before the onset of a huge thunderstorm, with flashing lightning and torrential rain.

## Lyn

Our original plan for Florida had been to walk inland on a route that would take us around Lake Okeechobee. Our friend, Coni Harris, hikes around this lake every year, and we had heard so much about it that we wanted to walk along one side. But with all of our delays we found ourselves walking through Florida in the heat of June and July, rather than April and May. Many people told us there would be breezes if we walked along the east coast, so when we came to State Highway 100, we turned southeast heading for the Coast Highway. This proved to be a very good choice.

The town of Palatka was one of our favorite towns in this northern part of Florida. Large murals adorned the sides of many buildings, and we stopped several times to admire and photograph them. Heading south out of town, we had to cross a bridge with a very high arch over the Saint John's River. Stopping at the top of the arch to look down, we spotted a pier beneath us with an eagle's nest. Mama eagle sat beside the nest, with her single eaglet perched inside. We watched and enjoyed them through our binoculars for several minutes.

The day we walked through Palatka was the day Ronald Reagan died at age 93. In our motel room the next few nights, we watched the news programs on television as they showed clips of his life. The country, even the world, was in a reflective mood as President Reagan's life was reviewed.

On Sunday, June 6 we went to Ormond Beach Alliance Church. It was Pastor Hoover and his wife Grace's last Sunday before his retirement. Deborah, the pianist, was the pastor's niece. His sermon that morning was on the unchangeableness of God. It was a reminder that God is still just as faithful as He was in Abraham's day, or in Paul's day. He has been there for mankind down through the ages. God has never changed, but people do change. God is dependable. People, on the other hand, cannot always be depended upon.

We met a man and his wife near San Mateo, Florida who really stand out in our minds. Ronni had parked in front of their place to wait for us. The owner came charging out to find out what she was doing there. She explained, and gave him one of our cards with all the information. Wally's reaction changed immediately as he realized she was not one of the local young drivers that always tore up the front yards of homes with their wild driving. In fact, we noted many signs in front yards telling people to stay out and off of their yards.

Wally and Dot invited us up to their house to have tea with them. They asked many questions about our walk. When they found out that Joni and I were from California, Wally mentioned that Dot had accepted Christ in California many years earlier under the teaching of Charles Fuller and the Old Fashioned Revival Hour in Long Beach. Now this was a radio program that I knew about. While I was growing up my family had listened to Charles Fuller on the radio every Sunday afternoon. I commented about the program's piano player, Rudy Atwood, and how he thrilled everyone who heard him with his hands running up and down the keyboard as he played. Wally and Dot couldn't praise his playing enough. For some of you older folks out there, the names Charles Fuller and Rudy Atwood will bring back lots of memories. The younger folks, on the other hand, missed a lot.

It was in this area that Cassie had run into the bushes to chase two baby armadillos we had spotted. For several weeks we had seen lots of armadillos, but they had always been dead ones—usually the losers in battles with cars traveling at fast speeds. Now for the first time Joni and I saw living ones, and they were just babies. What a thrill. But Cassie scared them off before we could get their pictures. There was another day soon after that we did get pictures of live armadillos along the road, when Cass wasn't with us.

One of our more memorable experiences with the police came in this part of Florida. State Trooper Larry M. had pulled up to see what we were doing. When we told him about our walk of prayer, he got out of his car and came around and hugged us each.

Dogs often followed us as we walked. Sometimes we had to drive them back to where they had begun following us. Other times we slipped into stores until they gave up and turned around, or we ditched them by jumping into the van for a while when our driver showed up at the right time.

One time we saw a poor old hound dog with ribs poking through, following along beside us, yet keeping her distance. Later in the day we drove back with food and water to find her. Spotting her, we stopped and Joni got out to set our gifts on the ground for her. But our stopping seemed to have spooked her and she ran from behind our van out into the road in front of an oncoming car. She had been hit. The cars paused long enough to allow Joni to go out to the street and carry her to the grass. There Joni sat, holding the poor dog as she took her last few breaths.

Later Joni told us that the poor dog seemed to have a lot of tumors in her abdomen. Perhaps she wouldn't have lived much longer anyway. We felt somewhat relieved that the dog was no longer in pain, though it broke our hearts to have to see this happen.

Then there was Cassie, who didn't walk a lot with us these days because of the heat. This one particular day Cassie had started out with us. When we had walked almost three miles, Cass suddenly spotted a squirrel and decided to take chase. Needless to say it took Joni by surprise and she was suddenly slammed to the ground. For awhile Joni lay there with the breath knocked out of her. Before she got up we assessed the situation. There was a cut above Joni's left eye where her glasses had been pushed into her face. Her small pack had been in front and she had fallen on it, giving her some pain.

We were soon off to the Florida Hospital Ormond Beach Emergency Room, where Joni had lots of attention. The doctor ordered a CAT Scan for her abdomen in case the pack had done some unseen damage. There was none, but we were thankful that they had checked, because later her stomach became quite painful with bruising that occurred from the fall. As for the cut above her eye, they literally glued it together and told her not to get it wet for the next five days. The Emergency Room staff, Theresa, Debbie, Charles, and Susan, were all efficient and friendly. By the next afternoon we were out on the road again for a short day of walking.

Not long after that we were walking through Korona Beach past a bar, when several men called out to us. They were laughing and offering us drinks, and asking where we were headed. Thinking they had a bit too much to drink, we ignored them at first. Then we thought that if Jesus had been walking by he wouldn't have ignored them. Since our purpose was to pray for America and walk as representatives of Jesus, we decided to go over and talk with them. As soon as they found out what we were doing they were very congenial. While some of them made it clear they didn't believe in prayer, they were still very appreciative of what we were doing. They allowed us to take their pictures. Then, as we headed on our way, one of them quietly asked us to pray for him.

A few days later we had a very similar situation when Chuck, Rick, Leo and John called out to us to come on over. Again we hesitated, but we knew that Jesus wanted us to go over to them. They too, acted very congenial toward us when they found out what we were doing. After some conversation and picture taking they bid us good-bye. As we walked away, they advised us not to walk any further in this area that night, saying that this was an area of drugs and prostitution. With a quick prayer to God for guidance, we called for Ronni to come pick us up, sensing that God had placed them there to warn us.

Certainly we believed that God was watching out for us. Not only did He protect us from harm, he also sent people to our aid when we needed them—and sometimes when we didn't know we needed aid. Edward checked the air in our tires and filled the one that was low. In return we prayed that God would provide Edward with a job. We just happened to see him the next evening again, and he told us that he just got a job and would be starting the next day.

# Chapter Thirty-Five

# THE BRITISH ARE COMING

### Lyn

Our walk took us past a beautiful African Methodist Episcopalian Church one day, and we decided to leave our Memorial Stone number 257 there for Ormond Beach. We really wanted to look around inside this intriguing building, but saw no one around. Then around back, we noticed two men next door, working in the yard. We asked them if they knew anything about the church, or where we might find someone to let us in. Once they found out who we were and what we were doing, one of the men said he would be happy to show us through the church. Inside was even more beautiful than it was outside, and we were grateful that Riley had been so kind as to take us through.

### Joni

For over a year Lyn and I had not seen an ocean. We California girls missed seeing the beaches and waves pounding on huge boulders. At last we had walked to the Atlantic from the Pacific. We just had to take a little time to put our feet in the water, and feel the sand between our toes.

Admiring the vast expanse of white sand, we decided to get in the van and drive the length of the Daytona Beach Strip. It was such a novelty to drive on the beach that Ronni, Lyn and I each took turns driving and taking pictures of each other.

Florida storms are not to be toyed with. Lightning strikes in this state are extremely high. For this reason we were very careful when we heard the thunder and saw the lightning flash. Several times we got caught in storms. Once we took shelter in a tire store. Actually, Cassie saw the open door and ran in after a clap of thunder frightened her. Tony welcomed us and even brought chairs for us to sit on while we waited for the storm to blow over. He sat and visited with us, and we learned about his earlier migration from Cuba.

Another time, while crossing a long bridge where a lake and the sea join, lightning began closing in on us, and we hurried to get to the other side where Ronni had the van. After waiting out the storm we went back to our walking. Only later did we realize that the storm had seemingly dumped buckets of water everywhere around, except the area where we had walked. We could almost visualize God's large umbrella over us protecting us from the wind, rain, and lightning.

## Lyn

On the 12th of June I met a cousin, Ike Tiner, for breakfast. He was staying in Daytona Beach on business. Ike and I made plans for us to come back later to share at the church he was attending while he stayed in the area.

(On June 30 our team drove from Fort Pierce back to South Daytona where we had dinner with Ike and his wife, Janice, who had come from California to be with him in Florida for a while. Then we went to Ike's church, White Chapel Church of God. Joni and I each shared from our experiences on the walk, then answered many questions from the audience.)

We moved from the Ormond Beach/Daytona Beach area after that breakfast on June 12th. Coni Harris had arranged for us to go to Mulberry to share in her church that Sunday, the 13th. Coni took us on a sightseeing tour, stopping at Gatorland, the only place we saw alligators up close. She also took us to see some antique airplanes. Ronni was enchanted and asked many questions of the docent. We saw Spook Hill, then drove through Kissimmee as we headed for Mulberry and Lakeland.

The service at Shepherd Road Presbyterian Church the next morning was quite memorable. Coni was invited up to introduce me, as I was the spokesperson for the team. Pastor Bob Hovey had allowed ten minutes for my sharing.

After I sat down the pastor got up to give his sermon. He looked at the pulpit, then around at the music pastor, then back to the audience. Finally he said, "All right, who took my sermon notes?" I quickly shuffled through my stack of papers and realized that I had picked them up with my notes on the way back to my seat earlier. Sheepishly I handed the sermon notes back to the pastor. For the next several minutes he quipped that previously nobody had realized he even used notes. He said he had always known one of these days someone would pick them up, but it wasn't until Coni's friend came that it

288

MT1   MT 2   MT 3   NE 1   NE 2

NE 3   NE 4   NE 5   NE 6   NE 7

NE 8   NE 9   NE 10   NE 11   NE 12

KS 1   KS 2   MO 1   MO 2   MO 3

AR 1   AR 2   AR 3   AR 4   AR 5

AR 6     AR 7     MOBH 1     MOBH 2     MOBH 3

MOBH 4     KY 1     TN 1     TN 2     TN 3

TN 4     TN 5     TN 6     TN 7     TN 8

TN 9     MS 1     MS 2     MS 3     MS 4

MS 5     MS 6     MS 7     MS 8     MS 9

MS 10    AL 1    AL 2    AL 3    AL 4

AL 5    AL 6    AL 7    AL 8    AL 9

AL 10    AL 11    AL 12    AL 13    AL 14

AL 15    AL 16    AL 17    AL 18    AL 19

GA 1    GA 2    GA 3    GA 4    GA 5

GA 6    GA 7    GA 8    FL 1    FL 2

FL 3    FL 4    FL 5    FL 6    FL 7

FL 8    FL 9    FL 10    FL 11    FL 12

FL 13    FL 14    FL 15    FL 16    FL 17

FL 18    FL 19    FL 20    FL 21    FL 22

actually happened. I laughed with the rest of the congregation over his remarks. He then preached from Colossians 1: 15–20 on "The Supremacy of Christ."

Following the service many people stopped to talk with us, and we took their pictures. One was with Pastor Hovey standing between Joni and me. Now he is a very tall man and made us look pretty small. I asked, "Just how tall are you?" His answer was, "I'm five feet, twenty inches."

From church we went with Coni to a local southern buffet named Picadilly, where we had a wonderful meal. Coni took us to see the Bok Tower nearby. This tower is built on the highest point in Florida—remember that one spot that is 345 feet high? We found out that the tower is located on 120 acres of land. It is made of 205 feet of stone and marble and has 60 bronze carillon bells, ranging from 157 pounds to 12 tons each. These bells continue to ring regularly.

Saying our good-byes to Coni, we headed for Melbourne, where we would set up headquarters for the next week. These days were very hot and humid, so that our skin was always sticky and glistening. Thankfully we had gotten used to it enough that we could walk straight through the day at times. It was nice not to always have to break for long periods in the middle of the day.

Since Daytona Beach, we had been walking on Highway 1, staying close to the Atlantic Ocean. Here the coastal breezes often helped make the heat of the day more bearable. We would be on this highway all the way to Key West, where we would finish our Journey.

On one of these very hot days we had stopped to take some pictures of osprey in their nests, when we noticed a man walking on the other side of the road. He was pulling a dolly loaded with what appeared to be all his earthly possessions. Curious, we crossed the road to talk with him. David told us he had been walking for about eight years throughout Florida. He tried to tell us how he lives and how we should live, but we weren't too keen on his ideas. Though he told us his ideas were biblical, they didn't fit the Bible we knew. It was the hottest part of the day and we were standing in direct sunlight, getting hotter and beginning to feel a bit woozy from the heat. We were sipping water as we stood there, but knew we needed to keep moving before one of us passed out. Finally we were able to break away. Walking helped a lot, as it stirred up the breezes around us just enough to cool us down. We kept drinking our water and began to feel better almost instantly.

## Joni

On Tuesday, June 15, we drove to Sanford Airport to pick up my twin brother John, who was arriving from England to join us for a week of walking. It was really fun to have him participate in the Journey with me.

Walking through Mims and Titusville, John noticed two armadillos. They were very much alive, and we were able to get pictures of them. While in this area we went to the manatee deck, to see if we could spot any of these interesting creatures swimming. Two of them were visible, though we could see only their noses sticking out of the water and their unusually large flat tails.

We ended our day at Harvey's Orange Stand, where a notice stated: "Closed while Mother Nature works her magic." On John's first day of walking, we stopped at 17.5 miles. He was very hot and tired. Although he is a marathon runner, coming from England, he was not used to this heat and humidity.

Going through Port St. John the next day, he and I dedicated this part of our walk to our mother, Alice St. John.

One touristy type thing we chose to do while John was with us was to visit the Kennedy Space Center. It was thrilling to watch the IMAX movie about the space program, "The Dream is Alive." Later we were disappointed when the unmanned rocket launch we had looked forward to seeing had to be scrubbed just minutes before blast-off, due to a lightning storm.

We were guests at a Rotary Club breakfast one morning at the Suntree United Methodist Church in the town of Viera. Tony, Lyn's friend, introduced us, and Lyn shared briefly about our Journey. The main speaker that day was from the local Humane Society, and being dog lovers, we found her presentation very interesting.

After the Rotary meeting, Tony took us on a tour of the church. The church administrator gathered most of the staff together and the senior pastor prayed for us. What a great experience! We also left a special Memorial Stone for their church.

On Sunday, June 20, we attended His Place Ministries in Melbourne. We met a few people on the way in, then took our seats. During the singing Pastor Terry Morris worked his way over to us and asked if he had heard right—that we were walking across America praying for the nation? He then asked if we would be willing to share with the congregation what we were doing.

This is a very "outreaching" congregation. A team of their people had just returned from the Dominican Republic the night before, and most of the service was given to this team sharing about how God worked in and through them on their mission journey. We were all impressed as Terry and his wife, Betty, along with their son, Jason, told of their experience.

We also found out they have a potluck lunch at the park after church. The members bring the food, and the homeless and others of the community eat with them, as they make an effort to mingle together and minister to those in need.

Watching TV that evening, we saw that an American in Saudi Arabia had been executed. The man's son lived in Port St. John, where we had walked yesterday. We were all very sorry and prayed for his family.

Still walking along Highway 1, we went along the Indian River waterway, full of sea birds and jumping fish. One very large heron caught a fish as we watched. There were also ducks, terns, pelicans, cormorants and osprey.

Continuing through Palm Bay and Malabar, we saw our first flamingo. Then there was the fascinating mailbox made of concrete and shaped like a manatee and her baby.

One beautiful morning we walked along the river through Grant, Roseland, and Sebastian. This was John's last day to walk with us. Lyn made copies of her week's journal to give to John. He had walked a total of 79.3 miles.

We drove him back to the airport, and I knew he would be happy to get on the plane just to get some rest! We hugged at the gate, and he turned and walked inside. I was so sad to see him go, but had enjoyed our week together. (John shares his thoughts about his experiences with the team in Appendix 8.)

### Lyn

We were nearing the town of Cocoa (not to be confused with Cocoa Beach) when we received a call from Dellie in California. She told us she would be meeting us in Miami to walk to Key West with us. JoAn from Canada was also planning to come back for the final weeks. It was exciting to think others would be joining us soon to walk with us through the Keys to the finish. We estimated we would reach Miami on July 7, and Key West on July 23.

My friends, Shawn and Bev, from Winter Garden, Florida met us near Melbourne and took us all out to lunch. We enjoyed this special time with them.

From June 23 through June 27 we would not be walking. Joni and Ronni would be staying in Orlando doing some touristy things like going to Epcot Center and shopping. I was flying to California for the wedding of Brenda, my eldest granddaughter, to Josh Calderon. The wedding was on the 25th, and I flew back to Orlando on the 26th to join Ronni and Joni at their motel.

On Sunday, the 27th, we drove to Fort Pierce, stopping at a church in Kissimmee for our time of worship. We chose the Bible Baptist Church where Pastor Joe Williams preached from Acts 2:41. It was a great service with a very friendly congregation. Charles and Beverly shared with us that he had three types of cancer and Beverly had the early stages of Alzheimer's. They had been married for 54 years and still looked happy and in love. We told them we would keep them in our prayers.

*Chapter Thirty-six*

# CASSIE "DINES" AT THE GOLDEN CORRAL BUFFET

---

**Lyn**

Getting back to walking, we soon found the Old Dixie Road, which took us off the busy highway for quite a stretch. This road took us through Vero Beach, where we left Memorial Stone number 268 at a fire station beside their Memorial Statue in honor of local firemen who had died in the line of duty. (A few weeks after the walk was over we heard from one of the firemen at the station. They had found our stone while cleaning up after two hurricanes had ripped through the area. Now they informed us that the stone was inside the station, where it is under glass for its preservation and to have it available for all to see.)

Several times we met small children or youth as we walked along. We remember one young man who especially wanted to be in our book. He was twelve years old, and figured we'd be famous someday. Well, Michael Hatch, we may not be famous, but we are happy to make sure you get in our book.

We have to break here to tell you about some of our embarrassing driving moments. Mine happened on a Sunday near Montgomery, Alabama. We were looking for a church. We pulled in at one, but found we were very early, so we decided to go for a snack before the service. Driving away I got in the left turn lane and waited for traffic. Ronni commented that she didn't realize it was legal to do that. Only then did I realized I wasn't in a left turn lane, but rather a lane meant for oncoming traffic. This was a bit embarrassing, since it was Ronni who pointed out my mistake. Ronni, you know, is from Australia, where they drive on the other side of the road.

Another time as Joni and I were walking we saw a familiar van—ah, yes, it was indeed Lady Van Go, stuck in the sand on the side of the road. It seems Ronni had misjudged the ground on the roadside, where she wanted to park and wait for us. The dirt turned out to be soft deep sand, and Ronni could not get the van to move. As we came along she tried to wave us on, but, of course, we had to stop and take pictures. Our very resourceful Ronni already had help on the way, and the van was quickly released from its prison of sand.

Joni always drove home to our night's lodging at the end of the walking day. This particular evening she drove up to make the usual U-turn to get to our motel in Fort Pierce. It was getting dark. As she was easing to a stop at the red light before making the U-turn, the light changed to green. Immediately Joni began her sharp turn as Ronni and I hollered "Stop." Too late. She was already up on the wide median strip before realizing her mistake. Fortunately Lady Van Go is fairly high from the ground and we bumped over the large rocks cemented into the median. Once we knew we were OK, I began to laugh, then Ronni, and finally Joni joined in the laughter. We pulled into our space in the motel parking lot and sat there holding our sides as we laughed with tears running down our cheeks. I think Joni gets the prize.

While walking in Fort Pierce we discovered an ice cream place on our route. Some of the flavors had interesting names, but my favorite was "Purple Haze." It was a berry ice cream with chocolate covered jellies in it—amazingly delicious. The store owner and a customer had noticed us as we walked in. We seem to stand out with our smashed hats, walking stick with the flag on top, matching shirts and sweaty bodies. People are always curious about this strange walking duo going down the road. As we left the store, we each gratefully accepted a bottle of water.

The town of Stuart was one of those places we just had to spend time enjoying. Its great fountain with the leaping swordfish was a major focal point, not to mention its cute, diverse shops. We stopped in a few of these shops and met several people. One store was a great place to get ice cream, and in this weather we were always on the lookout for that. However, it melted so fast we could barely keep up with it. We ended up a sticky mess. Of course, we just laughed and kept moving.

In Stuart we discovered we had somehow left the main road and gone quite a bit out of our way. Ronni was trying to find us, and we kept watching for her. We finally saw a Real Estate Office and knew they would have a map. The lady inside helped us figure out a way to get back on our route without a lot of backtracking. Finally we could tell Ronni a place to meet us that she could easily find. Soon we were all back on track, but we had wasted a lot of our walking time.

Ronni was not without her exciting experiences, and here's one we just have to let her tell. Use your imagination to hear her Australian accent as she talks.

## Ronni

The girls had started off from a little park that morning. Cassie and I waited there a while, then I went into the outhouse before driving off. I hooked Cassie's leash to the door handle on the outside of this restroom, then went inside.

A police siren sounded in the distance, and I could hear Cassie howling and scuffling to one side as she pulled on the door handle. To my horror I heard a "click" and found that Cassie, the "cheeky blighter," had locked the door from the outside. I looked for a way out, but saw that this outhouse must have been built to last 50 years, at least. "Crickey, mate," the temperature inside must be 120 degrees Fahrenheit. It was frightening!

In a panic I looked around and saw there was only one tiny vent and a skylight above me. A plastic wastebasket stood nearby and I turned it upside down to get high enough to bang at the skylight with my shoe. Just then the wastebasket gave in and dumped me onto the floor.

Fortunately I had my cell phone in my pocket, so I called 911. Once I'd explained my predicament, the dispatcher encouraged me to calm down and give her the name of the park I was in. I didn't have the foggiest idea what the name was! We were able to figure out where it must be, and the dispatcher finally assured me that an officer was on the way to my rescue. Just then I heard another "click," and realized that Cassie had pulled the handle the other direction, unlocking the door. I lunged for the door and opened it before Cassie could lock it again. The dispatcher was still on the line, so I was able to tell her I was now out, and OK.

Just then a policeman arrived and asked me if I was OK. I was bloomin' mad, and I asked him to "arrest" Lyn and Joni for leaving me there. He was ready to go along with this little joke, until he got a radio call to go to a more urgent emergency.

While my "toilet horror" was very scary at the time, I was able to laugh about it by the time I met the girls and told them this story.

## Lyn

One day we met a special little boy on his shiny red bicycle. He asked if we liked his bicycle, and we assured him we did. Next he wanted to know what we were doing, so we told him about our walk and gave him one of our cards to give his parents. Zach rode off and we continued walking. We hadn't gotten far when Zach came running to tell us his mother wanted to meet us. So we turned back to talk with Allana who was coming with her daughter, Rebecca. What a sweet family they were. Allana shared with us about a friend of hers in Washington state who needed a bone marrow transplant, and asked if we would add her to our prayer list.

Our first drawbridge, near Jupiter, was exciting. There would be several of these to cross in the days ahead. On one of them we stopped to take pictures as a tall sailboat headed toward the bridge. We had gone beyond the part of the bridge that went up, so we were comfortable standing there to watch the process. Bells rang and whistles blew, then suddenly a voice over a loudspeaker asked the ladies taking pictures to please step beyond the gate so they could lift the bridge. Oops! We quickly moved out of the way of the gate and they raised the bridge, allowing the boat to safely pass through.

The Fourth of July was a Sunday this year. We had been walking hard the previous few days and were ready for a rest day. We would soon be moving from Fort Pierce, so we chose the First United Methodist Church, not far from our motel. During the week before, we had placed our Memorial Stone here. Arriving for church, we were disappointed to see that the stone was no longer there. Someone had already removed it. This was the second stone we knew of that had been taken from its place.

We enjoyed the service in this beautiful old church building. Pastor Todd Stube preached from Matthew 5, and many people gave us prayer requests. One lady told us her husband had died two weeks earlier. Several widows in the church had already taken her under their wings to help her through this difficult time.

## Joni

The place we chose for lunch was the Golden Corral Buffet—all you can eat, and great southern cuisine. A thunderstorm struck while we were eating, and soon an announcement came over the restaurant loudspeaker: "A large dog has jumped out of the window of a green van and found her way into the restaurant. Would the owners please come rescue the poor dog." I rushed to where a crowd was gathered around Cassie. She was so excited she jumped all over me. Everyone was exclaiming over what a beautiful, smart dog she was. The manager gave me some roast beef to give her and very kindly turned off the alarm on the back door of the restaurant so I could take her directly to the van. By now the storm had passed, so she was content to stay, and I could return to finish my meal.

We chose not to attend any fireworks display. The thunder and lightning of the afternoon had been enough Fourth of July celebration for us this year, and besides we were very tired.

A large drawbridge took us over an inlet of the Atlantic into Palm Beach. Someone told us that Palm Beach is actually built on a large sandbar. This city was both beautiful and fascinating, from the large Episcopal Church with its coconut trees, to the hedges that were at least 15 feet, perhaps even 20 feet tall. These served well to hide the mansions behind them.

In the Palm Beach area we met Lynette. As we got out of the van and prepared to walk, Lynette came from one of the homes to let us know that the beaches there were private. Seeing us loading up our packs, she assumed we were heading for the beach. We could certainly understand that reasoning. After all, how often do you look out your window and see people walking across the United States? We explained our real purpose for being where we were. Smiling, she then told us we would be more than welcome to use her private beach. Then she noticed I was eyeing a coconut on the ground and told me I would be welcome to take it. I had been wanting to get a coconut for several days, so I thanked her and put it in the van. She was very pleasant, and we enjoyed talking with her.

We like interesting signs, and we saw a few along here. One sign proclaimed that Palm Beach would continue in 3/10 of a mile. Lake Worth took up the beach for this short distance, then reverted back to Palm Beach. There were other similar places, and we concluded that each town had to have their own special ocean front beaches.

Another sign stated that "Illegal Dumping is unl AWFUL [sic]." It seemed that even in places like Palm Beach, there were people who thought it was OK to dump their rubbish anywhere, though most likely it did not come from the people who lived there. It is always so sad to see people's junk just tossed anywhere. Still another sign read, "Sea Turtles Lighting Project." During the nesting season here, all street lights are turned off.

Since we were walking on a sandbar, it was not unusual to see large yachts anchored in the inlet between the mainland and the sandbar. Later as we walked across a bridge, we were able to watch water skiers, boaters and swimmers in a large area where ocean and inlet met.

## Lyn

Steve Clark invited us to a Florida Trail Association meeting on the evening of July 5th. Coni Harris, our friend from Mulberry, had put us in touch with Steve. Arriving right on time, we discovered that the meeting place had been changed. After asking several people we found where they had moved to, we walked in about 15 minutes late. After stopping to introduce us they continued their program, a slide travelogue about a trip to Patagonia by one of the couples. At the end we were asked to share about our walk, then responded to their questions.

It was an exciting day when we moved from Fort Pierce to Miami. We would have to make only one more move before the end of the walk! The Sleep Inn was convenient to the airport and had a shuttle bus. This was a plus, since we had two people flying in to meet us in the next few days.

On July 8, Dellie from Atascadero, California, flew in to join us for the remainder of the walk. For a few days she would be sharing our room. The room was now "Wall to wall people, beds, suitcases, and a "furry person."

With the heat and humidity, Dellie wasn't able to walk as much as she had hoped. Ronni was happy to have her ride along and keep her company in the van when the heat was too much for her. Once when a lightning storm hit we were able to take shelter in a high-rise condo where a guard let us in. People were always so pleasant about helping us in situations like this.

It wasn't unusual to meet people who were traveling from other places, but one day we had an especially interesting encounter. As we came out of a beach restroom in Lauderdale by the Sea, we were greeted by a smiling couple curious about the significance of our hats. After we explained our Journey, they asked a lot of questions. When we told them we were from California, they told us they were also. In fact, Richard and Annette were camp hosts at Mount Madonna near Gilroy, a place we have often loved to hike.

Hearing that our purpose for this walk was to pray, they told us their main reason for being in Florida was to check out information for a liver transplant for her brother. We promised to pray, and also to look them up sometime after we finished the Journey. (After coming home from the walk, we did get together with Richard and Annette and learned that her brother had had a successful transplant!)

My "Mr. Wonderful" was at it again. Arriving back at our motel, we were surprised to see a large bouquet on top of the refrigerator, with four candy bars among the flowers, one for each of us. The card attached said simply, "See you in two weeks!" What a special treat for four tired women.

At last we walked into Miami. We stopped often to take pictures of the impressive buildings. Just beyond Miami we enjoyed talking with a group appropriately named "Tree-mendous Miami." In a large strip under the elevated light rail system, they were planting Poinciana trees, with orange/red blossoms. We had been enjoying these lovely blossoms for several miles.

Dellie had graduated from the University of Miami "a few years before," so we made sure she was with us when we walked past the campus. It was a time of reminiscing for her as we stopped to look around and take pictures. Dellie and Ronni later drove back and looked around some more.

That was also the day that our friends, Scott and Kathy Stauffer, their three daughters, Sarah, Kelly and Karen, as well as Scott's dad, Jack met us for lunch. They took us to Pollo Tropical, a Cuban restaurant whose delicious food was a first for us. Then they also treated us to ice cream at Cold Stone Creamery. What a great time we had with this family.

# Chapter Thirty-Seven

# KEY WEST—JUST 123 MILES!

## Lyn

Sunday, July 11th we attended the First Presbyterian Church of Miami Springs. Soloist Myron Harden sang, "Here I Am, Lord." The pastor was on vacation, but we enjoyed a good message from the Reverend Jared Reed from Genesis 1:1 to 2:3: "In the Beginning, God."

Driving through road construction is seldom fun, but we enjoyed walking through it. It usually meant little traffic, and interesting conversations with the workers. They were often curious about why we were walking. In Cutler Ridge we met a worker from Jamaica. Another man told us that he and his family were feeling a real need to get back to church. We were thankful for these opportunities to share.

## Joni

I will never forget the time we were talking about Cassie's needs. I had been quite concerned about her with the heat and humidity. Even when she was in the van, it was difficult to find shade when Ronni wanted to park and go shopping.

Twice while we were eating at fast food restaurants, she had tried to get out of the van and into the restaurant. She hated sitting in the van by herself, so I often brought my food outside, along with a plain hamburger for her, and sat with her under a tree. I was also concerned about Cassie being caged up again on the long flight home.

As we talked about this, we walked past a bus stop where a woman was sitting reading a book. Lyn happened to notice it was a Bible, and felt compelled to speak to her. When we told Patrice about our Journey of prayer, she immediately stood to her feet, then asked if she could pray for us. We stood there holding hands, as she prayed a powerful prayer asking God to watch over us and bless us on this Journey. Saying good-bye, we told her that she was an angel sent by God to minister to us at a time when we needed it.

There were many times on this Journey when God sent someone to minister to us, especially when we were really in need physically, emotionally, spiritually, or financially. Our hearts were overflowing as we left Patrice and walked on, confident that

God would take care of Cassie. In fact, we felt lighthearted, and our feet seemed to skip along as if on wings.

It was later that same day we saw a very welcome mileage sign. The bottom line of the sign read, "Key West—123 miles." This was the first indication of actual mileage to the end of our walk! It was almost overwhelming as we realized how close we now were to the end. Tears came easily for the rest of the Journey, and sometimes we "whooped" in joy, or even pinched each other to see if this was real.

Soon after that sign we saw another, more sobering one. This read, "7 fatalities on the Florida Keys Road so far this year." As we drove past this sign to our start point each of the next few days, we would see this number go up. The last number we remember seeing was "12."

## Lyn

On July 12, JoAn Thomas flew from Canada to join us for the remainder of the walk. When we returned to our motel that evening we found her in her room and had a happy reunion. Dellie was happy to move in with JoAn, where she would have a real bed rather than a rollaway, plus room to move around. Of course, that greatly relieved our tight living conditions as well.

JoAn and Dellie had both expected to be able to do a lot of walking with us. However, they had not counted on the high humidity of Florida. JoAn had plenty of experience with humid weather where she lived near Toronto, but was surprised with how much worse it was in Florida. The two of them walked when they could, but were often quite content to ride in the air conditioned van.

Joni and I had adapted well to the heat and humidity. In fact we seldom took those long afternoon breaks anymore. Besides, we were so close to the finish that we were charged with new energy. We also decided that the water we frequently drank from the packs we carried on our backs had a lot to do with our extra stamina. We encouraged JoAn and Dellie to get some similar packs to keep from getting dehydrated.

We had water on both sides of us through the Keys. The beautiful blues and greens of the Atlantic and the Gulf sparkled in the sunshine, and the ocean water was almost hot as we splashed it over our arms. Key Largo provided the first of many beautiful sunsets we would enjoy throughout the Keys.

July 14 was our final moving day before finishing the walk. With five of us, plus Cassie, and all our luggage, we had decided to rent a second vehicle. To pick up the car we had reserved, Joni and I rode the shuttle from our motel to the airport in Miami. Even with two cars, finding space for all our "stuff" was tricky.

Before leaving the motel, we made reservations to stay here after we finished the walk, since most of us would be flying home out of Miami. The staff here had been incredibly gracious during our stay.

We really appreciated Ronni's thorough, thrifty ways as she checked over our motel bills. She frequently saved us from being charged for "extras."

We moved to Marathon, about mid-way on the Keys, and just before the Seven Mile Bridge. Finding a place for the five of us and a dog was not easy in this area. In general, everything was more expensive. We looked at several places, and many would not allow dogs. One place would have worked out great, except that we would have had to move elsewhere just for the weekend. That certainly wouldn't do. It was getting late, and we were tired and frustrated.

As some of us sat outside the Ramada Inn and discussed our options, Ronni was inside talking with the clerk. The clerk was adamant, but Ronni kept trying different tactics, until the manager came out to see what was going on. When Ronni explained what we were doing and what our problem was, the manager told the clerk to give us the space for the whole time at the "manager's special price." Ronni had come through for us again. That particular clerk never did seem happy with us, but the manager and everyone else treated us with great respect. We made it a point to be kind to her, but seldom, if ever, got a smile.

Moving days were often hard on us, and this one had seemed especially difficult. So it was great to get back to walking. A car was waiting at a red light at one intersection, and the young man called over to us asking, "Did you pick those clothes out yourself, or do they make you wear them?" We laughed and told him what we were doing. He just said, "Awesome," rolled up his window, and rode off into the sunset—or something like that. Joni and I had a good laugh over that as we looked at each other and realized what a sight we were. By now our hats were faded, battered and flat. Our clothes had become quite faded in this weather, and we were dripping with sweat. Our shorts pockets bulged with supplies we carried in them, making us look like squirrels with stuff stored away in our pouches. A fashion statement we were not. Perhaps the young man had good reason to wonder about our appearance!

In the Key Lime Products Store, where we stopped for restrooms, a clerk asked what we were doing today. We told her we were walking to Key West and her mouth dropped open. Then we went on to say that our walk had started in Washington state, and the mouths of everyone in the small store dropped open. Soon we had Jodi, Stephanie, Althea, Joel and David gathered around asking questions. We had a lot of fun with this delightful group of people. As we left, Jodi gave us water and candy.

The Keys are a great place to see large iguanas running wild, as well as palmetto bugs larger than some of the huge Montana grasshoppers. In fact, there were some iguanas that hung around the pool regularly at the motel where we now were staying.

The Islamorada Chamber of Commerce gave us a friendly welcome. They asked us to stop by the Free Press offices, where Steve Gibbs, the Senior Staff Writer, would interview us and take our picture. But first we chatted with them and got a little history of the area from Mary, Ilene, and Joe.

In the early 1900s access to the islands was only possible by boat. But by 1912 a railroad line had been extended from Homestead to Key West. Engineers and laborers had worked long and hard designing and building this incredible system of bridges. Then on Labor Day of 1935 a hurricane of great force hit. This destroyed the railroad, and in 1938 the Overseas Highway was built. Forty-two bridges connect this highway of the islands for 126 miles.

Later in our walk we came upon a very special memorial honoring the 300 people lost in the Florida Keys hurricane of 1935. This memorial was beautifully set into the local Keystone Rock, imbedded with imprints of shells.

Our excitement surged when we saw a sign proclaiming it was now fifty miles to Miami one way, and fifty miles to Key West the other way.

Soon after that we came to another memorial, honoring the multitudes who have lost their lives trying to flee from Cuba. These Cubans crossed the ninety miles of sea in rafts, inner tubes, or anything they could find that would float. Unprepared for the rough seas and storms they would encounter, hundreds, perhaps thousands, perished. This memorial also gave tribute to the many who did make it and are now free and contributing to their new homeland as teachers, business people, or political leaders.

*Chapter Thirty-Eight*

# CASSIE GOES TO CHURCH

**Lyn**

To us California girls, it was fascinating to look out over the Atlantic and see people wading out about half a mile or more, and not even waist high in the water. In some places, sections of the old bridge were still used as walking and cycling bridges, and also fishing bridges. It was awesome to walk across on these with absolutely no motorized traffic. Often people would have their tents set up for a shady respite as they spent much of the day out in the sun, fishing over the railing. Sometimes we found parts of fish in our path—even eels, or an octopus or two. Joni liked to pick up these long-dead critters and toss them back into the sea. Was she hoping they would revive once they hit the water?

Thankfully, humor was often part of our day. On one such day we met two men looking for their lost rooster. They seemed quite intent on finding this critter, but we thought it doubtful they would ever find it. To us, such a frantic search for a rooster seemed rather funny. Perhaps it was more than just an ordinary rooster.

July 18th was our last Sunday of the Journey, and our last Sunday on the Florida Keys. We were blessed to find Kirk of the Keys Presbyterian Church for services that day. It was difficult to find a shady spot to park for Cassie, and we ended up parking by a tree and leaving the side door open, with Cassie leashed on the twenty-five foot lead.

Inside the church we talked with Pastor James Kennedy and asked him if there were alligators in the canal outside. Joni was worried about one attacking Cassie. He assured her there were no alligators, but then encouraged her to bring Cassie inside for the service to get her out of the heat. He told us that many in the congregation were dog lovers, and they would understand. How we appreciated his kindness.

When the pastor introduced us during the service, he also explained that he had told us to bring Cassie inside. Everyone seemed delighted and we heard no complaints. Our canine mascot was happy to be inside with us, content to lie at Joni's feet most of the time. It was not the first time she had joined us in a church. She didn't even try to vocalize with the congregation during the music. Still, the chain around her neck rattled when she moved, so Joni removed the collar. Cassie took this as permission to roam, and headed right to the platform. Joni jumped up and caught her just before she walked up to pay the pastor a visit.

We stayed for refreshments after the service and visited with many of the congregation. What a great experience for our last Sunday. One lady in the kitchen asked us if we would like to take some chocolate chip cookies back with us. Would we ever! Well, she gave us all that were left, which was quite a bunch. She insisted that if she took them home they would just get stale. We were happy to keep her from ending up with stale cookies.

The Seven Mile Bridge was one we had been looking forward to. We had planned it so that we had two or three miles to walk before the bridge. Just before getting onto the bridge, we made sure to use a restroom conveniently located there. For the full seven miles we did fine without another restroom—one of our big concerns.

Another concern about this long bridge was traffic and walking space. But our concerns were unnecessary since it had very wide shoulders. Partway across we encountered road construction and had a whole traffic lane to ourselves! Perhaps our favorite part of this bridge was the high span in the middle where boats passed under. This beautiful arched span gave a delicate, graceful beauty to the bridge. All the way we enjoyed a nice breeze as well.

At Bahia Honda State Park, as we stopped to take a picture of the sign, a car pulled up and parked on the side of the road. A man got out and headed to the sign. Suddenly I realized this man was my husband, and rushed across to his welcoming embrace. I finally got my picture with Dave standing beside the sign.

Dave, though he had only arrived a couple of hours before, had already arranged for us to meet the staff of "US 1" radio station in the Florida Keys at 104.1 on the FM dial. We arranged to have an interview the next morning after 10 A.M. The station manager and crew were wonderful and we looked forward to seeing them the next day. It was now July 19th.

On Big Pine Key there are tall evergreen trees and fresh water. This makes an ideal home for the tiny Key Deer—unique to this area, and worth protecting. Unfortunately we never saw any of them, but figured it was just too hot for them to be out in the open at the time.

The next morning Rachel and Zach pulled up in their car and came over to talk with us. They had heard about us on the radio and were excited about finding us. It seems the dear folks at the station were already talking about us, and we hadn't even been interviewed yet.

Soon we arrived at the 4,000 mile mark for our walk! After a brief time of celebration and pictures, we went to the radio station. The interview gave us a great opportunity to let people in the area know about our Journey, and also our ending date and time. We encouraged people to come out on July 23 between 3:00 and 3:30 P.M. to meet us at the Southernmost Point of the Continental United States.

From that point on, we met more and more who had either heard our interview, or heard one of the many announcements made on this station about the approaching end of our Journey. At this point, it was not unusual for people to come out of stores we were passing just to say "Hi" and wish us well.

We liked a large sign we saw in front of one home. The sign read, "GOD bless our troops!" Diane and Mike had a son in Iraq, and we added his name to our prayer list.

When Sheryl and Patrick drove up, they told us they had been at Shepherd Road Presbyterian Church in Mulberry, Florida a few weeks earlier when we spoke there. Now they were vacationing in the Keys and were surprised, but thrilled, to see us again.

By the end of Tuesday, July 20, we had only 15 miles left to walk. That could easily be a one day walk, but we planned to walk eleven miles the next day, take Thursday off, and walk the last four miles in the afternoon on Friday.

During this time Joni had developed blisters again, not just on her feet, but also on her hands. We were pretty certain it had something to do with the heat and humidity. At this point, however, she didn't care about a crazy blister or two.

Arriving at Cow Key Channel, we called for our support vehicle and ended our next to the last day of walking. Dave picked me up, and Ronni, Dellie, JoAn and Joni went exploring.

It was just past noon, so Dave and I went to the Key West Diner for some lunch. As we did a little exploring, I told Dave not to drive anyplace where I could see the end point of our walk. I did not want to see it until we approached it on the final day.

## Joni

After leaving the two lovebirds, Dave and Lyn, to go off by themselves, we four "girls" went to a restaurant for lunch. We then went to Ernest Hemingway's House and Garden. His house was very intriguing and the lush garden was beautiful with huge trees. We also visited his writing studio. In the Gift Shop I bought some of his books and his biography.

We saw many descendants of his six-toed cats, still roaming the garden. All the cats had special names, like Charlie Chaplin, a black and white cat with a big black smudge across his nose.

As I was driving back on the Overseas Highway a tire blew out while we crossed one of the bridges. I found a safe spot to park and called Lyn and Dave. They soon found us. Lyn called the emergency road service and waited at the van with Dellie, while Dave took the rest of us to get Cassie from the kennel where I had left her for the day. The repairman found Lyn and Dellie, changed the tire, then we all met back at the motel.

Thursday, July 22, was a leisure day for all of us. We had decided to do some sight-seeing and enjoy some relaxation. There was a place in Islamorada we all wanted to go. There we saw the tarpon, a large fish, and bought sardines to feed them. Some of the tarpon were as long as five feet—maybe longer—with unusually large mouths and teeth. Ronni fed some, and one grabbed her hand and made it bleed slightly—trust Ronni. Cassie was allowed to go out with us to see these huge fish as they scrambled for food.

For the rest of the day we all went in two cars to Key West to shop and do the "tour-isty thing." I left Cassie in a kennel again, where she could stay cool and be well cared for. It was fun to spend time looking around and shopping for things to remind us of this momentous event in our lives. Lyn and I had an interview in the afternoon with the Key West Citizen reporter, and he photographed us at the Conch Republic Seafood Company.

## Lyn

At the end of the day Dave and I went to Shula's Steak House on the Beach to eat a celebration dinner. We all met back at the motel in Marathon, where we discussed the final details for our last day of walking, then headed to our rooms.

Friday, July 23—day number 438 of the Great American Journey. We didn't leave the motel until about 11:00 A.M. There were only four more miles to go! Shortly after we started walking, a man called to us from a tennis court we were passing. He wanted to know how far we had walked. We told him, "4,023 miles." His daughter asked where we had started. We talked for a while and explained our purpose, and how we were almost finished. He said he wanted to shake all of our hands, and took off running to catch some of the team that had walked ahead. His three children all followed. He then shook each of our hands, as did his children, and they wished us well as we headed on.

The whole team—Dellie, JoAn, Ronni, Cassie, Joni and I—walked together today. Dave would be at the end to greet us and also to meet people as they came to join with us in celebration. Clayton Thomas called to wish us well, and said he wished he could have come to see us end what he had seen us begin. (Clayton had met us where we were staying when we began the walk in Washington state, and had followed us via our web site throughout the walk.)

Finally we began the last mile of our Journey. A block or two from the end, Dave joined us to walk the final steps. It was a few minutes before 3:00 P.M. when we arrived, and people had already gathered to see us finish.

Among those waiting there to greet us was a man holding a big sign with a bouquet of balloons tied to it. We read the sign which said,

---

I was there to see you off in Blaine, WA May 12, 2003.
So now I am here to see you end it—15 months later!!
Your friend, Clayton

---

Gasping in shock we realized Clayton was actually there in person. We had been sure his phone call earlier had been from his home in Indiana. That phone call had served its purpose, to throw us off, so we didn't expect him. We were totally surprised, and what a thrill it was! Clayton then presented us each with a bouquet of roses.

People were there from a couple of local churches, plus some we had met on the road the last two or three days. We visited and took pictures, and cried. Joni went across the street with Cassie for a while, reeling from the shock of being done, and uncertain whether she was happy or sad.

### Joni

I could not believe our walk was over. I went up to Lyn, gave her a hug, and congratulated her on being the only member of the team to have walked every step of the 4,026.5 miles of the Great American Journey: 8,503,968 steps.

### Lyn

Dave had hired a videographer to capture our last steps to the end, as well as our time of celebrating there. One of the important things we did at the end was to place our final Memorial Stone number 288 in a planter near the Southernmost Point marker. (Dave shares his final thoughts about the Journey in Appendix 7; JoAn shares in Appendix 9; and Dellie shares in Appendix 10.)

Finally we headed out to eat dinner at the Key West Diner. Clayton accepted our invitation to join us in a great time of celebration and satisfying conversation. Joni and I still couldn't believe it was over.

There was one more night at the Marathon motel, then the trip to Miami, where the team would have one more Sunday church service together. Our time in Miami was a time of saying good-bye to each other, which was very difficult, especially for Joni and me.

We were all leaving Miami at different times and heading in different directions. Dave and I were driving Lady Van Go home to California and would be taking three weeks to re-adjust to life together with time to talk about the whole experience. Our departure came Sunday afternoon, after a time of prayer in Ronni and Joni's room. Joni and Cassie would be flying to San Jose, JoAn to Canada, Ronni to Canada to visit an old friend, and Dellie back to Atascadero.

The Great American Journey was over as far as the walking was concerned, but it was far from over in affecting our lives. Little did we know what highs and lows we would experience in the days ahead, as we adjusted to living a "normal" life again.

The End . . . and the Beginning

# EPILOGUE

## —*Home Again!*—

*"My whole being, praise the LORD;*
*all my being, praise his holy name.*
*My whole being, praise the LORD and do not forget all his kindnesses.*
*He forgives all my sins and heals all my diseases.*
*He saves my life from the grave and loads me with love and mercy.*
*He satisfies me with good things and makes me young again, like the eagle."*

—PSALM 103: 1–5 NCV

## —*Never The Same*—

### By Lyn

For Dave and me the next three weeks were a time to talk, reflect and rest as we traveled and visited friends and relatives along our route heading back to the home I had left over 15 months earlier. Eventually we arrived and began the task of settling down.

I'll never forget that day, Monday, August 16, 2004 as we drove back into familiar territory. There had been changes. New homes had been built nearby, trees had grown taller, yet overall it was how I remembered it.

But let me go back to the beginning of that Monday. It began at my sister's home in Lincoln, California. We had spent a few days with Gail and Jerry, catching up on each other's lives since I had last seen them. The biggest change was that they had moved from San Jose to Lincoln during my absence.

Late that morning we said our good-byes, and Dave and I headed for home. Hours later we drove into our driveway. I was in a daze as I walked in and looked around. After hugging our son, Russ, I sat on the floor with our two dogs, Wrinkles and Dimples. They sniffed and licked and jumped all over me. Any doubts I had about them remembering me vanished quickly. Russ' dog, Loki, sat back and watched with apprehension. For a while I just sat there looking around the room, playing with the dogs and talking with Russ and Dave. It was good to be back, but still I felt almost like a guest in someone else's place. My home had been "on the road" for over a year, and I was no longer sure where "home" really was.

A couple of days later Dave took me for a drive around town to see changes that had taken place during my absence, the most notable being the loss of some of the buildings that fell in the earthquake of December 22, 2003. Landmark buildings, including the acorn clock tower, had toppled, and two lives had been lost in the quake. Many other buildings had been damaged, and renovations were in progress. The parking lot at the town's library had a section fenced off because of an underground hot sulphur springs that had blown open during the earthquake. Our town had changed and I was struggling to take it all in.

Gradually I fell into somewhat of a routine, but things would never be quite the same. My life was quite different now. I had coped with so many changes and decisions on the Journey. Now I had Dave to talk things over with, and I could enjoy the comfort of him taking me in his arms.

But there was also a lot to deal with emotionally after the Journey. Walking across America had been a truly good experience most of the time. I had seen God work in incredible ways. Day after day our team had felt God's presence and had seen many people who were either encouraged by our walk, or who gave us encouragement. We on the team had spent hours praying together, laughing, talking and enjoying one another. There had been many good times, and a few bad times.

Now that I was home, I found myself thinking about those few bad times more than I wanted to. The good had far outweighed the bad, but my mind kept going back to dwell more on the bad than the good. There were times I had lost my temper and had said or done something that hurt others. Now I was filled with guilt for every one of those times. Certainly others had also lost their tempers, or said and done things that hurt one of us, but those weren't the times that bothered me.

I prayed and steeped myself in Scripture. I talked with my closest friends when the five of us went for our annual retreat. Marilyn suggested I go away for a few days completely alone and just spend time with God. The time alone was very helpful, and I dealt with a lot of things that were on my mind. Things were better after this, but still some feelings of guilt remained.

While it wasn't a deep all-consuming depression, my spirit lingered in a gray world of "why's," "what-if's" or "if only's." My mind wanted to go back in time and change the bad experiences, but that was impossible. This went on for months.

Finally on May 17, 2005, ten months after the Journey was finished, I was on my way to my ladies prayer group and Bible study. Driving along, my heart was heavy, and I longed for relief. I began to pray out loud, and ended with, "Please, LORD, help me."

Joanie, the leader of our Bible study group, had invited her son to come and share. It was the last day before we broke for summer. Mitch Janzen shared a little about his work with Youth for Christ, then led us in an experience that would change my life. Mitch asked us to close our eyes and use our imaginations to take us on a quest. With eyes closed I listened intently, as he took us step by step on this short journey.

Imagine you are walking down a long hallway. Picture in your mind the polished marble floor, and the columns that line either side. Each column stands tall and strong with richly embellished capitals and broad, firm bases. As you pass by each one you feel an urgency to keep moving forward, to see what great thing lies ahead.

Then, suddenly, you see in the distance two huge doors. They look heavy, and you wonder if you'll be able to open them. Still, you feel compelled to keep moving forward. As you get closer you notice two men standing by the door, one on either side. They seem to be guarding the doors, and you notice they are dressed in white, holding sheathed swords. As you slowly approach, perhaps trembling, one of them speaks to you. He tells you to wait, and wants to know by whose authority you dare come to enter these doors. You catch your breath and state that you are a child of the King.

Immediately the huge doors swing open. As you pass through them you marvel at their beauty. Each is made of beautiful wood, polished to a deep lustrous shine that brings out the rich colors and hues of the incredibly beautiful designs chiseled into the wood.

Now you continue forward as you enter a large room. On the far side you notice a wide platform with steps leading up to it. You keep moving toward this platform and soon notice a throne sitting in the middle of it. A bright figure sits on the throne, and you find yourself looking down, unable to look at the purity of the One clothed in bright light. Still, He bids you to come forward. As you approach, you fall to your knees and put your face to the floor. He speaks to you softly, yet crystal clear. His voice has a melodious quality to it as He asks what you want Him to do for you.

Now imagine yourself face down, summoning all your courage, as you ask Him to remove the burden you are carrying. This burden could be anything: the loss of a loved one, a fear that you are carrying around, bitterness that you know you need to get rid of, some sinful deed you are hiding, or guilt over some past wrong.

There is silence now as you wait. You feel his hand gently touch your back as he takes the burden. Instantly you know it is gone. Now He lifts you to your feet and sends you out with a newfound peace, and a freedom that you have not felt in a long time.

As we opened our eyes I felt such a strong peace. I wanted to sing, knowing that I was free from the guilt that had kept me in chains for the last several months. Mitch asked if any of us wanted to share what we had felt, and a few of us expressed what had happened in our hearts.

That burden has gone completely. A few times the enemy has tried to bring it up again, but quickly I am reminded that "He has taken our sins away from us as far as the east is from the west" (Ps. 103:12 NCV).

In the months, and now years, since the Great American Journey ended, we have shared our story with numerous groups—seniors, singles, various church groups, hiking clubs, service clubs, neighborhood groups, and home school classes. Each time we share with people, it's as though we are going back in time and are on the road again. We are thrilled to share the story again and again of what God did on this incredible Journey.

Shortly after we returned home Dave had a special charm made, which I now wear on a chain around my neck. It is a gold map of the United States with each state outlined. A line from Washington State to the bottom of Florida, showing our route, is anchored at each end by delicate rubies marking the starting and ending points of our Journey. People frequently notice it and comment about the beautiful, unusual pendant I wear. This gives yet more opportunities to share and relive the memories. Often it brings new prayer requests from these observers. And so the Journey continues, as we keep on praying and adding even more requests to our books of prayer concerns from across America.

Frequently we are asked if we plan to do anymore walking/prayer expeditions. The answer is always, "Yes." At the time of this writing, we are in the early stages of planning a prayer walk from Florida to the top of Maine. This will include time in Washington, D. C., praying for our government.

Perhaps five years or so after that, we are hoping to walk from the top of Maine to Tijuana at the California-Mexico border, continuing our prayers for America. We realize we are not getting any younger, but I am often encouraged by Caleb's words in Joshua 14:10, 11: ". . . So here I am today, eighty-five years old! I am still as strong today as the day Moses sent me out . . ."

I'm not so sure I'm as strong as I was when I did my first long distance walk, but as long as I am able, and as long as God puts it on my heart, I will continue walking and praying for our nation, my home state of California, San Luis Obispo County, and the city of Paso Robles, as well as the neighborhood where I live, bordered by Highway 46, Golden Hill Road, Union Avenue, and River Road. I do believe that when God gives us a task to do, He will also give us the ability and the strength to do it.

"The LORD bless you and keep you; the LORD make His face shine upon you and be gracious to you; the LORD turn His face toward you and give you peace" (Num. 6:24–26).

# —What A Great Adventure—

### By Joni

The flight from Miami to San Francisco was extremely cramped and tiring. I was so worried about Cassie, shut up in a cage all by herself in the hold of the plane. I had given her tranquillizers at the airport, but she was not used to being confined in such a small area.

Finally we were home at last. Cassie ran into the garden and rolled in the grass, then slowly made her way around every bush and tree, sniffing and peeing! I think she was remembering her favorite spots.

I just wandered through the house. It seemed so quiet and peaceful—and big. Maybe living in a 30 foot motor home made me appreciate individual rooms. It felt so great to be around familiar things again. I sat and looked at a photograph of my husband. Karl had died five years before, and I could hear him saying, "I always knew you were crazy!"

Let me return to the day we finished the walk. With Lyn, JoAn, Dellie, Ronni our driver, and myself heading towards the "Buoy" marker at Key West, it seemed so unreal. Had we really walked across America? There were so many hugs and tears, people congratulating us and asking questions, and more hugs and tears (especially from Lyn and myself).

Amid all the noise and laughter, I took Cassie to sit under a tree in a garden. I felt both elated and depressed. I asked myself, "What am I going to do now? What am I going to do tomorrow?" These questions went through my mind, as I sat looking out at the ocean and listening to the waves breaking on the rocks.

I sat and thought of all the hot humid days, the cold snowy days, the days of watching the trees turn red and gold, and seeing the spring appear with its riotous colors and perfumes. I thought of the disagreements that Lyn and I had, and the laughter that we had shared as we walked the hills, valleys, and long straight roads that seemed never ending.

My family met me at the San Francisco airport to welcome me home. It was so great to hug my daughter, Beth, and my son, Paul, and his wife, Lori. Scott, my eldest grandson, seemed to have grown so tall as he looked down on me from his six-foot-two-inch height. My red-headed grandson, Ryan, looked just as mischievous as ever as he gave me a big bear hug. Five-year-old Kyle was really eager to tell me about kindergarten and to show me he could read. My good friend Joan was there to drive me home. What a pleasure and a blessing to be surrounded by my family and friends.

Now I was home! What luxury! My own shower and toilet, my own big bed to stretch out on, and sleep for as long as I wanted! I gradually got back into a normal routine of housework, shopping, gardening and, of course, hiking with the YWCA group.

Often I just sat and let my mind wander right back to walking the highways. I thought of all the laughter and fun we had meeting people and praying with them. There was the joy of being alive and seeing this wonderful country, and of sitting on the edge of the road, laughing so hard about nothing. There were the beautiful times of prayer, and the peaceful feeling that God was so close and walking with us, always guiding us. He was always there keeping us safe.

Looking back over the 14½ months of the walk, I saw countless beautiful sights and met so many wonderful people. I stood on the crest of snow covered mountains, peering into distant valleys. I observed eagles fly and osprey dive for fish in pristine lakes. There were alligators and armadillos in their natural habitat, swift running pronghorn and grazing bison. I marveled at breathtaking sunsets and incredible sunrises, plodded beside acres of farmlands rich with wheat and corn, through endless prairies and deserts and along busy highways and lonely roads. The night skies were sometimes so black, yet lit with a million shining stars. I watched lightning streak across the sky and heard the thunder roar.

We met people from all walks of life. So many were generous and happy, but many were sad, lonely, and ill. These were the kinds of people we prayed for, and who prayed for us.

When I knelt in the sand with Lyn at the ocean and committed myself to this walk for the Lord, I knew there would be no turning back or leaving the Journey when I got tired or discouraged. Looking back, I feel the Journey led me to a closer understanding in my walk with my God. What a great adventure!

# —Sam's Story—

### By Lyn

As for Sam, her life has changed since the Great American Journey. After she left us, she went to live in Sweetwater, Tennessee, where her family had moved while she was on the walk. She went on to complete her high school studies, partly in Tennessee and partly in California.

For several years Sam had taught sewing to girls and boys of all ages, even to adults, in California. Many wanted one more opportunity to learn this skill from her capable teaching. So she spent several months there, moving from home to home (a week at a time), doing her "Sewing Camps."

Meanwhile she and Chip continued to "date" long distance. After months away in California, Sam and Chip decided to set a wedding date for July 31, 2005. Of course, Dave and I went for the wedding. It was a beautiful event held outdoors on the Harsh Farm. Dave had the privilege of giving the bride away.

Sam and Chip now live in Oak Ridge, Tennessee, where he works as a nurse, and Sam is beginning her nursing studies. Someday they hope to become missionaries to use their nursing skills to help those less fortunate.

It was a privilege to have Sam with us on this walk. Having a teenager along was an asset many times, as she was able to reach out to some in ways that we of the older generation could not. Her youth and vitality were a blessing as she walked tirelessly-or so it seemed. Her maturity was encouraging as she shared her insights with us.

To my granddaughter, Sam, I say, "Thanks, and I love you." "Don't let anyone look down on you because you are young, but set an example for the believers in speech, in life, in love, in faith, and in purity" (1 Tim. 4:12).

The following is part of a college paper written by Sam about our beloved Waliluke. It's a story with a sad ending, as she tells of what happened with Waliluke after she took him to Tennessee to live with her family. I think you'll find it a very fitting epilogue for our little black furry friend.

# —Waliluke—

### By Samantha Gruver

Waliluke and I left the Great American Journey in Arkansas to go home to my family. Leaving the team was hard, but Waliluke was always there to comfort me with a giant lick across my nose. He never adjusted to life in a house. Confused by the many rooms and doors, he often got lost. One day as he lay on our kitchen floor, he spotted a squirrel scurrying up a tree. Without stopping, he jumped right through our door, shattering glass everywhere. He wasn't hurt—just startled by the loud noise.

Then, only a few months after we came home from the walk, Waliluke was stolen right out of our yard! My little brother put signs up for him everywhere. The local newspaper even ran an article about him, but we never found him. This was devastating for me. He had brought joy to many of my days when, otherwise, I would have been depressed.

Losing Waliluke taught me to fully enjoy the friends God gives me now, knowing that, even though I may eventually lose them, I will have ultimately gained by loving and being loved. As Tennyson said, "'Tis better to have loved and lost / Than never to have loved at all."

*Appendix 1*

# MAY, 2003: CHRISTENING "THE CASTLE"

*Note: My son, Russ, visited and helped us three times. Here he shares about his first trip when he came with Dave.*

### by Russ Hanush

I've always loved the road, and I guess my Mom has too. This was her third Great Walk—the first being from Mexico to Oregon in 1983, and the second being from California to Canada in 1993. I had not participated in those adventures, but because I was currently on a sabbatical, I wanted to take the opportunity to join her in this one.

I knew my role would be limited to support, so when my Dad asked me to accompany him to deliver the donated motor home (which the team would come to know as "The Castle"), I was more than happy to help out.

It was sunny in California when we set out. The trip north was uneventful. My Dad and I took turns driving as we made our way up Interstate 5 through California, Oregon, and Washington. One thing I can never get over in all of my travels to the North is the drastic change in weather patterns as you cross from California to Oregon. It has always seemed to me that the border was originally chosen as the point where the sunshine ends and the clouds begin. Not so this time. The sunshine was with us as we crossed into Oregon, cheering us on and lending its encouragement to our mission. Beyond simply delivering The Castle, our secondary aim was to iron out any remaining problems, and learn the little tricks it would take to keep the motor home going for a full year. It had received a very thorough servicing, donated by Geoff Lyons in Paso Robles, California before we left. However, before that it had sat for years in storage, so we expected some trials. On that count our expectations were unfounded—to our great satisfaction. The Castle performed valiantly all the way to where we were to meet the team. The only problem encountered was that the automatic step from outside into the living area would not work consistently for us.

We met up with the team in Bellingham, WA. They had been walking for two days now. The sun was now a memory, the clouds draping us in a drizzle not uncommon to northern Washington. The team was all dressed in their rain gear—ponchos, hoods, and booties. Although lacking in sunshine, the drizzle itself contributes to the beauty of Washington. The pines and firs are thick, green, and full. People's lawns there are seldom brown. Since it was spring the flowers were in bloom, and I distinctly remember the smell of honeysuckle in the air.

After lunch with the team, my Dad and I set out to find a campground, which would be the team's first opportunity to try out the motor home. Since their plan was to move it once a week or so, we settled on a campground near Concrete, Washington on Highway 20. No one was home when we got there, so we parked and waited. Soon enough the owners came along and set us up in a spot. This was the first of many spots that would provide a temporary home to my mother and her companions for the next twelve months (or so we thought), as they made their way across America.

Over the next couple of days my Dad and I showed the interested team members what we had learned about their new home. Mom took on the dirty work of tending the sewage lines—something even I wanted nothing to do with. Joni took to the chore of packing up the insides and battening down the hatches. The rest of the team seemed content with their cabin back up the road near Concrete.

During these few nights, "The Castle" accommodated my Mom and Dad, and me. Joni joined the rest of the team in their cabins, for the sake of space. My niece Samantha, who would get to know The Castle very well, was not with the team yet.

There were a few items left on the list of repairs we wanted to accomplish before Dad and I left the team to their own devices and ingenuity in maintaining their new home. We set out to find a mechanic who could come out to the campsite to do the repairs. He addressed some plumbing issues, both water and propane.

Then the most persistent issue with "The Castle" reared its ugly head for the first time. Oh, it wasn't much at first, but eventually it would be the death of their new home. The first time my Mom tried to start the engine it simply refused. Since it had given us no problems on the trip up, we simply blamed her—wrongly, I might add. We worked on her technique, thinking it was flooded. We bought starter fluid and taught her how to use it, and that got it going. We thought it was no longer a problem.

My Dad and I headed back to the sunshine, taking Joni's car for the trip back. We were hesitant to leave them on their own, but knew that we had to do it. It was in their hands, but more importantly, in God's hands now.

One of the most blessed results of this visit occurred on the trip back when we stopped to visit my Grandmother, Elinore Hanush. Unbeknownst to us this was the last time we would see her alive. Because of that, this trip holds a special place in my heart, and I dedicate this passage to her memory.

*Appendix 2*

# DRIVER AND
# "JACK (OR JUDI) OF ALL TRADES"

NOTE: *It was a real blessing to have Judi drive for us and help us get organized that first month. You'll enjoy reading her thoughts about her time with us.*

### by Judi Cox

The Great American Journey was one of the most fun and meaningful experiences the Lord has allowed me. Not only did I get to see some new sights in this beautiful country of ours, but I also made new friends. I especially enjoyed meeting Lyn's family and friends. The trust, care, and fellowship of Christian sisters are some of the joys of belonging to Christ.

My main tasks during the short time I was with the team were to drive the van to the start of the walk each day, be available for errands, get groceries, medicines, dog needs, and RV provisions. I also washed, dried and folded clothes, and helped with meals. I fixed up the RV so it was more liveable, putting up curtains, hooks and towel bars, lining drawers, and whatever else needed doing.

One fun activity was measuring and drawing large 8" x 12" letters across the length of the RV that read "Great America Journey" with "praying for" vertically down the middle. Joni Balog got to paint inside the letters after I left (due to advancing cancer).

Besides driving across the gorgeous, awe-inspiring Cascade mountains and seeing Diablo and Ross Lakes, I got to visit Anacortes Island near Seattle, as well as Spokane and the mighty Grand Coulee Dam.

There were many funny incidents, but one in particular I'd like to share. JoAn Thomas and I had gone to Pioneer Park south of Ferndale, Washington. While looking at some old time houses we saw a dead mole. Later we saw "Mole's Funeral Home." We were really impressed that they cared so much for their tiny moles!

High points of the trip were the churches we visited each Sunday; the devotions and prayer time we had each morning; the friendly people we met on the way; unusual sights, like the numerous bunnies at Marblemount; and especially the camaraderie we experienced together on the walk. Yes, we had difficulties, like an overheated van, sewer stoppage, and others. But we all experienced the wonderful way the Lord provided for our every need.

## Lyn

Judi is still battling cancer, but continues to have a very positive attitude and deep trust in God. She has already expressed a desire to drive half-days for our 2008 walk up the east coast, and to walk half days if she is able.

# MEMOIRS OF MY WALK WITH "THE GREAT AMERICAN JOURNEY"

---

*NOTE: Though Anne was the oldest member of our team, she had loads of energy. She was always pleasant, and truly a valuable asset to the team. Enjoy her sharing about her experiences.*

**by Anne Foster** *(resident of Bear, Delaware, and the oldest person on the team)*

I was hiking with the Florida Trail Association around Lake Okeechobee—a 10-day trip—and got to make many new friends. When one friend, Coni Harris, heard I was making plans to go to California, she said, "I know someone you should get in touch with! She will be glad to do some hiking with you!" and she gave me a copy of Lyn's newsletter, with her address and phone number, of course, but more importantly the plans for walking across the United States. Oh, I want to do that, I thought.

I love to hike and walk (my favorite pastime), and how wonderful it would be to see the whole country on foot. But the most wonderful thing about the walk would be that we were doing it for a purpose, to glorify God by proclaiming Him when and where we could, and by earnestly praying for our country, for those towns we were passing through and for the people we met.

So I got to meet Lyn when I was on my trip to California, and what a delightful person she is. We hiked on some local trails she knew, and did a lot of talking about ourselves, getting to know each other. When we said goodbye, after a nice dinner with her and her husband Dave, she invited me to join the team. I was so thrilled that I had passed muster, and also I thought Lyn was a dedicated Christian, a good organizer, and would be fun to be with.

When I told my children of my plans, they advised me not to plan to do the whole walk, for various reasons. And then, also there were the finances. I could not afford to pay my way for the whole trip. Another reason, and probably the most important, was that my body most likely would not hold up that long! So I decided to be there at the beginning and walk for a month, hopefully through the state of Washington.

Well, we didn't get to finish the whole state in the month of May, but we almost made it. Maybe some of the other contributors to this treatise will explain the problems we had (mostly with the van), but the time we did have together was incomparable. I loved walking along the shoreline of Puget Sound. And then the cities, towns and little villages we went through were so charming. Many of the smaller towns had lists of their citizens who were serving in the Armed Forces. At this time the United States was in the midst of fighting in the Middle East. The churches we visited also gave us names of those in their congregation who were in the service. Our hearts went out to those who were anxious for their loved ones.

At first, the weather was comfortable, and our mileage was limited. As the month wore on, it got hotter, then colder (in the Cascades), then hotter again, and we had to walk in the morning, take a break, and then walk some more in the early evening. We got stronger as we went along, and maybe another journalist will give details of the mileage we gained.

The scenery was spectacular. The Cascades were awesome—still covered in snow. The town of Concrete was something else! We were there a week, and got to know the area. A famous author, Tobias Wolfe, went to school there, and I read one of his books from the local library. Big concrete silos are still standing in the town, memorials to what used to be. A beautiful lake and resort was a short distance to the north, and Grand Coulee Dam was not far to the south. The people were friendly, and during this time Dave and some others visited us and walked with us.

Then there was the town of Winthrop, made over to look like you were in the middle of the Wild West. Mostly I remember Lyn and I having ice cream cones, eating them while sitting in the saddle stools on Main Street.

At one point we had a visit with Lyn's family at a beautiful family compound on top of a hill, way out in the country along a dirt road. We don't have dirt roads in Delaware. This was a wonderful time of visiting with another lovely Christian family.

So-o-o . . . lovely walking, lovely scenery, lovely people—but most of all the lovely time we had each morning with our prayer and Bible study. Because we had so much to talk about from our Bible readings that we spent too much time at it, instead of getting busy with our Journey, so we put it off until later in the day. But there is nothing to compare with starting the day with Bible study and prayer with friends. Lyn, Joni, JoAn, Judi, Samantha: Thank you all for the inspiring times we had together.

So this is the lesson to be learned. When you do something for others, you get repaid much more than you give. I pray that many hearts were touched, that many believers were inspired by our efforts, that God blesses our prayers for our country, and that all were blessed as I have been.

★ ★ ★ ★ ★ ★ ★ ★ ★ ★ ★ ★ ★ ★

# AUGUST, 2003: BIG SKY MONTANA

---

*Note: Russ' descriptions here are fascinating as he tells of his struggles to get to us, and the help he was able to give us as we walked.*

## by Russ Hanush

It was time to hit the road again. Since my last trip to see the Team, I had moved to Paso Robles to help my Dad while Mom was on the road. Paso Robles has a very distinct microclimate that is perfect for wine grapes, but for a Northern California boy the heat during the summer is just oppressive, so I was anxious to go. From Paso Robles it's a pretty even distance, north or south, to Interstate 80 at the Nevada/Utah border. I had rarely taken the southern route before, so I decided to go south. This decision turned out to be a somewhat formative moment that would have its effect on me for years to come.

For the first leg of the trip I planned on stopping in eastern Nevada to see Great Basin National Park. I left in the late afternoon, so most of the drive would be at night when it was coolest. I hoped to reach Great Basin by late morning the following day. My first stop was for gas in Bakersfield, California. I gassed up and continued on. The sky was clear and it didn't seem unusual that the wind was kicking through the windmill farms as I went over Tehachapi Pass. When I got to Barstow I turned onto Interstate 15 just as the first drops of rain were hitting my windshield. It wasn't even enough to dampen the wiper blades, so I let the wind take care of it.

Off to my right there was a flash of lightning. My dog, Loki, flattened his ears and buried his head in the sleeping bag in the back seat of my truck. There was more lightning and lots of thunder. Then the rain began to pour. The wipers were certainly damp now as they worked at full speed to barely give me a view of the road. I thought about stopping, but the road was taking me over open hills and down through the gullies between them. The desert terrain was ripe for flash floods, and the high ground was prime for lightning strikes. I decided it was best to just keep going and time-average the combination of hazards. Visibility was really poor at this point so the going was rather slow, but I figured it was better to head for civilization than to be a sitting duck in a desert thunderstorm.

As the lights of Las Vegas came into view, so did the road. It was just about dawn and as the sun rose it chased away the clouds, making for one beautiful sunrise. I stopped for breakfast and then began that day's final leg north toward Ely, Nevada. I found a nice secluded campground outside the National Park and set up camp with the intention of making a day trip to the park the next day. My truck, however, had other plans.

I woke up the next morning, and as usual when camping, I opened the tent and lay there for a while listening to the birds sing, breathing in the fresh country air, and letting Loki roam. From this vantage point I could also see the ground under my truck —and it was soaked in fresh oil! I jumped up to see if it was mine. Discovering it was transmission fluid, I checked the level, only to find that it was near empty. I dumped in the spare quart I always carry and got the level back up onto the dipstick. I knew I had to get more, so I altered my plans, skipping the park and continuing on over to Ely instead. The bright side of this new plan was that it would give me an extra day with the team.

As I set off down the road I noticed the transmission was slipping; it didn't start out that way. Now I'm a pretty competent mechanic, and I understood the risks and rewards of what I was about to do. I prayed to God, verbalizing my hopes that it was His will that I continue on, rather than let this stop me. Now I was on "a mission."

Ely was still a good 60 miles away. I wanted to top off the transmission as soon as possible, but when I got there, it was nothing more than a gas station and a visitor's center with a scenic view of Great Basin National Park. They were out of the fluid I needed and directed me down the road to Elko. I was getting pretty nervous at this point, and the fluid level was just at the tip of the stick. As I made my way up over the pass to Elko I could feel the slippage getting worse. My heart was up in my throat, and my head was throbbing from the anxiety. I pushed on.

Finally, I pulled into Elko. The first gas station only had two quarts. This got me up to halfway between empty and full, but I wanted it full, with a spare quart or two for the road. I found a mini-mart with a good stock of fluid to round out my supplies, thanked God for his watchful eyes, and set off. When I pulled into West Wendover at the Nevada-Utah border for gas I checked my levels again. To my great consternation I found that I was losing fluid at an enormous rate. Once again the stick was dry. I stocked up with a case of fluid, with an eye for the long haul across the Great Salt Flats of Utah. I made a point of checking the level early and often from here on. By the time I reached Northeastern Utah I had a system down. All I had to do was stop every thirty minutes and pour in a quart, and that way the level was always somewhere between "full" and "add."

I couldn't find a campground, so I drove all night. I rationalized that driving at night would keep the transmission cooler, but it still took a quart every thirty minutes. Loki and I traveled across all of Wyoming this way. He didn't mind because he was getting to mark his territory in great detail all the way from Nevada to Montana. We made camp at the reservoir near Guernsey, Wyoming that night. I wanted to be fresh when I finally caught up with the Team.

The next day I met up with the Team at the KOA Kampground in Hardin, Montana. They were still out walking for the day, so I set up my campsite kitty-corner from theirs. At this point the Team consisted of my Mom, Joni, and my niece Samantha. With three women in the motor home and cooperative weather, I felt no need to infringe on their privacy. When they got back we said our hellos, talked about the camp, their day, and my rather eventful drive out.

The following morning I drove them to their previous day's stopping point just north of Billings, Montana. After I dropped them off I planned on getting some breakfast in town and then hitting some media outlets to try and generate some publicity for their cause, but God consolidated things for me.

As I pulled into the parking lot at Burger King there was a van with a broadcast antenna on top in the parking lot. I ordered my breakfast, looking around the whole time trying to identify the occupant(s) of the vehicle I had seen. There were not a lot of people in the restaurant, and certainly no one who jumped out as a news anchor. The most likely dressed person had his son with him, so I figured it was a long shot but asked him anyway. Sure enough, it was his truck. He had just decided to bring his son with him that day. He was excited to hear about my Mom's walk, and after we spoke he drove out to interview her on the road.

With such encouragement, this really got me going. I went to the local TV station, the major newspaper in town, and a couple of smaller outlets. One turned out to be a paper for legal notices, but he was still very interested in what the Team was up to. After lunch at the park with the Team I tried the radio stations—the ones I could find, at least. By the end of the day that market was saturated with stories of the three ladies walking across America.

Now I had a transportation problem to deal with. As much as I would prefer to stay on the road for months at a time, I knew I had to go back eventually, and my trip was never meant to be a long one. So the next day I had to begin dealing with my truck. This wasn't too hard in Hardin, Montana, because there were two dealers in town. I had known my truck was beyond what I was interested in repairing before I left. Once I added in a transmission that needed fluid every thirty minutes I knew I wanted to trade it in. Being a big fan of GM vehicles I started at the only GM dealer in town, Incredible

Chevrolet. They really lived up to their name. Now God had a plan for this all along, because if there was anywhere in the US that the truck was going to get maximum value it was deep in the heart of cowboy country. Incredible Chevrolet had two options for me, but neither was ready for their lot quite yet. They asked for a couple of days to see what they could accomplish for me. This worked out just right, as I had come up there with every intention of driving for the Team and getting to do some walking with my Mom.

I went back to the campground for the day. It was the week after Labor Day so the place was deserted, and I found it very easy to get caught up on laundry, showers, reading, and rest. When they finally got "home" that night they had an extra dog with them —Ohwashtadryabillywilliwalimathewmarklukejohn . . . or something like that. I never did get the name of that dog straight. I was glad when they shortened it to Waliluke!

The next two days I spent on the road with the Team. Joni had been driving the shuttle van, parking it, and walking back toward the rest of the team. I wanted to spend some time on the road with my Mom, but also felt that Joni should be getting to walk with the Team since she was a member, and I was just there to support them. I let the three of them walk together the first day. The day's segment took them through a construction zone and onto the Crow Indian reservation. As is typical of stereotypes, the Crow failed to live up to the (undeserved) reputation that preceded them. Their reception of the Team, and myself, was very warm. They were eager to share their culture and their spiritual needs with the Team, and we were all invited to join them at a tribal celebration reenacting a famous battle.

The second of those two days was spent on the road to St. Xavier, Montana, where "Big Sky Country" must get its name. The road wound off forever into the distance, finally meeting the sky some 20 to 30 miles away in each direction. This was the perfect setting we had been seeking for a team picture. After spending some time working on that, I walked a mile or two with them, then back to the van. As I drove, the terrain changed from open, rolling, grassy hills to tree covered rangeland. With the next shift in the landscape the opening words of "America the Beautiful:" "O beautiful for spacious skies, For amber waves of grain, For purple mountain majesties, Above the fruited plain . . ." were manifest before my eyes, for the hills faded into a scene of purple mountains. The earth that composed them was literally purple! I felt as though I was on hallowed ground and whispered a prayer of praise and thanks to God for sharing the wonders of his creation with me.

After such a gorgeous scene I found it quite regrettable the next day, my final day there, that I had to deal with getting a new car instead of being on the road with the Team. I went back to Incredible Chevrolet, but they weren't quite ready for me yet. After killing some time with test drives and paper work, I finally drove out of there in a used Dodge Neon, traded straight across for my broken down four-wheel drive truck. Not only did that Neon get me home, but it is still running strong three years later. It also took me out to see the Team one more time the next spring, but that's another story.

*Appendix 5*

# SWEET TEA AND ARTICHOKES

---

NOTE: *Sam was not with us when we walked through Tennessee, but I think you'll enjoy her descriptions of her new home state, as written for a college class. The trip she talks about at the beginning actually took place during the first week-and-a-half of our Journey.*

## by Samantha Gruver

Hey, Sam, wake up! We're flying over Tennessee. I opened my eyes and looked over at my mom, then out the airplane window. Everything below me was green and wet—nothing like the dry, rolling hills of California. I was a California Girl, and this was my first trip to Tennessee. Little did I know how completely different things would be in this green state with no beaches, or how observing those differences would change the way I thought.

The first differences I noticed were on the long drive from Nashville to Sweetwater. Interstate 40 was nothing like the freeways I was used to in California. There were tulips growing in the divider! There was almost no traffic, and definitely no traffic jams. Our Tennessean driver stayed at the speed limit, or just under it, the whole time. Why would someone want to move so slowly?! I was used to people rushing everywhere, going 80 miles an hour, when the posted speed limit was 65. Yet, I enjoyed the beautiful landscape so much more because we were moving so slowly. I began to wonder how much beauty I'd missed in California by trying to keep up with everyone else.

As we drove through the towns and cities along the way, I noticed a peculiar thing: there were no fences around the yards. Did people not want privacy from each other? I couldn't imagine being able to see into my neighbor's yard like that. What a thought: letting them see everything that happens in my yard! I didn't want to know if my neighbor got drunk every Friday night, or if he never mowed his lawn. Another odd thing about the houses was that they were all very different from each other. You might have one house that looked like it had been built in 1910 standing next to one that was built ten years ago. To me, it looked mismatched and tasteless to have homes so different next to each other. I thought about my home in Los Banos. It, like all the other houses surrounding it, had a red tile roof, light colored stucco on the outside, a little double driveway with a cement walkway to the front door, and a small front lawn with built-in sprinklers to keep it from turning brown in the dry air. What would it be like to have a house next door that looked different from mine? Once I got used to the idea, it was kind of cool to think that the differences in the appearance of the houses was a way of communicating who they were. The seven-foot-high fences and identical houses of California kept us from getting to know each other. It was more comfortable to stay under the illusion that we were all the same.

During our ten-day trip, my mom fell in love with the state, and only six months later, my whole family moved to the little town of Sweetwater in eastern Tennessee. The move was quite a culture shock. The winter was so cold, and to my five-year-old brother's amazement, it actually snowed! Spring was beautiful. The trees grew back their green leaves and the flowers began to bloom. Yet, to our dismay, it rained every day without fail. Not a drenching, freezing cold rain that lasted for hours like those in California, but a hard, warm rain that lasted no more than 30 minutes and left clouds of steam coming up from the asphalt. The short, warm showers became increasingly disappointing as the summer got warmer and more humid. I felt like the heat and "thick air," as I called it, was going to suffocate me. Oh, if only I could go home to the 100-degree, dry, windy summers of California! I found myself running outside when it started to rain, only to come back wet and disillusioned because the rain drops weren't cold and refreshing. Although I hated the idea of not having an air conditioner on such hot days, it forced me to go outside with a cup of ice water and simply enjoy the slight breeze blowing through the trees. Maybe it wasn't such a bad thing to stop and enjoy life once in a while, and not be so caught up in accomplishing things, as I had been in California.

One of the biggest differences I have noticed between California and Tennessee is the food. I grew up in a small agricultural town in the San Joaquin Valley of California with a population of about 30,000. Our town produced an assortment of dairy products, cotton, and many fruits and vegetables, including tomatoes, cantaloupe, honeydew, watermelon, and corn. We had no end to the supply of inexpensive, tasty fresh fruits and vegetables. I remember summers when my Dad would bring home a flat of fresh strawberries each night. My three sisters and I would give no thought to eating the whole thing in one sitting. In Tennessee, I go to the grocery store and pass up the strawberries because they cost $2.50 for one little box!

I have also discovered that many Tennesseans aren't familiar with as large a variety of vegetables as my California friends are. Take artichokes, for example. A year ago, I went to Kroger in search of artichokes. No one knew what I was talking about. I checked each time I visited the grocery store, and finally I found them, unmarked and in a corner. When I went to pay for them, the girl at the cash register gave me a weird look and asked, "Do you know what these poky green things are called?" Even worse, when I brought them home, I had to explain to my Tennessee husband how to cook and eat them. Later, he said, "I had never had one of those, and upon taking the first bite I never will again."

Food has been one of the hardest things for me to get used to in Tennessee. I can't stand how everything is deep-fried! When I took a bite of deep-fried squash, I could feel the grease turning to fat in my veins. The worst of all is sweet tea. It's shocking to take a sip of what you think is going to be bitter iced tea and, instead, taste only sugar. As my husband says, "It's not sweet tea unless it has so much sugar you could pour it over pancakes as syrup." I may not like the unhealthy side of the food in Tennessee, but it has taught me how I can get much more than a full stomach out of a meal when I share the enjoyment with friends and family as is the custom in Sweetwater.

I have learned a lot from the culture in Tennessee. When I first came here, I found it odd that people spent hours in the evening sitting on their front porches drinking sweet tea and watching the cars go by. Or that when a stop light turns green, it takes the car in front at least ten seconds to start moving again. As a result of this laid-back attitude, I am learning to slow down and relax. It is probably one of the toughest lessons I have ever learned (as evidenced by the speeding ticket I got two months ago).

In thinking through the many differences, strengths, and weaknesses of these two states, I cannot say that one is better than the other, or even that the people in one state are better than those in the other state. They both have their beauty and their quirks, their kind people and their unique culture. I truly love both. And although I love the mountains full of green trees and the selfless people of Tennessee, my heart will always be in California with the softly rolling, golden hills and the majestically peaceful beaches.

*Appendix 6*

# SPRING, 2004: SOUTHERN HOSPITALITY

*NOTE: The trip Russ made to meet us his third time is described here in vivid detail. You'll enjoy his thrilling account of the scenes that greeted him along the way, and then of the joy he gave the Team as he opened his heart to serve us in many incredible ways.*

### by Russ Hanush

The loss of Sam was a blow to the Team, but on the bright side, it gave me an excuse for another road trip. It didn't seem right for Mom to have to walk so much of the way alone, or for Joni to have to miss so much of the route in order to drive the shuttle van forward. I eagerly volunteered to join them. Since the last trip had been compromised by car problems, I threw a quick tune-up on the Neon; just spark plugs and an air filter. I packed up the car and was ready to hit the road.

My first stop was planned for Lake Havasu on the Arizona side. I had never been there, but had heard it's quite nice. Unfortunately the Arizona Department of Transportation had other plans for the unacquainted. I arrived in the midst of a major road construction project, and all of the road signs were down. If you knew where you were going, there was no problem, but for a first timer to the area it was very frustrating. After driving back and forth looking for the turnoff for hours, I gave up and decided to drive all night to make time. I got back on the freeway and headed east.

Apparently Arizona does not ticket semi-trucks, no matter how fast they are going. Every truck on the road was passing me like I was standing still, at 75–80 miles per hour. They would bear down on me, blinding me with their headlights. If I dared to get in the left lane to pass another motorist, the truckers would ride my bumper, blinding me with their lights in my side view mirrors, making it impossible for me to see when it was safe to get back over into the right lane. This went on for hours, and at no time did I ever see even one Highway Patrol in the entire state of Arizona. One trucker even went as far as to cut so close in front of me that the rear end of his trailer literally passed over the hood of my car!

It was also during this mad midnight dash across Arizona that the Neon picked up a heavy stumble in the engine. Since I had just replaced the plugs and filter, I knew that if it was anything I would be able to fix on the road, it would have to be the spark plug wires. I made the decision that I would head for the next big town, which happened to be Albuquerque, New Mexico, and from that point on I would get off the freeway and take back roads to relieve the stress of driving with those crazy truckers.

I pulled into Albuquerque in time for breakfast and got to the auto parts store just as they were opening. I got my plug wires and tried to change them in the parking lot, only to discover that they were indeed the problem. One of the wires was rotting away near the spark plug, down a narrow hole about six-inches deep. I knew it was going to take great care and patience to save the day. I decided to go ahead and live with the stumble until I got settled into a campsite further down the road, so I could take my time with the repair. At Santa Rosa, New Mexico, I turned south off the freeway, vowing to avoid it as much as possible from there on out.

My new route took me straight into the old stompin' grounds of Billy The Kid near Sumner Lake. I pulled into the campground at the lake in the early afternoon and set up camp. The lake was low and the campground deserted. Loki and I had it all to ourselves. The desert landscape provided little shelter from the wind that picked up in the afternoon, so that first night we had to do without a campfire. I hung tarps in the little shelter provided at the campsite and finally got it fancy enough to where I could light the camp stove. We had dinner, did a little reading by lantern light, and went to sleep.

The next day Loki and I did a little exploring. We went down by the inlet to the lake, where it looked like ancient lava flows had formed layer after layer of what were now huge slabs of rock. Over the hill behind our campsite we found an old explosives bunker built into the hillside. Imagining that this could have been Billy The Kid's hideout at one time or another, I tried to get inside to see what it looked like. Old timbers fallen from the roof were blocking the door, so I did the next best thing I could think of. I stuck my camera through the arm's width opening and took a picture. The flash must have startled them because all of a sudden a loud squeeking and whooshing broke the silence of the deserted campground. Bats! Lots of them! They flew out through the partially open door, darkening the sun and pushing Loki and me back in surprise.

That was enough exploring for one morning. We made our way back to our campsite and had some lunch. Then I set about repairing the Neon. Three of the plug wires gave no resistance and were easily swapped out. I saved the worst for last. When I pulled it, the connector separated from the wire, leaving a piece on the spark plug. It was too big to let me get at the spark plug to pull it out, but it was also too small to reach with any tool I had. I started digging through my gear to see what kind of options I could come up with to solve this little problem. String was too weak, and rope was too big to fit down the little hole. Then I saw it! I pulled the speaker wire off of the ghetto blaster I used to listen to my CDs, cut off about 18 inches of it, and stripped it. I formed a little loop with it, stuck it down the hole, hooked the broken connector and pulled. It didn't budge! I pulled harder and it still didn't budge. Finally, with all my strength, I braced myself and tugged as hard as I could. It sent me flying. Luckily the connector came out from under the hood with me. I went back to the car, put the last wire on, and fired it up—smooooooooth!

The next morning I broke camp and headed out in earnest to meet up with the Team. I cut across the Texas Panhandle where everybody has huge, perfectly manicured, yards. I drove through the Red River Valley and saw that the river really was red. Once I hit Oklahoma it was getting near dusk, so I found a campground at Lake Altus. This was a busy campground full of both families and hunters. One group of young hunters set up camp right next to me and started smoking their kill. They were a boisterous bunch, but the howling wind and the jets coming in low to the nearby airport drowned them out completely.

More than anything, it was the wind that drove me from my bed just before midnight. Unable to sleep through it, I decided to make the best of it and hit the road for another night of driving. The hunters' fire was just starting to die down and they were concerned that they were the reason for my leaving. They offered me deer jerky and asked me if I wanted to join them. I assured them it was only the wind, and that I was on a mission to meet the Team. I explained my Mom's walk across America and said my good-byes as I hit the road. After a few more hours of driving, I could feel the exhaustion coming on, so I pulled down a small dirt road and slept until sunrise. Oh, what a beautiful sunrise it was!

I stopped for breakfast in Lawton, Oklahoma, and made the Arkansas border by about noon. I made camp at Blue Lake just past DeQueen, Arkansas. The next morning when I went to pack up the car I was met with yet another challenge—a flat tire. I unpacked the trunk, put on the spare, and drove back to DeQueen. I found a station to fix the flat and got to talking about my Mom's journey with the owner of the station. She was also a great supporter of our troops and had arranged a mailing campaign in town to get letters and supplies to our soldiers in Iraq. We exchanged stories while my tire was being fixed, and then I headed back out to the campground. I could feel it as I got closer and closer to the Team. I was starting to get into the swing of this and felt good about spreading the word on my jaunt through the South.

I stayed one more night at Blue Lake, hoping to meet up with the Team in just over one day. I made my way through Arkansas and across the northwest corner of Mississippi, hoping to find a camp site there. Alas, there were no open campgrounds to be found until I was past Memphis, Tennessee. It was already nightfall and we had half a state to go, but I wanted to be rested up when I met up with the Team. I found a campground at Meeman-Shelby state Park, had dinner and a small fire, and hit the sack. After about an hour or so my neighbors from the next campsite over pulled in. They were talking and laughing enough to keep me awake. This time, however, instead of hitting the road I decided "if you can't beat 'em, join 'em."

I went over and started talking with them. I told them about my Mom's walk; we talked about music; we talked about physics; we talked about philosophy. They told me about their home in Indiana, I told them about California. Their names were Jim, Cody, Cara, and Justin, and they were about twenty years younger than me, but it was amazing how much we all had in common, even separated by such great geographic and chronologic distances.

The next thing we knew it was morning. We all had to pack up and go that next day, but rather than go our separate ways, "The Kids" decided to take the final leg of my solo journey to meet the Team with me. They followed me to Jackson, Tennessee, where we finally met up with the Team for lunch. We all talked for a while, took each other's pictures, and when they were ready to go we all said our good-byes. But only after deciding that my trip home, after my time on the walk, would take me through Indiana for a visit to their home town in West Lafayette; after all Indiana is just a hop, skip, and a jump out of the way from Alabama to California isn't it?

That first half-day with the Team was marked by a vicious downpour with thunder and lightning. I had planned on leaving The Castle to the ladies and camping in my tent while I was with them, but with the rain, and lightning, and whatnot, I decided to move into The Castle with them. On my first day driving with them I made it clear that I was there only to support them. I wanted Joni to get to walk as much of the time with Mom as possible.

It took a few days for me to get used to their method. The trick was to drive far enough so they could get some uninterrupted miles in, but not too far as to be simply leaving them abandoned on the side of the road with no support. The first three days I was with them took them through Jackson, Tennessee, then on south as far as Selmer, just shy of the state line.

Then came my first moving day with them. We decided that I would drive my car ahead, with enough of a lead to scout out a few campgrounds for The Castle. We ended up in Tupelo, Mississippi, the birthplace of Elvis Presley. It was a nice little RV park run by a very friendly lady named Jeannine, with the cutest little beagle that just followed her around everywhere she went. The Wisteria were in full bloom and all of Mississippi that we saw had a brilliant purple hue from all of the flowers and especially the bountiful Wisteria.

As the Team walked south from Selmer toward the Mississippi state line, the road changed from a four lane divided highway into a major freeway. We all had two problems with this: safety, and a lack of contact with the people in the towns we were passing through—although Mom didn't mind all of the extra cars she got to wave at as she walked. I began to find ways for them to get off the freeway and pass through the nearby towns so that they could meet the people. At first it just started out by taking them over to the frontage road that ducked behind a hill or two as it veered away from the freeway. Pretty soon we could no longer see the freeway, and little shops and people's houses began to come into view.

I was also getting better at finding good places to park the shuttle van while I waited for them. I liked to find hills so I could watch for the Team with my binoculars, or, as Joni had suggested, church parking lots were handy, with plentiful parking during the middle of the week. At one such church an elderly couple that pulled into the parking lot approached me. I explained about my Mom and Joni walking across America. The couple was thrilled to hear about their adventures and asked us all to join them for their seniors' luncheon. The pastor of their church, Morris, joined them for their luncheon and the subject turned to prayer requests for the community. This was when I first started noticing how bad the methamphetamine problem was in the South. Morris mentioned his ministry to the recovering addicts in his community, and, putting two and two together, I made the connection to the excessive amounts of traffic I had seen while parked near a schoolyard. The scope of that affliction was only just becoming evident. We returned to Morris' church for Palm Sunday services, but sadly, he was out of town, so we missed him on that visit.

As the Team walked further south and east I found more side routes for them to take. I started using a computer-mapping program, finding the best side routes with the shortest mileage; after all, they did want to finish sometime that year. The next few days took us closer to the Alabama border, and soon it was time to move The Castle again. This time we found a State Park in Alabama to camp at—Lake Lurleen State Park, named after Alabama's only female governor, the wife of former Governor George Wallace. It was there that we met Billy, the pastor of a Truckers' Chapel near Tuscaloosa.

As we moved deeper into the South I started having more problems with the places I was finding to park. In one spot between Vernon and Fayette, Alabama, people came running out of a house shooting guns. I had no way of telling if they were shooting at me or just trying to get dinner, but I took no chances and routed the Team away from that road. In a couple of other places south of Fayette I seemed to draw excessive attention just sitting there in a van for no apparent reason. The first time I just moved on to another spot. The second time I only became aware of how close I had come to having the cops called on me when I picked up the Team. I had noticed the stares when the same carload of people drove by—twice, while I was sitting there. Then, Mom and Joni told me that some people they had talked to up the road a bit were finally able to put two and two together when they heard how they were walking across America with a driver in a shuttle van.

Sometimes the mapping program was not so hot. One particular spur in Alabama led us into a dead end where the old road was being cut off by a new six-lane freeway still under construction. Luckily I had taken to pre-driving the route and was able to reroute them before they went too far out of their way. Other times the mapping program provided routing alternatives through country that the Team never would have had the pleasure of seeing without it. One such portion took us through West Blocton, just south of Tuscaloosa.

Before passing through Tuscaloosa, however, Easter Sunday came upon us. We were still camped at Lake Lurleen, and our neighbor Billy invited us to his Truckers' Chapel for Easter services. I was especially touched by that congregation, because of the contrast to the truckers I had been abused by on the freeway in Arizona. The experience provided some much needed healing for my soul from that terrifying episode.

When we got to Tuscaloosa, we met Jim Randall. He set the Team up with a spot on the "Good Day Tuscaloosa" show. Jim was a very accommodating host and took us all over town showing us the sites. After Mom and Joni's appearance on "Good Day Tuscaloosa" he took us to lunch and then on to the local arboretum. It was spectacular as arboretums go. The foliage was dense and green with exotic plants spread all throughout, and a viewing platform stretching out from a hillside to a view dozens of feet up in the thick trees. Jim wrapped up the tour of Tuscaloosa by taking us to The University of Alabama. Besides moving days, and Sundays, this was the only day off from walking my entire time with the Team.

After Tuscaloosa it was time to move again. This move took us to Jemison in central Alabama. By now I was getting really good at finding exciting routes for the Team to walk. By cutting a diagonal between two main routes I was able to save mileage, which equaled saving time, and keep them in the far back woods where, when you come to a town, you are literally immersed in it. The most memorable of those is West Blocton.

I had found a nice place to park near a creek that flowed under a bridge. As I frequently did, I let Loki out of the van and took him to the water to stretch our legs and let him have a fresh drink. To my surprise, when I came back up the bank of the creek, there was a police officer peering into the van. Being very careful not to startle an armed officer, I called out from across the street that I belonged with that van and could I help him? I handed him one of the cards that had come in very handy during these types of encounters and explained to him what I was doing there and what the Team was doing in general. He introduced himself as Ralph and explained to me what all the fuss had been about my parking the van along the roads through Mississippi and Alabama. It turns out it was related to the methamphetamine problem in those parts, as vans and trucks are used as mobile labs for manufacturing the drugs.

Once we had everything straightened out I told him that the Team was probably about at the other end of his town right now. Ralph and his brother Cliff, also a police officer in town, drove out to meet them. They picked them up, drove them back to get me, took us all into town to see if we could find the mayor and the police chief, and then took us to lunch where we met the pastor of their church Pastor Danny. The brothers had police business to tend to, so we ate lunch with Pastor Danny. After lunch he invited us to his church for services the next Sunday.

The next couple days of walking led the Team through some of the farthest back roads I was to take them on, providing some of the most spectacular views on this journey. Coming over one rise, the landscape stretched out in front of us. The view was probably a good 40 or 50 miles, and all of it covered about as solid as you could imagine with dense forest. There was a water tower sticking up out of the forest miles away, like a fly sitting on top of an expanse of green Jell-O.

Sunday came and we joined Pastor Danny's congregation for worship. Ralph and Cliff were there, and we met many more of the townspeople. They took up the most incredible love offering for the Team I had ever seen—even the little children were giving everything they had. We also enjoyed the pleasure of witnessing the burning of their mortgage that they had just paid off in full. Even with all of that, Pastor Danny's preaching was the high point of that visit. This man is truly gifted with the ability to inspire, and inspire he did. He taught The Word the way The Word should be taught; with fire and emotion, with highs and lows, with excitement and charisma. I was moved.

After that Sunday I had only a couple more days with the Team. We went through a town named Thorsby where we dedicated a memorial stone for my poor dog Thor, who had died of fright from fireworks a couple Fourth of July's ago. I spent most of my waiting time in the van planning out a route for them on the mapping program that would take them through to the Keys—and it worked for them all the way to Florida, where they changed to a coastal route

Finally the time had come. We had picked up Joni's friend Ronni from the Birmingham airport the night before, and now it was time for me to return home. Ronni was going to drive for them the rest of the way to the Florida Keys. It was heartbreaking to leave. I had such a great time being on the road and helping the Team. This had also been a well-taken opportunity to get to know my Mom better in a different environment then I had ever been in with her before, and Joni had become a true friend. The three of us had really formed a strong bond during those weeks. The Road tends to do that to you.

*Appendix 7*

# MY WIFE WALKED OUT ON ME

*NOTE: Dave's write-up will give you insights into his thoughts about the walk, his time at home without me, his visits with me on the walk, and the times with the team.*

## By Dave Hanush

I knew for some time that Lyn would be doing a walk across America. She had been in a 10-year cycle after she finished her walk up the Coast of Oregon and Washington. That walk had stopped at the Blaine, Washington USA-Canada Peace Arch. So I knew that there would be a walk in 2003 starting at the Peace Arch. The Oregon-Washington coast walk had also been a Prayer walk, so I knew that Prayer would be a significant part of the 2003 walk.

Shortly after the tragedy of September 11, 2001, when we saw thousands of our men and women going off to war in Afghanistan, and the fear and concern that seemed to engulf the people of America, it became evident to us that the purpose of this walk needed to be to "Pray for Unity in America, and for our servicemen and women around the world."

Oftentimes when I wanted to tell someone, or a group, about what Lyn was doing, I would start with: "My wife walked out on me." After getting the appropriate expressions of sympathy and concern, I would explain further that she was walking across America. As corny as it was, it made people remember us and the Walk. Three years later many people still comment about how they remember about that first "My wife walked out on me" comment.

One of those times was at our Church's Thanksgiving Service. People were standing up and saying what they were thankful for. Eventually I stood up and said something like: "I know this is a Thanksgiving service, but I need to say that after 43 years of marriage my wife walked out on me." At first there was a stunned silence, then gasps of sympathy, then giggles and laughs from those who knew of the Walk. Then I told how thankful I was for the Walk and the response that Lyn, Joni and Sam were getting along the way, and for their continued safety.

Even though I would have liked to be along with them on the Walk, I had to stay at home. I still have a significant tax and accounting practice and could not just take off for such a long time. So my job was to stay at home and handle the mail, e-mails and the web page (besides to earn the money to help pay for the Walk).

I am an accountant and not a web page type of person. I didn't have the slightest idea of how to set up a web page, so I enlisted some volunteer help. A friend got a friend of hers to design and set up the web page. Then when I gave them the first set of updates, they said that it would be too much for them to handle, and they turned it over to me. The pages had been set up, so I just had to learn how to update it and add new pages for the journals and other things. That was a very challenging task, and one that made me very much appreciate people who design web pages. I had the tools, and even the web page, but I know that I wasn't doing it the most efficient way. It was sort of like having a 55-gallon barrel of water and transferring it all from that barrel to another barrel, but using a teaspoon. I know that there were easier ways to do it, but I didn't have the slightest idea of what they were.

People often ask if I walked with them on the Great American Journey. My response is "Yes. I walked with them . . . for about a mile in Wyoming." Even though I did go to meet them five times over the course of the walk, I would find myself busy doing the driving, running errands, trying to make arrangements for newspaper or radio coverage, etc. But not being able to walk with them wasn't especially disappointing for me.

I did go to meet with Lyn on the Walk five times:

1) To Washington: The motor home wasn't completely repaired for them before they had to leave for the start of the Walk. So my son, Russ, and I drove the motor home to Washington when it was ready. We met them in Bellingham and then stayed with them a couple days in Concrete. During that time I had to teach Lyn some of the driving and safety tips for the motor home. We also tried to get them set up so they could get e-mails on their laptop. That never did work out.

2) In Wyoming: In September I flew to Rapid City, South Dakota, rented a car and drove to meet them in Gillette, Wyoming. It was beautiful weather and we had a great time being together for those couple days. Lyn and I took Saturday off to go to Mt. Rushmore and the Crazy Horse Monument.

3) At Christmastime: I went to meet the team in Missouri. I flew to Knoxville, Tennessee, and picked up my granddaughter Lois. We then drove from Sweetwater, Tennessee, through Nashville and Memphis, and on to El Dorado, Missouri. Lois and I were with them for a little over a week as they walked toward Springfield, Missouri. Then we took a break for Christmas at Branson. Lois and Samantha stayed in the Castle with Waliluke, and Lyn and I stayed at our WorldMark timeshare at Branson.

4) Alabama and Georgia for Mother's Day: This time I flew into Atlanta, rented a car and drove to meet the Team in Eufaula, Alabama. I had a couple days with them as they walked from Alabama into Georgia, then the "exciting" day of moving the Castle from Eufaula, Alabama to Albany, Georgia. As it turned out, this was the end of the road for the Castle. Along the way someplace it blew a valve or something—anyway it would be too expensive to repair it. On Mother's Day we visited Maranatha Baptist Church and the Sunday School class that President Jimmy Carter was teaching. After church we were able to get our picture with Jimmy and Rosalynn Carter.

5) To Florida at the end of the Walk: I again joined the Team for the final week of the Walk as they walked the Keys of Florida and finished up at Key West. Then after seeing Joni and Ronni off at the airport, Lyn and I took about three weeks to drive home, stopping in Albany, Georgia to rent a U-Haul trailer and load up all the things that they had stored from the Castle.

When we originally rented the trailer they had set it up as an eight-day rental. We told them that it would take us three weeks to get home, and they said, "That's OK. Just turn it in at Paso Robles when you get there." It was a special pricing deal for the eight days, and we assumed that the extra days would be at a higher rate. After the eight days we considered turning it in at a U-Haul place, then re-renting it for another eight days. But we thought we might have to unload the trailer, and we didn't want to get into that.

About two weeks later, in Green River, Wyoming we noticed that one of the tires was about to come apart. We called U-Haul and they said they would send someone out to replace the tire. Instead, they sent a tow truck that would pick up the trailer and take it up the road a piece and replace the tire there. On Sunday (the next day) we drove to the repair shop, but it was closed, and the trailer was sitting there with the same old tire. After several hours of calling U-Haul, we were told that the trailer had been reported as stolen, because it had not been turned in at the end of the eight days! So essentially, they had confiscated the trailer. No one was in the 24-hour U-Haul Service Center who could authorize extending the rental time, so we had to wait until Monday.

When we went back for the trailer, it turned out that the repair shop was actually a U-Haul facility. We explained what had happened, and he said that frequently happens. The people who rent the trailers don't understand, or don't tell the people of the restrictions. He made several calls and got everything straightened out, and rented the trailer to us for another eight days (enough this time), and we even got the special pricing for the deal. However, there weren't any tires of the right size in town, so he sent us on to the next town for the tire replacement. When we got there, they had the tire changed and we were out of there in about 15 minutes, no problems.

Lonely? Over the 14 months that Lyn was gone many people would ask, "How can you stand it with her being gone that long? Don't you get lonely?" My general response was something like, "Yes, I miss Lyn and I do get lonely. But when I feel like that, I think of the families of the servicemen who are fighting in Afghanistan (like one of our neighbors). Many of them are gone for longer times, and they are also worried if their loved ones will even survive. Or I think of some of our friends whose spouses have died. Now they are lonely. I can handle this "short" period of absence, especially when we do meet several times throughout the Walk."

What about the house? Shortly before the Walk began we learned that our son, Russ, was going to sell his house and needed another place to live for a couple years while he worked on a research project and wrote up his thesis of the project, so we invited Russ to move in with me while Lyn was gone. This would prove to be an invaluable experience for all of us. It wasn't nearly as lonely around the house with someone else there. Russ was always available to take care of the dogs when I went to meet Lyn. Also, we knew that someone would be around and available in case I had any medical emergencies (nothing was considered potential, but it was something that concerned Lyn).

Then there was the Mississippi River. When Lyn and Joni were finishing Arkansas and moving into the boot heel of Missouri, they were heading for a crossing of the Mississippi River at New Madrid, Missouri. This was in early March, and there were news reports about the Mississippi River nearing flood stage. About this time Russ rushed into my office and said that the news had just reported that two women had been swept away from their motor home in the floods of Missouri. Of course this made us very concerned.

It took several hours to verify that Lyn and Joni were in fact OK, and that the women who had been swept away were in a different part of Missouri (they, too, were OK). But that made us very concerned about their situation. I followed the flood news closely for about a week, as it was predicted to hit flood stage at just the time they were planning to cross the Mississippi on a little barge ferry. As it turned out, they crossed on the very last crossing of the ferry, and the flood actually hit that night after they were safely out of the area. But this scare helped us to encourage Russ to go out and drive for them a little earlier than he was originally planning.

Miami: July, 2004. I started this trip with a weekend at Harmony College West (a Barbershop training weekend at Redlands University). I had commuted to Redlands with a group of other Gold Coast Chorus members. Uncertain about just when Harmony College would be finished on July 18, I had reservations on a later flight from Ontario

Airport. My flight was from Ontario to Las Vegas, then on to Miami, with a layover in Las Vegas of about four hours.

As it turned out, Harmony College finished several hours earlier than I had expected. The guys dropped me off at Ontario Airport several hours before my scheduled flight to Las Vegas. Fortunately, because of all the transfers that had been scheduled, I had been able to pack four weeks of provisions into one carry-on bag. As I entered Ontario Airport, the line to go through the security checkpoint was extremely long. Even though it was over four hours before my scheduled flight, I decided to go to the departure area to see where it was. Besides, there were no really comfortable waiting areas outside the security area.

When I got to the departure area I found that the waiting area there was also very cramped, with very limited opportunity for refreshments. Wandering around the gate area, I found that an earlier flight to Las Vegas was still waiting for departure, and decided to try for the earlier flight. It was far from full, and because I had no checked luggage, I was allowed to switch to the earlier flight. As a result, I had an eight hour layover in Las Vegas waiting for the scheduled flight to Miami. But the waiting area in Las Vegas was much larger than the one in Ontario, with numerous cafes and restaurants, plus many fascinating people to watch. The eight hour wait in Las Vegas was very interesting, and much more comfortable. I was even able to get several naps during that time.

The arrival at Miami Airport went smoothly, and getting the rental car was very quick. I picked up a map and some directions for getting out of the airport, heading south on Highway 1 to meet Lyn in the Florida Keys. Going through Miami it seemed that I was on the wrong road—I had assumed that Highway 1 would be a freeway. But I knew I was going the right direction—south—because the mile marker mileage was decreasing as I went.

All too soon it started pouring tropical rain. Along the way I had to make a restroom stop. It was hard to see in the downpour, but I noticed a fast-food place and quickly pulled in. After eating, I pulled back onto the highway and resumed my trip toward the Florida Keys. After about 20 minutes things began to look familiar, even though I had never been to Florida before. Then I realized that the mileage markers were going up instead of down. It finally dawned on me. I was going north on Highway 1 instead of south. I was headed back to Miami. When I left the fast-food place I had gone the wrong way getting back onto the highway. Even though I was all alone, I was embarrassed and chagrined as I had to turn around. Then as the rain cleared up, I "enjoyed" that 20-minute section of Highway 1 a third time.

Whenever I went back to meet Lyn along the Walk, I always tried to surprise her, even though she knew I was coming. So I would try to get there earlier than I figured she would expect me. Then I would drive the expected walk route to try to find them. (On these trips, this was always exciting to me, even though on many of Lyn's previous walks this same endeavor would usually be very frustrating, trying to find her along the way.) But because I wanted to surprise her, I made a special effort not to call her to find out just where they were.

Eventually I found them at Bahia Honda State Park taking pictures of the park sign. So I pulled in and parked the car. Then I walked up behind Lyn and offered to take a picture of her with the park sign!

*Appendix 8*

# MY SMALL PART

---

NOTE: *John Colechin is the delightful twin brother of Joni Balog and lives in England. In June 2004 he joined our team to spend a week walking with us in Florida on the Great American Journey. He blessed us with his persistence, his humor, and his accent. Thanks for coming, John. It meant a lot to us. This is his account of that week.*

## by John Colechin

In November, 2002 I was on vacation with Joan (called Joni in this book) and we were walking in the Grand Canyon. She told me that she and Lyn were setting off the next year to walk across America. I was really astounded that she was attempting such a task, and have to admit that I had doubts of them achieving their goal. So I rashly said, "Let me know when you reach Florida, and I will come and join you," never realizing at the time that I would actually have to do it.

At my home in England I had a large map pinned to the wall, showing their route across America. As I monitored their course across the continent, by the spring of 2004 it was obvious that I would have to make plans to fly to Florida. In Paso Robles, Lyn's husband, Dave, was the co-coordinator for the walk, and via e-mails I had to arrange with him a suitable rendezvous with Joan and Lyn. The task was for me to arrive at a convenient airport, with connecting flights from London, where they could meet me with minimum disruption to their walking schedule, and—most important—return me a week later to catch my flight home. To arrive too early or too late would require them driving long distances to meet me. Dave's predictions put Joan and Lyn in the vicinity of Cape Canaveral in mid June and Sanford Airport, Orlando seemed the best option. So on the 15th of June I found myself boarding a flight at Gatwick for Sanford, to begin my small part in their Great American Journey.

Most flights from England to Florida are holiday flights, and mine was no exception. It was filled with families going to their villas, or on a fly-drive, and they would be visiting the major attractions like Disney and Epcot. I wondered what they would think if I said that I was not visiting any attractions, but intended to spend the whole week walking with two elderly women and a dog. As the comfortable flight progressed, doubts and fears came into mind. I am fortunate that I have always enjoyed good health and remain fit through participating in sports over the years. I have also been a marathon runner and a keen cyclist, and developed, quite independently from Joan, an interest in walking. But I had never walked in temperatures and humidity likely to be encountered in Florida, and I had not walked consistently day after day. Would I be able to keep up?

I put these fears out of mind as we approached our landing, and then thought, what if no one was there to meet me? Had my communications with Dave gone astray and not been relayed to Joan and Lyn? My only route out of Florida was a return flight in seven days time. Sanford is a nice quiet airport without the hassle that you find at Heathrow or San Francisco. You collect your luggage, stroll leisurely through customs, walk out a doorway, and step into the Florida sunshine. Waiting for me was a welcoming party of four.

Joan was first to greet me. Although we have lived 6,000 miles apart for at least forty years, we are just as close now as when we were children growing up in England. We have met up many times over the years, both in England and America. Meeting is always happy, and parting always sad, but we never say "Goodbye," only, "See you soon."

The second person to greet me was Lyn. We had met before in California, where she and Dave made me very welcome in their home. They are an extremely nice, genuine couple, and you can't help immediately liking them.

The third member of the group was Ronni. I had never met her before, but I knew she was a close friend of Joan's from Australia. Ronni was everything you would expect—a no nonsense, straight talking Aussi to be sure, and she gave me many laughs during my visit. She was the driver, and she drove us each day to our start point and took us back to our base in the evening. She did have the habit of occasionally wandering to the wrong side of the road, but she would quickly recover if I shouted, "Ronni, you're on the wrong side." On another occasion she found what seemed to be the perfect parking place, a nice grassy area with a concrete strip to park on. I had to point out to Ronni that I thought she was in someone's front garden. There was also the time when she drove into a gated community with a private golf course, only to be stopped by a security guard. Putting on her best Australian accent she told the guard she was a golfer and would like to visit the pro shop. Needless to say the guard sent us on our way. Ronni's contribution in driving was invaluable, and Joan and Lyn's task would have been more difficult without her.

So who was the fourth member meeting me at the airport? It was Joan's faithful German Shepherd, Cassie. I had met Cassie before at Joan's home in San Jose, but was wary of her, as she could regard me as an intruder and is very protective towards Joan. But we bonded very well, and I think she realized that I was not a threat. I don't know if she recognized me at Sanford, but we soon became good friends again.

On leaving the airport we headed to Melbourne, our base for the week. Joan and Lyn had spent the previous year living in a motor home. It was cramped and sometimes unreliable, and they called it "the castle." I was not looking forward to living in it for a week. I think a more appropriate name for it would have been "the shack." Fortunately for me, but not for them, the motor home broke down prior to my arrival, after a year of faithful service. So my base, whilst I was in Florida, was to be a motel room, with a proper bed, a shower and air conditioning. That's what I would call a palace.

Melbourne is a small town about halfway down the east coast of Florida on US 1, adjacent to the Indian River. On checking in at our motel in Melbourne, the manager was interested that I came from England. He told me he liked drinking English tea and invited me to join him at some time for a cup. Unfortunately, when I was there he wasn't, and so our paths did not cross again.

It had been a long day, an early morning check in at Gatwick, an eight hour flight and a five hour time difference. I had been awake for twenty-four hours and I was ready for some sleep. Tomorrow I would start walking into the unknown.

The daily walking routine in Florida had been well established by Joan and Lyn long before my arrival, and a typical day would be an early breakfast, four hours walking during the relatively cooler morning, a three hour break during the hottest part of the day, and then another four hours walking in the late afternoon and early evening. Sounds easy enough! Breakfast at the motel meant taking your tray to the small dining area and loading it up with cereals, fruit juice, coffee and muffins and eating a hearty breakfast in your room.

The next task was to load up our shuttle van with all the things we would need for the rest of the day—anything you forgot you went without. Loading the van meant stepping out of the air conditioned sanctuary of the motel into the heat and humidity of Florida—a real shock. Our start point for that first day was at a place called Mims, about 40 miles north of our motel in Melbourne. Lyn had meticulously recorded the spot where they had stopped walking the previous day, so that not even one step of the highway would be missed. Those first few hours were very hard, your clothes quickly became saturated due to the high humidity, and drinking plenty of fluids was essential. The roadway was very hot, and the heat transferred up through your walking boots and into your feet, making ideal conditions for blisters.

Cassie would take the first opportunity, when meeting up with Ronni, to climb back into the van and rest in the shade. Cassie had her own area in the van with food and water. We could also use these meeting points to refill our water bottles from the van's onboard refrigerator. The route took us past lush green vegetation, along the edge of the Indian River, a haven for fish and fowl. I would seek out many shaded spots with cool breezes. A few miles out to our left on the horizon were the ever present launch buildings at Cape Canaveral. By midday we had reached a convenient park area with picnic tables and an inviting lake, but also a sign which said 'Beware of Alligators.' Ronni had also been busy buying our lunch, which consisted of cold meats and cheese, huge tomatoes, fresh bread and bananas.

During the hottest part of the day we did our best to keep cool, and we went to a viewing platform by the river to watch for manatees. We managed to spot some of these very strange creatures. I was also spotted by the local mosquitoes, which Joan called the "no-see-me" flies. Repellant spray from a friendly tourist helped a lot.

Soon we were walking again to achieve our daily mileage. At the end of the day Ronni would meet us and we would drive back to our motel, first having recorded the finishing point and verifying the mileage. After a stop for an evening meal, it was back to the motel. With a shower to remove the sweat and grime of the day, and some clean clothes, I sat there very pleased with myself. I had survived; I hadn't collapsed with sunstroke or suffered any blisters, and we had covered 17 miles. I was looking forward to tomorrow.

The pattern of all our days was very similar. The start point for today was a place called Titusville. A Roman settlement came to mind, but then I realized this was America, not England. A daily routine for Joan and Lyn after about an hour of walking would be morning prayers. This was a very informal event, carried out while walking, where they reflected on the past day and the day still to come. I was always invited to join with them, but I felt comfortable to walk on and leave them to their own thoughts. They had, after all, come a very long way together, and their journey was still not yet over.

Another regular routine that had started at the beginning of the walk was for them to leave a large stone at appropriate locations, with a message written on it stating who they were and why they were there. Stones of a suitable size were difficult to find in Florida, but in Titusville we passed a company selling aggregate. A plea from Lyn to the owner of the company resulted in him giving her enough stones to complete their journey. Ronni was hastily summoned, and we loaded the van with the generous gift.

During the day we walked through a small community called Port St. John. Joan and I were delighted to find such a place and wanted Lyn to take a photograph of us beside the town's nameplate. I think Lyn was a bit bemused by our behavior until we explained that St. John was our mother's maiden name. We then renamed the place Mom's Town, or in English, Mum's Town.

For our midday break we drove toward the Atlantic coast to visit the well known resort of Cocoa Beach. Then back to walking, this time through busy roads choked with homeward bound traffic. Lyn would wave to many cars. A stop for dinner, then back to our motel base to prepare for another day tomorrow.

Our early breakfast today was a break from the usual routine. Through a contact of Lyn's, we had been invited to a Rotary Club breakfast at the Suntree Methodist Church. The Church was a very impressive modern building set in a beautiful location. The Club and Church made us very welcome. We had a nice breakfast and enjoyed the speaker's lecture. We hoped they also enjoyed Lyn's brief talk on what we were doing. We still managed to set off to our start point at Rockledge by 9 o'clock.

It was a very hot day, probably the hottest of my week. The ever present view of Cape Canaveral on the horizon was now seen not in front of us, but over our shoulder, as we gradually moved a bit farther south each day. For lunch today we met up with some friends of Lyn's, after which we were close enough to Melbourne to rest in the coolness of our motel rooms.

It was a scorching hot afternoon, so not until about 5 o'clock did we resume walking. The coolness of the evening made for a very pleasant walk, and as dusk arrived we called up Ronni to come and collect us only 4 miles from our motel. We stopped to buy a Subway sandwich to eat back at the motel, a very enjoyable way to end an enthralling day.

Another hot day, and another early breakfast, but we only had to drive 4 miles to our start point. There was also a big psychological bonus in that this morning we would walk past our motel and continue on southward. Today's walking took us through some of the best scenery of the week, past marinas and beautiful waterfront homes.

One very secluded street had private river bank mooring decks and boats to match. It was the sort of area where strangers stood out, and Ronni driving around in the van attracted the attention of the residents. A police patrol car stopped her, but she quickly convinced the policeman that she was not a burglar or a thief when she told him why she was there. She then told the policeman that it would be a good idea if he "arrested" three suspect walkers a couple of miles up the road. The policeman agreed with her ploy, but before he could reach us, he was summoned on the car radio to investigate some real crime. It's sad to reflect that some of the outstanding scenery and homes we saw that day were devastated by hurricanes later in the year. With 15 miles completed, and lightning flashing in the distance, we called for Ronni to come and collect us.

Today was Sunday, a rest day from walking. Joan and Lyn made a point of attending church on Sundays in the area they had spent the week in, and so after a later breakfast I joined Joan and Lyn for the morning service in the local church in Melbourne. It was to be a moving experience. The church was like no other I had been in. The minister was casually dressed in jeans and tee shirt; his wife played guitar and sang; a three piece group replaced the organ, and the hymn book was an overhead projector. They were a friendly and modern congregation who made us feel welcome, and they were interested in what we were doing.

The minister and some of the congregation had just returned from the Dominican Republic, where they were helping to build a school. Several members gave very emotional accounts of their visit and the poverty they encountered. One said that when an American invites you into his home, it's to show you how wealthy he is, but when a Dominican Republican invites you into his home, it's to share with you what few possessions he has.

Although this was a rest day, there was laundry to be done before setting out to have Sunday lunch. This was Joan and Lyn's only excess of the week. We ate at a very nice restaurant in Cocoa Beach before visiting the Kennedy Space Centre. This was my first visit to the centre, and I found it most impressive. The highlight was to be an unmanned launch that evening, and we listened over the public address system to the countdown. Unfortunately, with minutes to go, the launch was canceled due to pending bad weather. Driving back to the motel, we encountered the worse storm I had ever been in.

Monday, with no sign of the previous nights' storm, was to be my last day of walking in Florida. We were now back to our usual walking routine by starting where we had stopped two days earlier. It was a pleasant waterfront walk through places with names such as Grant, Roseland and Sebastian. A roadside nameplate said that Sebastian was a town of nice people and a couple of old grouches. The grouches in our group posed for a photograph at this sign. We picnicked on a pleasant grassy area by the river and then sought refuge from the sun in an air conditioned Wal-Mart, so I got the chance to do some shopping before going home. After our final session of walking, Lyn again recorded the exact finishing spot and checked the mileage. That evening back at the motel Lyn gave me a copy of her journal notes for the week I had spent with them. I thought I had walked about 80 miles, but no, Lyn said it was 79.3 miles, and if I wanted it to be 80 miles then I would have to walk another 7/10 miles before going home. I was happy with 79.3.

The next morning we checked out of our motel. Joan and Lyn walked for a while, and then we all drove to Sanford Airport to drop me off for my flight home. I was at the back of a long queue at the check-in, as there was only one desk open. Once again Ronni was to surprise me. Sensing another desk was about to open, she grabbed my suitcase and strode to the desk just as extra check-in staff arrived, and I now found myself at the front of the new queue. Cases now checked in and boarding pass in hand, it was time to leave. I said good-bye to Lyn and thanked her for letting me be part of their walk. I said goodbye to Ronni and thanked her for all she had done as our driver. I said my usual "see you soon" to Joan, walked through a door marked Immigration, and my Great American Journey was over.

In the departure lounge I reflected on my week. It had been exhausting and uncomfortably hot, and I wondered: why do people go to Florida for a holiday? I enjoyed every moment of the experience, even though I did not see any alligators, but the memories will stay with me forever. I would have regretted not taking part.

I think that when you take on a challenge, it is part fitness and part determination, and I knew that Joan and Lyn had the determination to reach Key West in a few weeks' time. Twelve hours after leaving Florida (temperature 92 degrees) I was back home in South East England (temperature 62 degrees), looking again at my wall map that charted their progress. My 79.3 miles seems very insignificant, and you really have to walk with them to appreciate the enormity of their achievement. Lyn and Joan were very tired, but also very determined and excited as the finish drew closer.

*Appendix 9*

# THANKS FOR THE MEMORIES

*NOTE: It was a joy to have JoAn along at various points of this Journey. She was a special asset in the winter when she blessed us with her "Snow" knowledge. Her laughter was always a joy to hear. Meeting and talking with people she met brought great rewards. Enjoy her account of the different times she was with us.*

## *by JoAn Thomas*

When asked to add something about my experiences on the Great American Journey to this book, my first thought was, "This task could evolve into a book in itself." Thinking about it brought to mind our experiences and the lovely small towns and communities we passed through, many with catchy or unusual names, like Sedro Woolley, Concrete, Twisp, Kettle Falls, Osawatomie, and Cudjoe Key, to name a few.

A need for brevity, plus a deadline, meant that out of the nine or so weeks I spent with the team, only a few experiences could receive a special mention. These are by no means the only memorable ones, but will serve as an example of what I experienced right across the country.

The policeman who stopped his cruiser in an intersection, halting busy lunch-time traffic, to allow me to take a photo of the town's sign surrounded by flowers against a backdrop of mountains.

The avid gardener who promptly cut two of his prize roses and presented them to Anne and me when we stopped to smell and admire. I pressed my rose and have it in my photo album.

Evie, who because she thought I didn't have a red shirt for the final day of the walk, wanted to give me, quite literally, the red shirt off her back (she did have a spare white one). Readers, she makes the best sub I've ever eaten. When in Florida look for her sub shop at Cudjoe Key.

All the people along the way who fed and watered and encouraged us, waved and honked as they drove by us, or who stopped and asked whether we wanted a ride (we didn't accept rides, but the offers were much appreciated).

Anne, who walked and talked many a mile with me and found the snow-covered trail to the absolutely breathtaking vista from Washington Pass Lookout.

Judi, our driver in Washington State, who shared my cheese and rather stale crackers atop Washington Pass. It was moving day, and the van's engine had overheated. While we waited for it to cool, we were entertained by a friendly jay who cleaned up our crumbs.

Sam, who brought a breath of youth to our group of seniors.

Ronni, our last driver, who enjoyed along with me many an extended "Happy Hour," watching outstanding sunsets and sometimes intriguing storm clouds over the Gulf of Mexico.

Dellie, my gentle roommate, walking mate and sightseeing mate while in the Keyes and who, after many tries at bribery with food, finally caught a glimpse of the hotel's iguana.

Joni, who made it all the way in spite of blisters and colds and tried very hard to like buffalo meat—to no avail.

Lyn, whose idea it all was, and who walked every step of the way without getting us lost. Well, maybe once necessitating only a very slight detour.

To all of you, I'd like to say thanks for the very special memories. It truly was a great American Journey.

*Appendix 10*

# MIAMI NOSTALGIA

---

NOTE: *Dellie joined us for the last portion of our Journey from Miami to Key West. Below are her memories of this adventure.*

## *by Dellie Chapman*

Joining Lyn, Joni, and Cassie in South Florida, I was filled with nostalgia and a desire to accompany these dedicated women the last 163 miles of a 4,026.5 mile walk across our vast land, praying, witnessing, and meeting fellow Americans of all walks of life.

The nostalgia was in returning to Miami, Florida where I lived from 1955–1960, graduating from the University of Miami with a degree in education.

There were many changes over the years, such as the elevated rail, and the palm trees, which are now taller than the school buildings. The school used to be in open space, but now is surrounded by buildings, stores, and fast-moving traffic.

The other nostalgia was visiting my uncle's grave at the Hebrew cemetery. He was the patriarch of the family, living until age 95.

I was aware of the heat and humidity in July, but was not accustomed to it, so it began to take its toll.

Some of the highlights of my three-week adventure were walking on Highway 1. One day the skies were a threatening dark gray, which turned into a gusty thunder and lightning storm. I was thrilled at becoming drenched in that warm climate. Wise Cassie led us to shelter, which turned out to be a tire repair shop. Lyn was relieved as she witnessed a bolt of lightning on a chain link fence, filling her with apprehension. The shop's owner, who was from Cuba, told us interesting stories of his life there and of leaving for America years ago. When he found out about the mission of this walk, he took a large cross from his neck and told us of his faith. He was very gracious.

One Sunday we worshiped at a Presbyterian Church in Marathon, and the welcoming, dog-loving, pastor invited Cassie inside where she could rest in the comfort of air conditioning during the service. I saw quite a few surprised faces. After the spiritually uplifting service we fellowshipped for a while with the friendly congregation.

One day Lyn and Joni were interviewed on the radio in one of the Keys. Afterward, it seemed as if everyone on the Highway knew who we were. Many honked and waved. One lady ran out with bottles of cold water, which was an absolute godsend. She owned a café, and we decided to have lunch there. We were treated like royalty, enjoyed the food, and were surprised at being charged only half-price. We brought some excitement into that area.

The Seven Mile Bridge walk began very early on a beautiful morning. Since the heat and humidity sapped some of my energy, I decided to walk the old part of the bridge, about a two mile round trip. There was no traffic and I was pleasantly comfortable with the Atlantic Ocean on one side and the Gulf of Mexico on the other. That was the best part of the Keys. Lyn, Joni, and JoAn, my great roommate from Canada did the seven mile section.

One of my favorite tourist attractions on the Keys was feeding fish to tarpons on a pier. They practically took them out of my hand.

Key West brought back memories. In the 50s it was a sleepy, small fishing town. Alas, progress changed it dramatically. As you enter there are motels, restaurants, a chain pharmacy, and other businesses. It was funny to see chickens wandering around. Cassie would have liked to give them a merry chase.

Four miles to go to the end of the trail. On the last mile we were in the old section that I remembered. It was a happy, yet sad occasion for Lyn and Joni as we came to the southernmost point of the continental U.S.A., Key West, Florida, Home of the Sunset.

Quite a few people whom we had met several days earlier made it a point to be there, especially a man named Clayton who saw them off in Blaine, Washington. That was an exciting surprise for Lyn and Joni.

After it was all over we toured a bit. The annual Ernest Hemingway look-alike contest was in progress. It was amazing how many men there were. We enjoyed walking and window shopping in an area similar to the French Quarter in New Orleans. We also stopped by Mr. Hemingway's house.

We came upon a huge kapok tree, with a root formation like elephant legs. The Mayans believed if they climbed this tree, they would climb to heaven when they died. I am content that my faith in Jesus Christ will get me there without that strenuous effort.

Many times I rode with the van driver and Cassie. Ronnie was from Australia. I found her to be witty and delightful company. All in all, it was an unusual and fun adventure.

One thing I don't miss, besides the heat and humidity, are the huge, nocturnal palmetto bugs (roaches) that fly and crawl faster than you can imagine.

Praise the LORD, we all flew home safely. Lyn and Dave casually drove the faithful van westward, stopping along the way to visit friends and relatives.

# GREAT AMERICAN JOURNEY
## 2003 PRAYER LIST

- *To all those across America who asked us to pray*

- *To all we waved to as we walked the highways of America*

- *To every church we visited*

- *And to every individual we talked with, may God bless and keep you:*

Concrete Bible Church

Mark and Audrey

Joel

Greg

Maggie

The Fathers Ranch

Town of Republic

Brenda

Baby Larissa Ann

Free Methodist Church of Colville

John and Lynn

Diane

House of Prayer

Ken

Judy and Steve

Elizabeth and Rhett

Cabinet Mountain Bible Church

Pastor Happ

Three young men in Thompson Falls

John and Phyllis

Gil

Johnny and Carrie

Bill

Ed

Harold

Buster

Barbara and Red

Arlee Alliance Church

Ted

Mark and Mike

Les and Betty

Timberwolfe

Three Feathers

Jessica

Andrew, his Wife and Child

Governor Judy Martz

Chris and MaryEllen and family

Clarke and Ruby

Pat

Steve

Rex

Robin

Warren

Dr. Bob

Jason

Steve

Tom

Walt

Vicky

Jeff

Harden Open Bible Church

Richard and Zillah

Russ

Donald and Donald

Aliza

Mike and Ken

Marty

Rachel

Vera

Kevin and Kari

Kenton, Kieran, Karson and Katriel

Greg

Nate

Ken

Alfred

Elliot

Hershel

Makalia

Gutrerre

Sherry

Candy

Felica

Ray

James

Pastor Patrick and
Sharon

Levi

Larrisa

Vidal

Jenny

Patricia

Darlene

Matt

Joy

Vicky

Bob and Bonnie

Quinton

Ann

Hardin Middle School

Gina

David

Charrelle

Scott

Jamie

Dorothy

Robert

Morgan

Michael

Diana

Vera

Veranda

Franklin

Derek

Andrew

Myriah

Tristan

Manuel

Katlynn

Shalimar

Bryndon

Angelo

John

Kaleb

Hillary

Chris

Nathan

Dan

Stacy

Grace Bible Church

Berean Bible Church

Pastor Gary and Bev

Les and Joyce

Living Outreach
Church

Pastor Joel

Jim and Connie

Willie

Connie

Josh

Chadron First
American Baptist
Church

Pastor Richard

Anna

Jeremy

Georgia

Lloyd

Three Peaks Christian
School

Brad

Danielle

Melanie

Justin

Joel

Becky

Joey

Cody

Deanna

Sharon and Dennis

Bruce

Fran

Jennifer

Teens for Christ in
Miltonvale

Matt

Randy

John

Randy

Kenny

Brian

Miltonvale Kids Club

First Christian Church
in Clay Center

Paxico United Meth-
odist Church

Pastor Brian

Skyline Heights
Christian Faith
Center

Pastor Galen

Dan and Judy

Betty

Kenton and Lisa

Baby Sam

A.J. and Theresa

Jay

Paso Robles earth-
quake

Marilyn

Julia

Jerry

Anacker children from
Russia

Grand Old
Gospel Hour

Ginger

David and Melissa

Tahlia and Sylvie

David

Cowboy Church in
Branson

Pastor Al and
Norma Jean

Randy

Kevin

Justin

Karen

Ronnie and Cheryl

Deborah and Marian

Deborah and Chantel

Robert and Eva

Genevieve

Nancy

Kay

Nancy

Norma

Bill and family

Roxie's grandson,
Cameron

Christina and "Crew"
at Wendy's

Sarah

White Oaks Baptist Church

Pastor Sam

Jewel and Jean

Tom and Rolene

Jamie and Mary at Dairy Queen

Wayne

Malinda

Bob

Elnora Free Will Baptist Church

Pastor Jaral

Jerry and family

Bill and Hazel

Margie

Victory Independent Baptist Church

Pastor John

Nancy

Philip at Brinkley's Auto

Clearlake Freewill Baptist Church

Robert and Marilea

Kendall

Relton and Loyse

Hope and Harmony Churches

Judi

Sheila

Theresa

Carla

Dry Bayou Baptist Church

Pastor Stan and Hazel

Susan

J.R.

Blake

James

Bobby

James and Kim

Whitney

Tatum

Omar

Lisa

Minnie

Rhonda

West Hickman Baptist Church

Pastor Brent

Tim and Karen

Andrea, MaryEvelyn and Amy

KingDom SeeKers Ministries

Pastor Larry and Theresa

Old Country Store

Clark

Paige

Pam

Saltillo First Baptist Church

Gary

Micah and Amy

Keysha

Dwana

Ann

Karol

Tammy

Baldwyn First Christian Church

Pastor Morris and Lynn

Bekka

Andrew

Joe and Joan

Sidney

Jeanette

Tom

Truckers Chapel Outreach

Pastor Billy and Debbie

Lori

Pastor James and Diane

World Outreach Ministries Christian Center

Pastor Elworth and Jessie

Sunshine Outlet

Charles and Billie

Katey and Alex

Ramona

Jim

Doctor Harold, Veterinarian

Sheryl

Brenda

Debbie

Elaine

Jim

Mt. Carmel Baptist Church

Pastor Danny

Ralph

Cliff

David and Dawn

David

Jessica

All Roads Auto Shop, Brian and Cindy

Crestview Baptist Church

Pastor Larry

Kirk

Vince

Graham

Paul

Eddie and Dianne

Margaret

Steve

WALB-TV

Kathryn

Dalton

Jerome

Mama Gina's Pizza Ristorante

Shyenne

Scott and Pam

Sandy

Faye

Julia

Carol

Ramada Limited

Evelyn

Norma

Jimmy

Tony

Darryl

Teresa

William

Steve

Sheri

Randy

B.J.

Evelyn

Jodi

Betty

Norma

Mairi

Wayne

First Christian
  Church,
  Pastor Hugh

Ray

Four young men at
  Korona Beach

Edward

Bob

Shelley and Christo-
  pher

Lady and
  husband and
  dog in car
  accident

Clayton

Roger and Mary

Chuck

Rick

Les

John

Ian

Shepherd Road Pres-
  byterian Church

Pastor Bob

Ron

Brian and wife

His Place
  Ministries

Pastor Terry and Betty

Jason

Bible Baptist Church

Pastor Joe

Charles and Beverley

Ike, Janice and Floyd

Fatima

Souad

Marcus

Kissimmee United
  Methodist Church

Jerry and Carol

Susan

Shawn and Bev

Bob

Joan

Loretta

Douglas

PopPop

First United Method-
  ist Church, Pastor
  Tod and Christina

Mark

Doreen

Judy

Lillian

Allana

Zack

Rebbecca

Joan

Richard and Annette

Earline

Luis Palau Ministry

Lee's Summit
  Presbyterian

Pastor Dave and
  Rhonda

Phillip and George

Bear and Christy

Amanda

Jamie

Oliver and his
  daughter

Kim

Tracy

Coleman

Hazel

Vince

Linda

Stan

Randy

Hayley

Joyce Abrahamson,
  missionary

Judi

Baby Riley

McKenzie

Diane

Jim

Bonnie

John and Rosemary
  Kane, missionary

Gary and Robyn
  Peterson, Esther
  and Josiah

*We continue to keep you all in our prayers. May God bless each one of you.*

# MILITARY PRAYER LIST

## To all the men and women serving in our military:

*We salute you! And to your families, our love and prayers are with you. Thank you for your sacrifice. "The battle belongs to the Lord."*

| | | | | |
|---|---|---|---|---|
| Havilah | Derek | Connie | Tristan | Charles |
| Dale | David | Luis | Mark | Daniel |
| Matthew | Jans | Chris | Chad | Andrew |
| Marie | Phillip | Scott | Scott | Jason |
| Tom | Aaron | Josh | Holly | Kenneth |
| Mark | Andrea | Ian | David | Donald |
| Jon | Matthew | Jeff | Siya | Amber |
| Eric | Corey | David | Ignacio | Alfredo |
| Jed | Gary | Jason | John | Cyril |
| Aaron | Andy | Ron | Trevor | Franklin |
| Eric | Steve | Toney | Daniel | Jason |
| Jimmy | Ryan | Jackie | Shaun | Leanne |
| Nickolas | James | Byron | Derek | Donald |
| Jonathon | Calvin | Jimmy | Jon | William |
| Johnny | Jonathon | Keith | Joaquin | John |
| Grant | Trey | Eric | Jesus | Allen |
| David | Jimmy | John | Brent | Michael |
| Brandon | Jonathon | Jeremy | John | Charles |
| Missy's brother | Burt | Eric | Robert | Nicholas |
| Shawn | Matt | Jeff | Julio | Ty |
| Robert | John | Jeremy | Brad | Craig |
| Duke | Dustin | Jeff | Kona | Michael |
| Chris | Jackie | Joseph | William | |

| | | | | |
|---|---|---|---|---|
| Michael | Robert | David | Kathleen | 122nd Corp |
| Patrick | Felicia | Daryl | Sone | Neil |
| Jorge | Thomas | Sam | Eric | Dennis |
| Edward | Bruce | Cameron | Lili's son | Clayton |
| Philip | Sheldon | Tyler | David | Jamie |
| Randy | Meagan | Pedro | Alan | Mark |
| Nancy | Gary | Daniel | Bret | Lyle |
| Ronald | Bart | Christopher | Evan | Jon |
| Scott | Jon | Shawn | CJ | Chris |
| Edward | Steven | Raymond | Leah | Joe |

*May God bless and keep each one of you, and may you know the peace that only God can give.*